INSURGENCY
PERSONALITIES AND POLITICS OF THE TAFT ERA

STUDIES IN HISTORY, ECONOMICS AND PUBLIC LAW

Edited by the

FACULTY OF POLITICAL SCIENCE
OF COLUMBIA UNIVERSITY

NUMBER 470

INSURGENCY

*Personalities and Politics of
the Taft Era*

BY

KENNETH W. HECHLER, Ph. D.

NEW YORK

RUSSELL & RUSSELL · INC

1964

To

WILLIAM ALLEN WHITE

ACKNOWLEDGMENTS

INSPIRATION and assistance for this study has come from so many sources that it would take a book in itself to express adequate appreciation. In addition to the fifty men and women listed in the bibliography under " Personal Interviews," hundreds of farmers, laborers, politicians, professors, business men and newspaper editors have aided me with their first-hand knowledge of the movement called " Insurgency."

I want to thank a few of these individuals for the special aid that they extended. I spent four gorgeous days in the cool of the Blue Ridge Mountains as the guest of Senator Miles Poindexter. He opened his rich file of correspondence on this period, and we talked far into several nights on all phases of the progressive movement. Miss Fola La Follette provided the greatest single stimulus for this study, and gave unsparingly of her time and energy in helping me to crystallize my ideas about her father's career and philosophy. Long hours before an open fireplace with Senator Joseph L. Bristow gave me an intimate picture of the great character of one of the leading Insurgents, and the kindness of Senator Bristow and his son enabled me to make use of his previously untouched letters and documents.

I had the good fortune to receive a vast amount of encouragement and advice from that genial editor of the *Emporia Gazette,* William Allen White, to whom this study is affectionately dedicated. One of Mr. White's fellow Kansans, Representative Victor Murdock, spent three days giving me his astute comments upon the personalities and actual mechanics of Insurgency.

Representative John M. Nelson of Wisconsin and Senator George W. Norris of Nebraska dropped their many duties to describe to me the sidelights surrounding the collapse of Speaker Cannon, and two great biographers, Alfred Lief and Henry F. Pringle, gave me many leads and suggestions which proved of value.

7

Numerous others assisted in various ways—indefatigable Sarah Davidson of the Minnesota Historical Society, cheery " Ken " Colton of the Iowa State Department of History and Archives, hospitable Addison Sheldon of the Nebraska State Historical Society, and the entire staff of the Manuscript Divisions of the Library of Congress, State Historical Society of Iowa, State Historical Society of Wisconsin, Indiana Historical Society, Kansas Historical Society, New York Public Library, New Hampshire Historical Society, and Connecticut State Library.

In the academic field, I owe an inestimable amount to the constant inspiration of Professors Allan Nevins, Howard K. Beale, Frederick J. Manning, Lindsay Rogers, and especially Schuyler C. Wallace.

ROSLYN, NEW YORK,
APRIL 15, 1940.

TABLE OF CONTENTS

CHAPTER I

WHAT DOES INSURGENCY MEAN?

ALTHOUGH the word " Insurgency " was not generally used in American political life before the turn of the present century, the kind of intra-party warfare it has come to describe is probably as old as man's attempts to govern himself and his neighbors. Absalom plotted against his father, King David; Demosthenes orated against the Greek government for signing what he considered an unworthy treaty; Mark Antony broke up the triumvirate of Rome; Kossuth led the Magyars in a revolt against the Hapsburgs; more recently Trotsky is warring on Stalin.

Early in the history of our own country John Randolph of Roanoke turned his oratorical invective upon the Jeffersonians and led a group of strong states rights rebels known as " Quids." Sectional, economic and personal grievances, along with statesmanlike regard for questions of principle, have caused numerous rebellions from political party authority ever since. A few revolts stand out boldly, such as the determined battles of the young Republicans for internal improvements during the Madison-Monroe era; the National Republican, Whig, and Calhoun defections from Jackson's leadership; the Radical Republican resistance to Lincoln and Johnson; the Sumner-Edmunds opposition to the annexation of Santo Domingo and other Grant measures; the Liberal Republican and Mugwump splits away from Grant and Blaine; the mutiny of protectionist Democrats under the lead of Gorman, and the silver forces marshalled by " Silver Dick " Bland, enraged at Cleveland's stolid insistence upon a revenue tariff and the gold standard; the revolt of the " Sons of the Wild Jackass " against the conservative Republican leadership of the '20s; and the anti-spending and anti-labor rebellion of the Garner Democrats against the New Deal.

" Insurgency " was employed with most frequency during the administration of President Taft from 1909-1913, when a group of dissentient Congressmen representing the more progressive wing of the Republican Party disobeyed the dictation of the House and Senate leaders on questions of procedure and specific pieces of party legislation.

During the three years before the formation of the Progressive Party in 1912, the lines of the Republican Party were frequently shattered along the congressional front. Few chapters in the history of Congress are so fraught with intra-party conflicts as the period of the Taft administration, when the political turmoil exceeded in acrimony and extent the recent conservative Democratic revolt within the New Deal ranks.

The origin of the term " Insurgency " as applied in American politics is obscure. The surviving Insurgents of the Taft period all declare that the word was little used before the campaign of 1908, and did not come into common parlance until after Taft became President on March 4, 1909. It had been used during several minor revolts before the major revolution of the Taft administration got under way. One of the lieutenants of Senator William B. Allison of Iowa applied the term opprobriously to his political opponents within the Republican Party as early as 1901.[1] The contemporary press and news magazines used the word freely during 1902 and 1903 to describe a group of Congressmen from the beet-sugar producing states who refused to vote for Theodore Roosevelt's tariff reciprocity with Cuba.

Doubtless the word " Insurgency " as applied to internal politics was carried over from international law, in which field it is used to describe the state of armed rebellion that precedes recognized belligerency.[2] Revolts within parties had been flaring up throughout the nineteenth century; but the activities of the Cuban " Insurgents," which filled the newspapers toward the

1 N. M. Hubbard to W. B. Allison, March 26, 1901.
2 The Three Friends, 166 U. S. 1.

end of the century, led American political writers to use a striking word in a new sense.[3]

The revolt of the Taft period appears unique when we consider that before 1909 political rebellions were characterized by
the general name of the issue or the group under which the issue
was projected. We speak of the Whigs of Jackson's era, the
Liberal Republicans of Grant's time, and the Gold Democrats
who seceded from the Democratic majority under Bryan. On
the other hand, the rebels of Taft's day came to be known by
the name of revolt itself—Insurgency.

Four journalists share the honor of making the term an accepted word in the layman's political vocabulary—Mark Sullivan, writing in *Collier's Magazine,* Ray Stannard Baker of *The
American Magazine,* Judson C. Welliver of *The Washington
Times,* and William Allen White of *The Emporia Gazette.* This
quartet, especially Messrs. Sullivan and Welliver, drummed on
the aims and ideals of the congressional Insurgents in the
months between Taft's election and inauguration, and thus
made the American public distinctly conscious of the existence
of this faction of the Republican Party.

What were these aims and ideals? In brief, they constituted a
determination on the part of these Congressmen to carry out
what Theodore Roosevelt had affectionately termed " my policies." Opinion differed as to what precisely " my policies "
were, especially upon the subject of tariff revision and rules reform in the House of Representatives. Yet the Insurgents
pushed blithely forward, displaying the same moral fervor
that had characterized Theodore Roosevelt. They charged
into battle against their wicked opponents with the same reckless abandon as had Roosevelt, and sometimes they found themselves even warring against the very forces the former President had defended. It mattered little to the Insurgents that while
he had been in the White House, Roosevelt made no serious
effort to lower the tariff or check Speaker Cannon's power;
the important thing was that Roosevelt's crusading spirit ap-

3 Mark Sullivan to Kenneth W. Hechler, November 3, 1938.

pealed to those Republicans who recognized him as the steadfast opponent of blind reaction within the party.

In the House of Representatives, the Insurgency of the Taft administration was directed largely toward limiting the power of Speaker Cannon. Through his prerogative of appointing committee personnel, his domination of the committee on rules, and his arbitrary power of recognition on the floor, Speaker Cannon had gained a control over the House which by 1909 assumed autocratic proportions. The majority of the Republican Party backed Cannon, but a group of approximately twenty-five Insurgents regularly fought his personal dictatorship. The number of anti-Cannon Congressmen ebbed and flowed, now diminishing as the leaders tightened the screws of discipline, now increasing as sentiment in the country turned against Cannon. The high tide of Insurgency came on March 19, 1910, when the Insurgents rallied forty-two Republicans to join the Democrats in passing a resolution that stripped the Speaker of most of his personal power.

The war on Cannon was the prime issue of the House Insurgents; but they also had minor skirmishes with the regular party leaders on the Payne-Aldrich tariff of 1909, the Mann-Elkins railroad rate bill of 1910 and the Pinchot-Ballinger conservation quarrel.

In the Senate,[4] the Insurgents strayed from the Republican leadership on three major issues. In its acrimony and disruptive effects, the Insurgent revolt in the Senate against the Payne-Aldrich tariff was closely comparable to the House battle on Cannon. Effective railroad regulation, an issue raised by the Mann-Elkins bill, was another Insurgent concern. The question

4 One of the leading House Insurgents contends that "the Senate insurgency has been identified in hay-wire history with the House insurgency. The two were entirely different breeds of cats." Victor Murdock to Kenneth W. Hechler, October 6, 1939. But another Kansan maintains: "It was a revolt against the leadership in the Senate by men who believed that the policies advocated by the leadership were in the interest of certain great financial and industrial concerns, and against the welfare of the masses of people." Joseph L. Bristow to Kenneth W. Hechler, December 9, 1939.

of Canadian reciprocity in 1911 stirred up the opposition of from six to twelve Republican Senators on the various schedules. Less important Insurgent issues in the Senate were conservation and the postal savings bank question.

This study will attempt to appraise the historical and geographical roots of the congressional Insurgency of the Taft administration; to analyze the rise and development of Insurgency in connection with the principal public issues upon which it manifested itself; and to describe the personalities, organization and tactics of the Insurgents and their opponents. The searchlight will constantly be directed upon what caused men to break away from their party and how they went about it.

CHAPTER II

HISTORICAL, GEOGRAPHICAL AND ECONOMIC ROOTS

THE hotbed of Insurgency was in the agrarian states of Kansas, Nebraska, Minnesota, Wisconsin and Iowa. The movement overflowed into the Dakotas and Indiana, and there were also traces of it in New England and on the Pacific Coast. But in large part it was a middle-western agrarian protest differing little from similar waves of discontent that had risen in this area during the last quarter of the nineteenth century. The political and economic upheavals led by such men as Tom Johnson in Cleveland, Hazen Pingree in Michigan, and Joseph Folk in Missouri were likewise forerunners of the congressional revolt of 1909. Indeed, before going to Congress most of the Insurgents led progressive revolts in their home states.

The basic conflict between Jeffersonian agrarianism and Hamiltonian industrialism provided much of the inspiration for Insurgency. The Insurgents retained Jefferson's faith in the common man, his social idealism, his distrust of urbanism, his concern over political tyranny, and his deep confidence in agriculture as the backbone of a free nation. But Jefferson's dreams did not materialize, and by the dawn of the twentieth century, America was ruled politically and economically by the exponents of the industrial doctrines of Alexander Hamilton. Therefore the Insurgents undertook to graft the principles of Jefferson on to a twentieth century economy, exchanging in the process the Jeffersonian tool of limited government for the Hamiltonian tool of a powerful government. This was but a natural development, since the Insurgents hailed from those agricultural states which we would not expect to be wedded to the basic economic and political ideas of Alexander Hamilton. Despite the fact that Jefferson was the spiritual godfather of the Democratic Party, his agrarian interests were so similar to those of the Insurgents,

16

that it is not surprising to find one wing of the Republican Party gaining inspiration from his beliefs.

Besides the Jeffersonian influence, other pre-Civil War agrarian movements helped to shape Insurgency. The debtors' rebellion led by Daniel Shays after the close of the Revolutionary War differed from the Insurgents' uprising in that it demanded inflation. Yet the two movements accurately reflected the seething unrest in their mortgage-burdened constituencies. Andrew Jackson's dramatic war on the Second Bank of the United States, coupled with his full-blooded belief in practical as well as philosophical democracy, had counterparts in the opposition which the Insurgents of the Taft era manifested toward an excess of absentee financial control by eastern interests, and in their advocacy of direct democracy.

The Civil War gave rise to a host of political and economic problems whose repercussions were felt in the Insurgency of half a century later. Out of the war came a united West to match the political regularity of the " Solid South," and not until agrarian unrest reached its acute stage did the West break loose from Republican moorings. The Union soldiers who took advantage of the liberal provisions of the Homestead Act of 1862 to migrate westward after Appomattox, carried with them the political slogan, " Vote the way you shot." As the veterans of the Grand Army of the Republic came to dominate middle western politics in the post-war years, they added a solid bloc of votes to the Republican column.

The G. A. R. hegemony had begun to fade by the turn of the century. Yet the influence of the veterans and their kin remained powerful enough in 1896 to keep Iowa, Minnesota, and Wisconsin within the Republican ranks even though the election of that year was the most clear-cut sectional conflict since the Civil War. The influence of the political consequences of the Civil War on the Insurgent movement is clear: within those states where the Republican Party was strongly intrenched, it became expedient for political leaders such as La Follette in Wisconsin, Dolliver in Iowa, and Murdock in Kansas to seek

outlets for their ideals through the medium of the Republican
Party, rather than through a moribund Democracy.

The economic consequences of the Civil War were even more
far-reaching. Most of the economic battles that the Insurgents
fought may be traced to problems which the Civil War set in
motion, or to maladjustments aggravated by the great conflict.
The war sealed the doom of the southern planter aristocracy,
thus eliminating from Congress a group that had upheld the
Jeffersonian point of view. Northern Representatives, largely
concerned with fostering the Hamiltonian ideals of expanded
industry and high finance, were given free rein. The customary
post-war aftermath of moral looseness in official circles, specula-
tion and a rampant spirit of exploitative individualism bolstered
the new industrialism.

The years between 1865 and 1900 saw the virtually untram-
meled growth of pools, monopolies, trusts and holding companies with nationwide ramifications. In their hungry quest for
self-sufficiency and profit, these economic giants began to lay
their hands on the natural resources of the country. At this
point they touched a sore spot with the agricultural communities. In an effort to alleviate some of the tremendous economic
maladjustments accentuated by the Civil War, the Insurgents
made trust-busting, conservation, and a fairer distribution of
wealth their principal aims.

Related in some of its phases to the problem of concentration
of control in industry was a whole series of evils which arose
from the rapid development of the railroad systems in the post-
war years. As the railroads, aided by large governmental sub-
sidies, marched across the continent, they proceeded to establish
political and economic control over the territory through which
they passed. They ruthlessly gained domination over municipal
and state governments through such simple devices as making
heavy campaign contributions; distributing free railroad passes
to legislators, judges, and other interested parties; packing
assessment boards; or even bribing officials outright. Free passes
distributed to newspaper editors and preachers helped to bring

dividends in a friendly press and pulpit. The advantages to the railroad owners were those of low taxes on railroad property and freedom from governmental regulation. The absence of control resulted in abuses, including exorbitantly high rates, based upon overcapitalized stock; railroad domination of warehouses; rebates to economically powerful shippers; and absurdly low rates at competitive points which were offset by extortionate rates at other points along the line. This caused the hue and cry against rate differentials between long and short hauls.

Railroad regulation, which began with the Granger movement of the seventies, resulted in some remedial state legislation. The Wabash case [1] forced the federal government to attempt some curbing of railroad abuses in the Interstate Commerce Act of 1887. In the first decade after its passage, the act was considerably weakened by the Supreme Court, which limited the rate-making power of the Interstate Commerce Commission, emasculated the clause prohibiting a greater charge for a short than a long haul, and upon numerous occasions reversed the rulings of the Commission.[2] What teeth there were in the Hepburn Act of 1906 may in large part be credited to men like Senators La Follette and Dolliver, who later became known as Insurgents.

Insurgency in 1910 was vitally concerned with railroad abuses. Albert B. Cummins and Robert M. La Follette entered the Senate fresh from a series of notable triumphs in Iowa and Wisconsin, where as governors they had smashed railroad control of politics within their states and had established effective boards of regulation and control. Joseph L. Bristow entered the Senate in 1909 fortified by decades of experience with the machinations of the Atchison, Topeka & Santa Fe Railroad in Kansas politics. A native of Salina in central Kansas,

1 Wabash R. R. v. Illinois, 118 U. S. 557, curtailing state power to regulate interstate railroad commerce.

2 E. g., Cincinnati, New Orleans & Texas Pacific Ry. v. Interstate Commerce Commission, 162 U. S. 184; Interstate Commerce Commission v. Alabama Midland Ry. Co., 168 U. S. 144.

he knew the sentiment of his section, which was bitterly opposed to the railroad's rate discriminations in favor of Kansas City. And to the House of Representatives came Miles Poindexter, who, as a resident of Spokane in eastern Washington, chafed under the rate discriminations of the Union Pacific Railroad in favor of the city of Seattle on the coast. Men of this type joined hands in 1910 to attack and amend in the interests of increased effectiveness the Mann-Elkins railroad bill, a measure originally recommended by the Taft administration.

The gradual depletion of frontier lands in the years following the Civil War created the conservation issue; the Ballinger controversy of 1909-1910 brought it to a head. There was no fundamental difference between the aims of Taft and Ballinger on the one hand, and Pinchot and Roosevelt on the other. The two sides disagreed merely on tempo and methods.[3] Yet the dispute afforded the Insurgents an opportunity to dramatize the conservation issue.

The heart of Insurgency lay in the difficulties experienced by the farming communities of the Middle West. Immediately after the Civil War, a westward trek resulted in the settlement of the extensive Great Plains region. With new areas constantly being brought under cultivation, the center of corn and wheat production moved westward from Iowa and Wisconsin. Increased cultivation made agriculture less profitable. New scientific methods of farming, including the employment of machinery, came into wide use.

With the expansion of acreage devoted to agricultural uses, the spinning of the railroad network, the application of scientific practices and the increasing mechanization of agriculture came new difficulties to confront the post-Civil War farmer.

---

3 Henry F. Pringle wisely comments: " The persons of the Pinchot-Ballinger drama were varied types, but they had certain traits in common. Each was certain that truth and justice lay on his side of the controversy. Each was somewhat impervious to facts which might cause him to alter his views." Henry F. Pringle, *The Life and Times of William Howard Taft*, Vol. I, p. 470.

More capital was needed, especially for machinery; and, particularly in the happy decade after 1865, farmers mortgaged their land to meet the demands for capital. This resulted in a seemingly permanent debt burden, and western debtors soon developed a deep hatred for eastern mortgages. The farmer's debt problem was aggravated by the appreciation of the dollar's purchasing power as the price level fell.

The unbounded optimism voiced by James J. Hill and his fellow empire-builders resulted in the encouragement of western settlement which in turn led to an overproduction of agricultural commodities and consequent falling prices. Another factor in the farmer's difficulties was the tariff-protected prices he had to pay for his machinery and equipment. Inadequate banking facilities increased the interest rates, thus aggravating even further the problem of the debtor farmer.

The railroad problem was, of course, closely intertwined with the whole farm problem, and was first approached in the Granger movement of the seventies. Until the rise of Insurgency, the course of the agrarian revolt in the post-Civil War years was measured by, and consequent to, the rise and fall of prices of agricultural commodities. Rising prices in the late seventies caused the collapse of the Granger movement. It was succeeded, however, by the Northwestern Alliance, the Populist Party and William Jennings Bryan, all of whom offered their solutions for agricultural distress in the decades following the disastrous drought of 1887.

The Northwestern Alliance had its main strength in Nebraska, Kansas, Iowa, Minnesota and the Dakotas—almost precisely the same area in which the Insurgents later found their power. If questioned today, most of the Insurgents of the Taft era would deny that their program had any close connection with Populism. But La Follette in his *Autobiography* justly acknowledges that he was influenced by the Populists; and a realistic observer states the case well in saying: " The Insurgents caught the Populists in swimming and stole all of

their clothing except the frayed underdrawers of free silver." [4]
And when Senator Bristow of Kansas was at the peak of his
power as an Insurgent, the widow of " Sockless Jerry " Simpson wrote to him: " I want to congratulate you on the stand
you have taken in this reform. I can see the work my Husband
stood for, steadily going to the front." [5]

It is true that the Populists were more radical in their demands than were the Insurgents; but broadly speaking, with the
exception of the currency, they were interested in the same
issues. Both groups clamored for railroad regulation, conservation, more equitable taxation, postal savings banks, more
direct democracy, and the rights of the individual against the
depredations of the " plutocracy." The Populists represented
the same interests in the Democratic Party that the Insurgents later represented in the Republican Party.

The climax of the post-Civil War agrarian discontent was
reached in the bitter election of 1896 which found Bryan, in
the words of Vachel Lindsay, " smashing Plymouth Rock with
his boulders from the West." Bryan's ideas, except those on
silver and the tariff, were later to be taken over by the Insurgents. The Insurgents were protectionists and did not subscribe
to the Democratic theory of a tariff for revenue only; but they
beat the tom-toms of rebellion against the 1909 attempt of
the Republican leaders to foist upon them a tariff allegedly
beneficial to eastern industries.

For its fundamental economic implications, the Bryan movement was more significant than the Insurgency of the Taft
period. The Insurgents were less concerned with basic issues
than were their predecessors, although their pronouncements on
the floor of Congress were every bit as solemn. This is clearly
shown by the circumstance that the financial community joined
hands to defeat Bryan while it regarded the Insurgents' activities with relative unconcern. In 1896, according to the indus-
trialists and financiers, the issue was whether the country

4 William Allen White, interview, September, 1938.
5 Mrs. Jerry Simpson to Joseph L. Bristow, October 3, 1910.

could be saved from the menace of Bryanism; and the Republican coffers were filled to overflowing to support Mark Hanna's campaign of " education." Although the issue at stake in the midterm elections of 1910 seemed a grave one to the politicians of the Republican Party, it would have taken several Mark Hannas to whip the monied interests into the state of genuine alarm for the safety of the country that they had shown in 1896.

In tracing the way in which the roots of Insurgency grew, we must not underestimate the importance of the work of the muckrakers. Books like Frank Norris' *The Octopus* and *The Pit* helped to stir up feeling against the railroads and the wheat speculators; Winston Churchill in *Coniston* and *Mr. Crewe's Career* set the pace for the Insurgent movement in New England. It was with the appearance of the competitive low-priced magazines, however, that muckraking reached its high point. *McClure's* carried Ida Tarbell's exposé of the Standard Oil Company, Lincoln Steffens' devastating articles on municipal corruption and the alliance between business and politics, and Ray Stannard Baker's series on "The Railroads On Trial." *Everybody's* published Thomas Lawson's " Frenzied Finance," Charles E. Russell's attack on the beef trust, and Judge Ben Lindsey's articles on criminal law and juvenile delinquency. The *Cosmopolitan* carried David Graham Phillips' somewhat lurid descriptions of " Treason in the Senate."

The muckrakers were denounced as muck-makers by Theodore Roosevelt; but by their dramatic and thorough exposure of abuses they quickened public opinion and tilled a fertile breeding ground for Insurgency.

It was the whirlwind enthusiasm of Theodore Roosevelt, however, that provided the real flint and steel for the Insurgent movement. Combining in equal proportions the attributes of St. Paul and St. Vitus, as Lord Morley so well put it, Roosevelt dramatized the issues of railroad regulation, trust-busting and conservation, all of which later formed a part of the Insurgent program. His legislative achievements were greatest in the field of conservation; his trust-busting was confined to some isolated attacks on specific combinations; his efforts at railroad regulation found expression in the Hepburn Act of 1906, which, however, failed to reach the La Follette goal of physical valuation of railroad properties as a basis for rates.

Thus Roosevelt's greatest contribution to Insurgency did not lie in his concrete legislative achievements. Rather, it was his moral crusade against evil, his raising of the ideals of the Populists, Bryan and the muckrakers to the level of respectability. " Could you act as my atty. (sic) in an application for an injunction to keep the President from taking the rest of my platform? " Bryan asked a Republican friend in 1906.[6]

Viewed in its historical setting, Insurgency was one aspect of the progressive movement that aroused America from the turn of the twentieth century down to the World War. Whereas the progressive movement enlisted social reformers, champions of the rights of labor, and scions of the business world advocating a greater sense of responsibility to the public, Insurgency confined itself to balancing the scales which had been weighted against agrarian interests. The battleground of the progressive movement was largely the city hall and the state capitol, while Insurgency launched its significant attacks in Washington. Likewise the geographical roots of Insurgency were for the most part in the wheat and corn-producing regions of the Middle West, whereas the progressive movement spread all over the country.

Yet it is conceivable that Insurgency might have enveloped or united with the program of the progressives in the East and the Far West, as indeed it did in 1912. For example, if Governor Hiram Johnson of California or Governor Robert Bass of New Hampshire had been in the national legislature during the Insurgent uprising, there is no doubt that they too would have battled against Cannon, the railroads, and corporate control of politics in general. In campaigning for the governor-

6 William Jennings Bryan to William E. Chandler, December 12, 1906.

ship of California, Johnson had denounced the pervasive control of the Southern Pacific Railroad in state politics, just as Insurgent Senator Bristow had campaigned in Kansas on an anti-railroad platform. As Governor of California, Johnson instituted a wide program of progressive reform, including the initiative, referendum and recall, direct election of Senators, extension of the power of the state railroad commission, conservation legislation, woman's suffrage, an eight-hour law for women, employers' liability, and a short ballot.

Bass rose to power in New Hampshire with the aid of the persistent agitation of ex-Senator William E. Chandler and novelist Winston Churchill. Like Johnson and the Insurgents, he gained office by campaigning against the domination of the railroads in politics; in this case it was the powerful Boston & Maine Railroad which Bass attacked. He succeeded in procuring for New Hampshire a direct primary law, anti-lobby legislation, and laws limiting the issuance of free passes by the railroads and strengthening the regulatory powers of the state railroad commission.

Was Insurgency in the West similar to the unrest in the East and Far West which resulted in the elevation of Bass and Johnson to the governorship? In the opinion of Governor Bass there was no essential difference between the two. He wrote to Senator Bristow of Kansas:

. . . the problem I have to face is fundamentally the same as that which you have met so successfully in Kansas although the methods which I shall be forced to adopt may be somewhat different in detail. Our people in New England are, as you say, more conservative but at the same time they are out of patience with political control by an organization which is subservient to the great monied interests of one sort or another. The practical problem is to define the issue clearly without running counter to the conservatism of which you speak . . . I feel strongly that we are all working to the same end, whether our field of activity lies in the west or in the east. Furthermore I feel very strongly that it is most unfortunate to have any sectional lines drawn in the contest, which is being waged to wrest the control of our Government from the great vested interests.[7]

It may be concluded that generally the eastern and far western progressives were striving for the same ends as were the Insurgents. Yet the program of the Insurgents was more restricted to agrarian difficulties and did not attempt to consider labor problems. Another difference lay in the temper of the people. Even within the group of Insurgent states, Senator Bristow discovered that the people of Indiana were far less militant in their Insurgency than were the more progressive voters of Wisconsin and Kansas.[8] But outside of the Middle West it was extremely difficult to stir up as much enthusiasm for progressivism, and the progressives who attempted to put across their program in other states had to tread lightly lest they be branded as dangerous radicals who were more interested in revolution than reform.

7 Robert P. Bass to Joseph L. Bristow, June 7, 1910.
8 Joseph L. Bristow to Mrs. Bella C. La Follette, October 10, 1910.

CHAPTER III

THE DECLINE AND FALL OF "UNCLE JOE" CANNON'S EMPIRE

1. The Rise of the Speaker's Power

WHEN Moisei Ostrogorski, the distinguished Russian political scientist, came to this country early in the twentieth century, he expressed to several Congressmen his amazement at the power which had been concentrated in the hands of the Speaker of the House of Representatives.[1] In no other country in the world, he declared, did a presiding officer of a legislative body use his prerogatives in such a partisan manner.

Long years of steady accretions of power underlay the position of the Speaker of the House. In the First Congress, he was authorized to appoint the committees of the House.[2] In the years that followed, as the power of both the Speaker and the committee on rules was growing, the committee became closely identified with the aims and purposes of the Speaker. In 1841 the committee on rules was given the right to report at all times; in the same year Speaker White ruled that a simple majority vote, rather than the two-thirds required in the years prior to 1841, was sufficient for the House to adopt reports of the committee. When the House felt that the parliamentary experience of Speaker Orr of South Carolina would strengthen the committee on rules, Orr was designated a member in 1858, thus cementing the growing alliance between the Speaker and the committee. Orr's appointment set a precedent, and every Speaker from Orr to Cannon was appointed to the committee on rules.

Little objection to the accumulating power of the Speaker was heard, however, until the rules instituted by Speaker Reed had been in operation several years. Irked by the obstructive

1 John M. Nelson, interview, February, 1939.

2 C. A. Atkinson, *The Committee on Rules and the Overthrow of Speaker Cannon*, p. 8.

tactics of his Democratic opponents, Speaker Reed jammed through two significant rulings in 1890. He refused to entertain a motion that he deemed to be dilatory, and included in a quorum count those members who were present but would not answer to their names.

The power of the committee on rules increased with the use of the special order, which was a report from that committee designating the specific time when legislation should be considered by the House and regulating the extent of debate and the number of amendments permissible. Working with the committee on rules, the Speaker could check the type of legislation to be considered, and guide its course through the House.

Gradually, as the membership grew and the pressure of business increased, the Speaker assumed more and more discretion as to whom he should recognize from the floor.[3] Thus on the eve of the Insurgent revolt, the Speaker's hand was tightly on the throttle.

2. Opposition to the Rules Prior to Speaker Cannon

Before the advent of Speaker Cannon, objections to the dominating power of the speakership had arisen in a series of outbursts which steadily increased in volume, but it was not until 1893 that any serious Republican criticism was made. In that year, Colonel William P. Hepburn of Iowa fired the first shot of a long denunciatory fusilade against the rules which did not cease until he left the House in 1909.[4] In 1896, Hepburn offered an amendment to Rule XIV, directing the Speaker to recognize the first person rising. Hepburn dropped the proposal when a Populist eagerly came to his support.[5]

Continuing his criticism in the next Congress, Hepburn spoke for seven minutes in the committee of the whole, but was ridiculed by Sereno Payne. Sarcasm was the most potent wea-

3 Chang-Wei Chiu, *The Speaker of the House of Representatives since 1896*, pp. 197-201.

4 *Congressional Record*, 53 : 1 : 1147.

5 *Ibid.*, 54 : 1 : 578.

pon that the regular Republicans possessed in fending off attacks on the rules, and they used the weapon with telling effect.[6]

Undiscouraged, Hepburn continued to inveigh on the floor against the excessive power of the Speaker, and in the Republican caucuses his protests were even more vehement. But the Iowa Representative was such a stickler for party regularity that he "yielded with that implicit obedience that I hope I shall always be able to yield"[7] whenever the question came to a vote.

The first full-throated cry against iron-bound rules burst upon an amazed House on April 17, 1902. Francis Cushman of Washington, a tall, angular and ungainly individual with windmill arms and a stingingly satirical tongue, rose to deliver a diatribe which made even the later Insurgent onslaughts seem tame.[8] Representative Cushman's outburst came on the heels of efforts made by the House organization to jam through a reciprocity treaty that was inimical to the American beet sugar interests. He quickly shifted his attack upon arbitrary procedure in general to the rules of the House in particular.

"The Calendar! That is a misnomer," exclaimed Cushman. "It ought to be called a cemetery. (Laughter) For therein lie the whitening bones of legislative hopes."[9]

Cushman promised to deliver a future speech on the subject that "will be so hot that it will have to be printed on asbestos paper and tied to a hand grenade for distribution," but he never carried out his threat. Although one of Cushman's Insurgent colleagues used his biting criticisms as campaign material seven years later, the Washington Representative disowned his earlier remarks.[10]

6 *Congressional Record*, 55:3:1953-4.   7 *Ibid.*, 56:1:7.

8 Victor Murdock, however, concludes that "history will give contributions like that of Cushman heavy accent. But Cushman was very much clowning." Victor Murdock to Kenneth W. Hechler, October 6, 1939.

9 *Congressional Record*, 57:1:4320.

10 Miles Poindexter, interview, November, 1938.

Cushman's speech, nevertheless, made a decided hit even with the Republicans, who flocked around and congratulated him afterward. The next morning a tribute to this pioneer Insurgent appeared in the *Philadelphia Press*. This progressive paper published a full-length picture and a three-column headline honoring the first man who dared the anger of the regular leaders by denouncing their most effective tool for passing party legislation.[11]

3. The Advent of Speaker Cannon

When Joseph G. Cannon took office after the sudden retirement of Speaker Henderson in 1903, he molded the rules of the House of Representatives so that it became easier for the majority party to push its legislative program through the House. In addition, he used the office of Speaker in such a fashion as to give its holder the greatest amount of power ever possessed by an American legislator.

The quiet which generally characterized Cannon's first two terms as presiding officer was due in large part to the personality of the new Speaker. Unlike the cold-blooded Reed or the colorless Henderson, his immediate predecessors in the chair, Cannon achieved an extraordinary amount of purely personal popularity among his colleagues, Republicans and Democrats alike. " Reed was a great man," said Cannon early in his term, " but he didn't keep close enough to the boys." [12] Accordingly, " Uncle Joe " nursed along the members of Congress as carefully as a precinct boss would take care of the voters in his district, and employed strikingly similar methods.

The new Speaker burnished the same tools that other occupants of the chair had used in building up the power of the speakership over 125 years. He summarily removed several recalcitrant members from committee chairmanships and drew the reins of leadership closer to himself by packing the

11 *Philadelphia Press*, April 18, 1902.

12 " Speaker Cannon: A Character Sketch," *Review of Reviews*, December, 1903, pp. 673-676.

key committees with his loyal supporters. With increasing frequency he politely ignored members rising for recognition on the floor,—men who had not previously come to the Speaker's office and confided their plans to him in advance. He developed his strategic post as chairman of the committee on rules to hasten action upon whatever legislation he chose, and to choke off troublesome amendments or lengthy debate. It was not so much that Cannon forced legislation through the protesting House as that he dried up the stream at its source and blocked those bills to which he and his party associates were opposed.

It was " Uncle Joe " Cannon's economic and social philosophy that first aroused the western Congressmen against his autocracy. The question of power in itself did not greatly excite the average Congressman; but power exercised for reactionary economic and social ends seemed downright pernicious. It was no coincidence that the largest number of Insurgents hailed from Wisconsin, a state which Robert M. La Follette had wrested from railroad and corporation control at the turn of the century. Anxious to extend the reform movement from Wisconsin to the national legislature, these Representatives chafed the most under the yoke of Cannonism.

Cannon did not have the brilliant magnetism of Speaker Blaine that caused men to serve him blindly, nor the sound intellect of Speaker Reed that led men to admire and respect him. Men loved Cannon because he was one of them, but when crises arose they found that the ties of love were lighter than the ties of magnetism and respect.

Another weakness of Cannon's was his refusal to acknowledge the rising tide of unrest in the Mississippi Valley. At the height of rebellion, a communiqué from headquarters read: " The Speaker stands pat on his declaration that ' this country is a hell of a success'." [13] This was his reiterated answer to all who were agitating for progressive legislation.

His unflinching adherence to the *status quo* of party regularity was the ultimate cause of Cannon's downfall. He was

13 *New York World*, May 8, 1909.

an able politician, adept at the art of give and take, yet he had a supreme contempt for those who stood for other principles at the expense of strict party regularity.[14] When the first crisis over his power arose in 1909, Cannon yielded to the earnest entreaties of his friends, bowed ever so slightly, and retained his power. But when the final test came in 1910, he ignored his advisers, refused to bend, and was broken.[15] Never did he sense the seriousness of the opposition, nor would he admit the sincerity of their aims.[16] He insisted upon driving the machine, even if he had to go over the cliff in it.

4. DEVELOPMENTS IN THE SIXTIETH CONGRESS, 1907-09

The fires of Insurgency smoldered throughout the Sixtieth Congress, which opened in December, 1907.

The first detailed attack upon the rules and their operation by a Republican Insurgent was made by John M. Nelson of Wisconsin on February 5, 1908. In contrast to the sporadic outbursts which had previously characterized the opposition to the growing power of the Speaker. Nelson's speech was coldly analytical and factual. He made a plea for the return of those rights, powers, and privileges of the individual member that had been surrendered to the Speaker, and noted in detail the sources of the Speaker's personal power, attacking the " sword of Damocles hanging over the head of every member who dares rebel against the established order."

The speech contained the first direct plea to Theodore Roosevelt for support of the Insurgents in their fight to reform the rules. Nelson expressed fear that Roosevelt's legislation would be chloroformed, and brought a burst of applause when he exclaimed: " President Roosevelt has been trying to cultivate oranges for many years in the frigid climate of the Committee of Rules, but what has he gotten but the proverbial lemons? "[17]

14 L. White Busbey, *Uncle Joe Cannon*, p. xviii.

15 James E. Watson, interview, December, 1938.

16 Joseph G. Cannon to James S. Sherman, Nov. 19, 1908; Cannon to George Perkins, March 22, 1910.

17 *Congressional Record*, 60: 1 : 1652.

Meanwhile the other Insurgents were gaining courage. Victor Murdock of Kansas demanded a larger committee on rules which would be appointed by the entire House, and which would hold public committee hearings.[18] George Norris of Nebraska quietly presented a resolution amending the rules. But the rules were so ingeniously devised that an infinite amount of study revealed no loopholes through which such a resolution could be brought to the floor.

5. Personalities Among the Rules Insurgents

Before proceeding to an intensive study of the events leading up to the curbing of Speaker Cannon's power, let us glance at a few of the outstanding personalities engaged in the fight against the Speaker.

A. GEORGE W. NORRIS

The entire legislative career of George W. Norris of Nebraska, both in the House from 1903 to 1913, and in the Senate since the latter date, has been characterized by independence. " I would rather be right than be regular "[19] has been one of his guiding principles. Whenever his ideals have clashed with partisan considerations, he has never hesitated as to which should have superiority.

Unlike that of many of the other Insurgents who scathingly attacked Cannon, Norris' fight for reform of the rules had not one drop of personal bitterness in it. Upon numerous occasions, Norris carefully drew a distinction between Cannon himself and the system which Cannon directed. In other words, he doggedly fought Cannonism, but did not utter any harsh words against Cannon.[20] He assiduously preserved this distinction throughout the fight for rules reform, and led the band of Insurgents who refused to back the Burleson resolution declaring the speakership vacant.[21]

18 *Ibid.*, 60 : 1 : 2837.
19 Alfred Lief, *Democracy's Norris*, p. 333.
20 George W. Norris, interview, December, 1938.
21 *Infra*, pp. 75-76.

Of all the defects in the rules and in their administration, Norris felt that the gravest was the power of the Speaker to appoint committees, thus enabling him to build up a personal machine. If this power were taken away, claimed Norris, the rules could be administered equitably, no matter who was Speaker.[22]

Norris, too, was greatly concerned over the economic aspects of the situation, and expressed to the President a fear that the House committees had been constituted so as to choke out railroad legislation, the control of industrial corporations, publicity in campaign expenditures, conservation, control of the issuance of injunctions and other progressive legislation.[23]

Historians have generally accredited Norris with the leadership of the entire Insurgent movement in the House of Representatives. The movement for rules reform was a unified protest which spread throughout the country, and Norris cannot accurately be termed the sole leader. But he was the man who sensed the presence of an Achilles heel in the hitherto impregnable armor of the regular Republicans, took advantage of the parliamentary opening with his carefully framed resolution, and led the Insurgent forces to victory in their final clash with the Cannon machine.

B. EDMOND H. MADISON

" He isn't spectacular like Vic, but he is level-headed, clear-cut, and has got the nerve to stand," wrote one of Edmond H. Madison's colleagues in comparing him with another Insurgent, Victor Murdock.[24] Madison of Kansas fought shoulder to shoulder with the Insurgents until his death in August, 1911. A judge before his election to Congress, he maintained his judicial poise in Washington and did not make his Insurgency nearly so obnoxious to the regulars as did many of the bolters.

22 George W. Norris, " The Secret of His Power," *La Follette's Magazine,* January 8, 1910.

23 George W. Norris to William Howard Taft, January 10, 1910.

24 Joseph L. Bristow to Fred C. Trigg, March 20, 1909.

It was Madison's middle-of-the-road course that endeared him so much to Theodore Roosevelt, who called him " one of the best Insurgents." [25] Even Taft, who usually regarded Insurgents as akin to anarchists, found qualities in Madison that commanded his admiration. When the party axe fell upon the other Insurgents, Madison's committee posts remained conspicuously undisturbed.

" Your course and Murdock's is very generally approved," a loyal constituent once told Senator Bristow, " but the Judge's (Madison's) insurging is not the kind that fills the bill. It is too homeopathic." [26] But Bristow, looking down benignly from his Insurgent perch in the upper house, thought differently:

Ed Madison is really the hero of the crowd . . . He could have gone along in a quiet way, made himself agreeable to the powerful machine leaders, and avoided any trouble. But he has preferred to take a decided stand for what he thinks is right, and as a matter of fact he is taking his life in his hands when he does it, and he realizes that. . . . He won't vote against Cannon, because he doesn't think it is the proper thing to do under the circumstances, but he doesn't feel that Cannon has a right to dictate to him how he is to vote in regard to the rules of the House.[27]

Although he represented the famous Seventh District in western Kansas which had sent " Sockless " Jerry Simpson to Washington in Populist days, Madison was the kind of man whom conservatives describe as having both feet on the ground. He lent to the Insurgent movement a touch of respectability which was, at times, sorely needed. He smoothed off the rough edges, and upon more than one occasion " poured gentle oil on the turbulent waters " of Murdock's rebellious attitude.[28] It hurt the regulars deeply to lose a man like Madison, since he seemed to possess all of the temperamental attributes of a born stand-

25 Theodore Roosevelt to Theodore Roosevelt, Jr., August 10, 1910.
26 Rod Elward to Joseph L. Bristow, December 13, 1909.
27 Joseph L. Bristow to Harold T. Chase, March 15, 1909.
28 Victor Murdock, interview, February 1939.

patter. But he stood fast with the Insurgents, and never could be diverted from his course.

Shortly before Madison's death President Taft called him to the White House and tried to win the Kansan over to the regulars. " He'll never sway me," Madison told George Norris, " and I'll stick with you forever . . . " In Norris' words, Madison " was always true blue." [29]

C. JOHN M. NELSON

Representative Burleson, the chief political bargain-maker of the Democrats during the rules fight, often described John M. Nelson of Wisconsin as the outstanding personality among the Republican Insurgents.[30] As secretary of the Insurgent organization, Nelson called meetings and arranged *modi vivendi* with Democrats on specific issues. In these roles he laid a vast amount of groundwork for the later success of the Insurgents.

A close admirer and supporter of Senator La Follette, Nelson held the same philosophy as La Follette, and he regarded the House rules as one of the biggest obstacles in the path of progressive legislation.[31] He revealed this attitude in his first speech on the rules in 1908, when he expressed solicitude for the treatment that Roosevelt's policies had received at the hands of the Speaker.

Nelson typified the group of Wisconsin and Minnesota Congressmen, augmented by a few scattering individuals from other localities, who were the left wing of the Insurgent group in Congress. If Speaker Cannon had deftly guided his steamroller in the interests of genuine progressive legislation, it is quite probable that Nelson and his ultra-liberal associates would have put their tongues in their cheeks and backed a despotism that was benevolent. It was not the means that the House machine employed, but rather the ends toward which the efforts

29 George W. Norris, interview, December 1938.
30 Victor Murdock, interview, February 1939.
31 John M. Nelson, interview, February 1939.

of the standpatters were directed that aroused Nelson's group
to Insurgency. This difference separated them from the class of
Insurgents who were more concerned with arbitrary power in
itself.

D. VICTOR MURDOCK

Victor Murdock of Kansas was the most spectacular and
dynamic of the Insurgents. The pungency of his comments,
coupled with his striking personal appearance, invariably made
him stand out from the crowd. As chairman of the publicity
committee of the Insurgent group, Murdock obtained for the
rebels a tremendous amount of space in the press. A newspaper
editor himself, he had the knack of sensing a good news story,
and he appreciated the great value of good publicity in building
up support for the movement in the home constituencies
of the Insurgents. Indeed, his skill in obtaining publicity was
so great that jealousy among his colleagues frequently caused
him to be shunted into the background for expediency's sake.

Murdock was a rugged individualist, and therein he differed
from many of his Insurgent colleagues who welcomed the trend
toward collectivism in government. Economically, he was fighting against concentration of wealth and power, and for this
reason he belongs with that group whose intellectual leader
was Senator La Follette. Politically, however, he was much
closer to Gussie Gardner and Hamilton Fish, those blue-blooded
easterners who opposed Cannon not because of his reactionary
economic philosophy, but because he thwarted the free expression of will on the part of the individual Congressman.

Murdock felt keenly that the system of legislative control in
the House of Represen atives was a denial of the true representative principle. Murdock has described his attitude as

... merely reflecting Jonathan Edwards' philosophy that nothing
should come between God and man, in maintaining that nothing
should come between the people and their representatives. We insurgents felt that Cannon and the rules committee interposed an

obstacle between the people and the free expression of their will through their representatives.[32]

His ideal was a Congress run along the lines of a town meeting, in which all Representatives could freely voice their opinions, with only a minimum of organizational control to prevent bedlam and chaos. Party ties have always weighed lightly on Murdock as on Norris and his independence of thought made it inevitable that he should ally himself with the Insurgents.

In one important respect, however, Murdock differed from Norris. He was equally hostile to Speaker Cannon personally and to the system of Cannonism. When Norris led his band of Insurgents back into the regular fold on the Burleson resolution deposing Cannon, Murdock with a war whoop led his eight last-ditch colleagues in a futile fight to remove Cannon from the chair. Murdock said thirty years after the battle:

> There was never anything the matter with the rules themselves; it was the way in which they were administered. Put in the speakership a man with progressive principles and your difficulties would have been immediately solved.[33]

E. MILES POINDEXTER

Miles Poindexter of Washington added a great deal of moral strength to the Insurgent movement when he entered the House in 1909. Poindexter did not push to the forefront of the battle immediately, but his cool logic served the Insurgent cause well during the final pitched conflict in 1910.

Poindexter opposed with equal vigor the autocracy of Cannon and the Speaker's hookup with favored economic interests. Shortly after the fight started he wrote:

> In my judgment, it is an anomalous and unconstitutional situation for the presiding officer, who is supposed to be an impartial arbiter of parliamentary proceedings, to be at the same time the leader of the majority party with the distribution of all the patron-

32 Victor Murdock, interview, February 1939.
33 Victor Murdock, interview, February, 1939.

age of the House, including a vast number of committeeships at his disposal.[34]

His interest in the re-establishment of representative government, however, was not nearly so strong as his steady opposition to the alignment of one branch of the party with the forces of special privilege. Five weeks before Cannon went down to defeat Poindexter wrote:

No man who ever preceded the present Speaker of the House ever put that great office upon the low and contemptible basis of a mere personal and business agency. You will find that without exception those leaders of the reactionary wing of the Republican Party are corporation and special interest men.[35]

Poindexter's opposition to Cannon was aroused by the disinclination of the Speaker to foster the Roosevelt conservation policies,[36] as well as by Cannon's lack of sympathy " with the dominant and progressive elements of the Republican Party, and with the great spirit of reform which is pervading the entire country." [37]

Thus Poindexter's Insurgency differed from Murdock's in this respect: whereas Murdock recognized the economic factors extant in Cannonism, he was concerned mainly with the political ideal of the preservation of a truly representative form of government; although Poindexter took cognizance of the threat which Cannonism bore for representative government, he was interested primarily in divorcing the control of the privileged segments of society from the engines of government.

When asked today whether, in retrospect, his Insurgency was directed against the political autocracy of Cannon, Poindexter replies:

34 Miles Poindexter to L. A. Vincent, March 17, 1909.
35 Miles Poindexter to J. N. Maybury, February 9, 1910.
36 Miles Poindexter to William Howard Taft, November 10, 1908.
37 Miles Poindexter to Norman Hapgood, November 17, 1908.

On the surface this was a political battle, the various stages of which seemed purely political at the time. But back of it all were fundamental economic considerations, like adequate conservation of natural resources, and the proper enforcement of the anti-trust laws. Ultimately, Insurgency had an economic basis.[38]

F. CHARLES A. LINDBERGH

Rather silent and self-contained personally, Charles A. Lindbergh of Minnesota was nevertheless one of the most advanced of the Insurgents in his economic thinking. To him the fight against Cannon seemed to mean the opening of the dam that the House organization had erected against progressive legislation. Early in the conflict he wrote:

The rules are being used to the advantage of a certain few. The strongly centralized capitalistic interests of the country desire a centralized power in Congress such as the present rules permit of, because that central power can be reached with less difficulty than the House membership. It is in the interest of trusts and monopolies to keep politicians so organized as to make it possible to create a dominant central power and build up a mutuality of interests with it; for, to achieve their ends and prevent legislation for the people, all that is necessary is to reach those in control.[39]

Lindbergh believed in party government and appreciated its necessary rôle in the organized presentation of individual ideas; yet like most of the Insurgents he never allowed a matter of deep conviction to yield to the claims of party regularity. He had no inherent distaste for the caucus as a means of securing a cohesive expression of party opinion. But he objected strenuously when the caucus was reduced to an *ex post facto* ratification of prior decisions of the party leaders, especially when those decisions were designed to benefit interests outside of Congress.

One of the nine radical Insurgents who voted to depose Cannon, Lindbergh nevertheless harbored no malice against

38 Miles Poindexter, interview, November, 1938.
39 C. A. Lindbergh to *Little Falls Daily Transcript*, March 10, 1909.

the Speaker personally. " Even those who opposed Cannonism could not refrain from admiring the grand old fighter," said Lindbergh scarcely two weeks after the bitter battle of 1910; but ". . . . as Cannon is for machine rule, I did not allow my feelings of admiration for his great fight to give approval to Cannonism." [40]

Temperamentally, Lindbergh was very much like Senator Borah in his absolute independence of outside influences. He never could have assumed the leadership of the Insurgent group in the House, because he did not know the meaning of the word compromise. He would never have been able to assimilate the vast number of clashing ideas and plans which arose from the individual Insurgents, and to map out a unified course of action; he could not have indulged in any give and take with the Democrats, yielding here and making a concession there in the interests of the ultimate goal. There was too much " principle " in Lindbergh's blood for him to play the game of petty politics. Consequently, whenever Victor Murdock started making calls to line up Insurgent votes, he always passed by Lindbergh's office without a knock, for he knew where Lindbergh would stand on any issue that arose.[41]

As John M. Nelson puts it, "When Lindbergh stood with you, he was with you until Hell froze over." [42]

G. CHARLES N. FOWLER

Smooth, erect, sharp-featured and eloquent, Charles Fowler of New Jersey appeared almost too dignified to be an Insurgent, and indeed he can hardly be classified with any other members of that group. Against Fowler more than any other Insurgent Congressman, the charge that personal pique motivated his rebellion seems justified.

In the spring of 1908, the high Republican moguls were considering the passage of emergency currency legislation to

---

40 C. A. Lindbergh to *Little Falls Herald*, April 1, 1910.
41 Victor Murdock, interview, February, 1939.
42 John M. Nelson, interview, February, 1939.

relieve the tension caused by the panic of 1907. At this time Fowler, as chairman of the House committee on banking and currency, was strenuously advocating issuance of 250 millions of credit currency to strengthen the bank reserves. Speaker Cannon shied away from Fowler's scheme, and an entirely different piece of legislation was introduced in the Republican caucus, where it was passed upon two different occasions. Fowler still refused to report the party bill from the committee on banking and currency. Thereupon, the House leaders arranged to have Representative Vreeland of New York introduce a companion bill to one that Senator Aldrich was sponsoring in the upper house. To top it off, Fowler was shorn of the chairmanship of his committee.

Quite apart from the validity of Fowler's subsequent observations on the rules, or the justification for his displeasure, it is clear that his Insurgency dated from his rebuff. On all other issues, Fowler remained a typical conservative Republican.

6. Insurgency Crystallizes

What caused Insurgency, heretofore confined to isolated attacks, suddenly to take form in the Sixty-first Congress and break forth in an angry rebellion? For one thing, during the spring and summer of 1908 newspapers and magazines stirred public opinion against Speaker Cannon's treatment of the Appalachian-White Mountain Forest Reserve Bill. This conservation measure had been passed by the Senate, only to be entombed by Cannon in the committee on judiciary, over the protest of a majority of the House.

The Republican presidential nominee, Taft, began to feel that Cannon and his rules placed the party in a rather anomalous position inasmuch as the platform was progressive.[43] Then too, Theodore Roosevelt was uneasy as the House became more refractory.[44] Moreover a third great G. O. P. leader, Senator La Follette, let the members of the Wisconsin delegation in the

43 William Howard Taft to W. R. Nelson, August 25, 1908.
44 Theodore Roosevelt to James S. Sherman, September 9, 1908.

House know that he considered rules reform and the overthrow of Cannon as one of the most pressing problems that faced the country.[45]

As the elections of 1908 approached, sentiment against the Speaker grew even stronger. Taft sensed the opposition to Cannon which was stirring in the west and, believing that it would be politically inexpedient for " Uncle Joe " to cross the Mississippi, prevented Cannon from campaigning in Kansas.[46]

The country was in a ferment. James A. Tawney in Minnesota had a bitter primary election fight to retain his nomination, a fight waged largely on the issue of Cannonism.[47] Clarence B. Miller triumphed over J. Adam Bede in another Minnesota primary contest, winning by professing opposition to Cannon. Over in Wisconsin, Irvine Lenroot, fresh from a period of distinguished service in the speakership of the La Follette-controlled Wisconsin legislature, defeated Representative John J. Jenkins in a primary campaign waged on the Cannon issue. Insurgents Boyd, Hinshaw, Norris, and Kinkaid announced during the Nebraska campaign that they would not vote for Cannonism, and in a strong Democratic year with Bryan leading the ticket, all survived except Boyd.[48] Poindexter swept Washington in a campaign during which he and the Democrats both denounced Cannonism, and similar triumphs were registered by Murdock and Madison in Kansas. A new crop of young Iowa Insurgents rode into office on the political coat-tails of Senator Albert Cummins. Only four losses occurred in the House among those who were generally inimical to Cannon's rule.

The results of the election heartened the Insurgents and stirred some action in the lame-duck session of Congress which met in December of 1908. Meanwhile, however, the regulars

45 John M. Nelson, interview, February, 1939.

46 William Howard Taft to Charles F. Brooker, September 12, 1908.

47 T. E. Knatvold to Lewis Knutson, September 8, 1908 (James A. Tawney papers).

48 *Nebraska State Journal*, November 26, 1908.

moved to close their ranks and prepare for the impending struggle. They were optimistic over the huge majority that Cannon's own Danville district gave him,[49] and regarded this as a counter-balance for the adverse primary vote in the Northwest. In mid-November, Speaker Cannon was confident that if Roosevelt and Taft were favorable or even kept hands off, there would not be much of a struggle.[50]

With expert finesse, James S. Sherman and James A. Tawney moved to win over Theodore Roosevelt and President-elect Taft. Roosevelt soon became convinced of the impossibility of defeating Cannon, and advised Taft of the danger of making the attempt.[51] Early in December Taft decided to abandon his efforts to defeat Cannon, and assumed an attitude of benevolent neutrality toward the Speaker.[52]

After the 1908 election, the opponents of Cannon presented a sorry spectacle of disunity and cross purposes. Fowler of New Jersey was busily writing his friends in an effort to gain the speakership for himself. Madison of Kansas threw his influence behind Townsend of Michigan to supplant Cannon. Hinshaw and Poindexter started a boom for Burton of Ohio, and when they broke the news to Taft the President-elect must have winced slightly, for Burton was already engaged in a strenuous campaign for the senatorship against Taft's brother. Anybody seemed to suit Steenerson, of Minnesota, while the Iowa Insurgents lay low and announced they would support Walter Smith as a stalking horse against Cannon, at least until the smoky haze cleared.[53]

Not only were the Insurgents disorganized as to the man whom they would favor to replace Cannon, but they entertained a large variety of plans as to how the reformation of the rules

49 James S. Sherman to James E. Watson, November 9, 1908.

50 Joseph G. Cannon to James S. Sherman, November 19, 1908.

51 Theodore Roosevelt to William Howard Taft, November 10, 1908.

52 William Howard Taft to Horace Taft, June 27, 1909; Mischler Diary, p. 4016.

53 Arthur Vorys to William Howard Taft, November 16, 1908.

should be accomplished. Hepburn suggested that the Speaker be given power to appoint only one-third of the personnel of committees.[54] Other Insurgents wanted the Speaker to name at least three-fifths; and Norris proposed that the Speaker be given no appointive power whatever. To other members, the power of recognition seemed the secret of the Speaker's dictatorship. Some of them favored lessening his control by scheduling one day a week for a regular call of committees that wished to bring up legislation. Others felt that a rule to discharge bills from committees would release the key log in the legislative jam. Still others believed that if the Speaker were removed from the committee on rules the dictatorship would be ended. Political strategy should have dictated a firm cohesion as the prime necessity of the Insurgents, but they failed to come to any agreement and thus lost much of their bargaining power.

From the beginning of the rules fight down to 1910, the Insurgents continued to be puzzled as to what tactics they should pursue. They had but one opportunity at the beginning of each session to bring the question before the House. If they were defeated then, it meant two years of barren fencing with the regulars. For an ordinary resolution amending the rules was naturally referred to the committee on rules, where it had as much chance of being reported as a rule directing Speaker Cannon to abandon his cigar. " Ah, it is easy to get into the Committee on Rules," mused Hepburn, " but by what hoist and by what petard would we get out of the Committee on Rules? " [55]

Soon the Insurgents came to realize that excessive individualism was going to lead to the failure of their cause. Accordingly, meetings were held to draw up a common plan of action. By the middle of January the many proposals that had been offered for amending the rules were boiled down to two ob-

---

54 *New York Tribune*, December 4, 1908.
55 *Congressional Record*, 60 : 2 : 2655.

jectives: the election of committees by the House, and the establishment of a calendar day for a call of committees.[56] As a further piece of strategy, a determined campaign was launched to woo the new Congressmen taking office after March 4.[57]

On the floor, the most masterful criticism of the rules was made by 76-year-old Colonel Hepburn of Iowa.[58] Hepburn had been objecting off and on for sixteen years to the growing power of the speakership,[59] but his innate conservatism held him in check. In February, 1909, however, he was a defeated lame duck and could give free vent to his feelings, even to the extent of praising the Democratic national platform of 1908. Hepburn vigorously criticized the one-man rule of the Speaker over legislation and he observed that all constituencies but the Danville, Illinois, district were disenfranchised. Hepburn's speech, coming as it did from a man who had established a high reputation within the party, carried great weight with the other members of the House.

Soon after they organized the Insurgents suspected that there were some fellow travelers in their ranks.[60] A showdown came in February. Twenty-nine of the rules reformers joined in signing a resolution which called for (1) the abolition of the Speaker's power to appoint committees, (2) the institution of a committee of nine of the majority and six of the minority party chosen by members of the House and divided into fifteen geographical groups which was to act as the committee on rules and also to select the standing committees of the House, (3) the establishment of a " Calendar Tuesday " on which day the committees would be called in alphabetical order for the presentation of legislation. This plan, the brainchild of Norris, was somewhat like the proposal that he had introduced quietly

56 *Wichita Eagle*, January 19, 1909.

57 Victor Murdock, Everis A. Hayes, George Pearre to Miles Poindexter, February 9, 1909.

58 *Congressional Record*, 60: 2: 2653.

59 *Supra*, pp. 28-29.

60 *New York Tribune*, January 7, 1909.

in the House a year before and was to introduce amid tumult
and uproar a year later.[61] The other Insurgents, unwilling to
touch the Speaker's power of committee appointment, seceded
and eight members signed a resolution providing for the establishment of Calendar Tuesday alone. Both of these resolutions
were introduced into the House.[62]

Three days before the end of the Sixtieth Congress, the
regulars sprang a surprise counter-attack in an effort to widen
the breach between the mild Insurgents and the radical Insurgents. Dalzell suddenly rose to move passage of a resolution
that bore striking resemblance to the one advocated by the
eight luke-warm Insurgents.[63] Indeed, the only differences between the earlier resolution and the new proposal were that
Dalzell would make the calendar day for the call of bills from
committees Wednesday instead of Tuesday, and allow Calendar
Wednesday to be set aside by a majority instead of by a two-
thirds vote.

No evidence has yet been uncovered to determine who
actually induced Speaker Cannon to negotiate this compromise.
Keen politicians who sensed that rebellion was in the air at
the time believed that if Speaker Cannon had yielded a little
more at other periods of the uprising, the Insurgents might
have been quelled completely.[64] Cannon himself found the new
reform much to his liking, as he claimed it abandoned the
" pretense " of having to deal with a constant stream of seekers
after recognition.[65] The Calendar Wednesday proposal of
March 1, 1909 by no means served as an adequate sop to the
dissident Republicans. But it did force the fuzzier rules reformers from the periphery of the progressive group and line

61 *Nebraska State Journal*, February 11, 1909.

62 *New York Tribune*, February 10, 1909; *Congressional Record*, 60: 2: 2116.

63 *Congressional Record*, 60: 2: 3567.

64 Shelby Cullom, *Fifty Years of Public Service*, p. 449; James E. Watson,
interview, December, 1938.

65 Joseph G. Cannon, " The Power of the Speaker," *Century Magazine*,
June, 1909.

them up definitely with the regulars, thus solidifying the shattered remainder of the Insurgent ranks.

Time during the debate on the Dalzell compromise was distributed as follows:

For		Against	
Dalzell	2 minutes	Williams	3 minutes
Scott	5 minutes	Hepburn	5 minutes
Olmsted	1 minute	De Armond	4 minutes
Payne	2 minutes	Norris	2 minutes
Campbell	2 minutes	Gardner	2 minutes
Townsend	8 minutes	Murdock	2 minutes
		Clark	2 minutes

The table above shows what an important part the Insurgents played in the tensely-fought struggle. Dalzell apportioned fifteen of the twenty minutes at his disposal to those men who had bolted the Insurgent group and had reentered the regular group: Scott, Townsend and Campbell. And Democratic leader Williams, realizing the value of Republican criticism of Republican rules, apportioned eleven of his twenty minutes to Hepburn, Norris, Gardner, and Murdock.

Norris and Murdock were particularly biting in their denunciation of the compromise. Norris branded the resolution as "the most comical parliamentary joke that has ever come down the legislative pike. In its application it is a homeopathic dose of nothingness. Are we men or is this a kindergarten?" [66] Murdock drew guffaws by his assertion that " this is a Trojan Horse . . . and sticking out of the paunch of that horse I think I see several notable cold feet." [67]

On the final roll-call, the regulars squeezed their measure through by a meager five-vote majority, 168-163.[68] Twenty-six of the twenty-nine radical Insurgents who had signed the Norris resolution stood by a solid Democracy. All eight of the signers of the Calendar Tuesday petition were won over to the

66 *Congressional Record*, 60: 2: 3570.
67 *Ibid.*
68 *Ibid.*, 60: 2: 3572.

regular side. Had the radical Insurgents been able to hold them, the regulars would have been overturned.

Meeting in Hepburn's committee room immediately after the vote, the Insurgents agreed that Cannon's was a Pyrrhic victory, and that his five-vote majority was too slim to be safe against the onslaughts of the Insurgents and Democrats when the new Congress opened on March 4.

The Insurgents had good reason to feel confident, and Cannon yearned for his erstwhile whip of the House, Jim Watson, who had left Washington to conduct a losing campaign for the Indiana governorship in 1908. Worried, Cannon dispatched a telegram to Rushville, Indiana, imploring Watson to return and supervise his impending fight for the speakership, which would take place when the new House organized in the special session after March 4. Watson's aptitude for political intrigue was keen, and he sympathetically appreciated the personal feelings of men and the motives which move them. He immediately hurried eastward bearing the hopes of the regulars in what was to be one of the bitterest battles of American legislative history.

7. A Gloved Hand Pours Oil on Troubled Waters

The story of how Speaker Cannon retained his power in 1909 has never been told in its entirety, and not all of its details probably will ever be completely available, so closely did its ramifications touch the personal interests of many individuals. The story contains all the raw material for a first-class politico-economic novel. There was the huge corporation straining for a higher protective tariff on oil; the Tammany chieftain who had promised the corporation help—in response for what *quid pro quo* we know not; the glove manufacturer who knew the path both to the throne of the House of Representatives and also to Tammany Hall; the meat-packers, the railroads, utilities and sugar interests, whose activities cut across party lines; the Speaker of the House who shivered for the maintenance of his scepter while the minority leader openly wept to see his own men embroiled in the conspiracy. The charges of the Insurgents and the regular Democrats were met by arrogant counter-charges by the regular Republicans and the bolting Democrats. The full details are not available, but a few fairly definite patterns emerge.

Numerically the Insurgents were in a stronger position as they looked forward to the special session of Congress in March, 1909. In the new crop of Congressmen came nine who immediately took their stand against the regular organization. In addition, two hitherto regular Wisconsin Representatives went over to the other side, thus boosting the Insurgent strength to thirty. When the Sixty-first Congress opened, the Republicans had 219 and the Democrats had 172 members. If the Insurgents could induce 24 of their potential adherents to unite with a solid Democratic vote, this combination could force a revision of the rules.

Confidently, the Insurgents moved to line up the White House behind their cause. Several days before Roosevelt went out of office, Nelson, Gardner, and Madison called upon him to seek his support.

Roosevelt greeted the trio with his choicest toothy grin, venturing, " Well, what can we anarchists do now? "[69] The outgoing President took a keen interest in the details of the Insurgents' proposals, cautioning that the committee on ways and means should be preserved intact so as not to interfere with the prompt passage of the impending tariff bill.

" I'm for you," he proclaimed, " but I don't see just how I can help. At present I'm like the Bedford mate on the steamer; what is expected of me is silence and damn little of that . . . I don't know how Taft is going to stand on this . . . I'll write you a letter which you can't publish, but which you can read to your friends, and it will show where I stand." [70]

On the day before he left office, Roosevelt sent word that Gardner and Nelson must come to the Capitol at once to see

69 John M. Nelson, interview, February, 1939.
70 *Ibid.*

him. There the Wisconsin Insurgent and Lodge's son-in-law found the President busily signing bills, with President-elect Taft talking to friends in another corner of the room. Roosevelt then said that he could not write the letter that he had promised, but upon a plea by the Insurgents he agreed to intercede with Taft for them. Taking the two by the hands, he led them over to where Taft was sitting. Probably the retiring President did no more than introduce them to Taft, for when Madison related the story to Taft two years later, the latter denied that Roosevelt had ever actually interceded in behalf of the Insurgents.[71] If Roosevelt did speak a word of encouragement for the rebels, we may assume that its import was lost on Taft in the steady buzz of conversation and hurried rush of outgoing officeholders calling to pay their respects.

Taft took Nelson aside to the window, and tried to smooth things over in his genial manner, protesting that such a fight as the Insurgents planned would split the party.[72] The brief conference ended abruptly.

Cannon was not greatly worried about not being re-elected, because he knew that the Norris wing of the Insurgents was opposed to making a fight upon him personally. But the prospect of being reduced to impotence in a post where he had once been a czar led Cannon to search for ways and means to stem the rising tide. He warned President Taft that the rules rumpus would destroy the machinery for passing the tariff bill.

Frank P. Woods, a surviving member of the Insurgent Republican delegation from Iowa, relates that the opponents of Cannon came close to winning Taft over to their side:[73]

Before Congress convened I was invited by President Taft to meet at the White House at 10 o'clock in the evening to meet Vice President Sherman and Frank Hitchcock, the incoming Postmaster General. We were in this conference about two hours and

71 William Howard Taft to Mabel Boardman, April 15, 1912.
72 John M. Nelson, interview, February, 1939.
73 Frank P. Woods to Kenneth W. Hechler, September 9, 1939.

reached the final agreement that the President would see Mr. Cannon and have him agree to a conference over a few items in the rules for their adoption. If Mr. Cannon agreed to this, and the President seemed to think he would be able to get him to do so, the President's secretary was to phone me at once and I was to select from our group some one for the conference, but the next day rather early in the day Frank Hitchcock phoned me that instead of the President converting Mr. Cannon, Mr. Cannon had converted the President.

Taft then made his feelings undeniably clear to the undecided Republicans on the fence and the Insurgent strength started to slip. On March 10, Nelson, Gardner and Madison, the Insurgent board of strategy, called on the President to attempt to convince him that they planned no interference with tariff revision.[74] The Insurgents found Taft in a militant mood. He became angry and criticized the coalition that the Insurgents had made with the Democrats. He implied that Cannon was supporting him on the issue of tariff reform and that a fight over rules would destroy his pact with the Speaker. He raised his voice and denounced the Insurgents in a way that Archie Butt " thought would lead to a rupture,"[75] but then he broke down and tried to laugh off his anger gently. Madison reported that he never saw such a sudden transformation within a few moments.[76] The Insurgents left the White House puzzled, but convinced that Taft was using his influence against them. We must not forget however that it was political expediency rather than personal conviction that was shaping the President's course toward the Insurgents. Thus after a canter on the speedway with Bourke Cochran on the day following his tiff with the Insurgents, Taft confided to Archie Butt : [77]

74 *Wichita Eagle*, March 10, 1909.

75 Archie Butt, *Taft and Roosevelt: The Intimate Letters of Archie Butt*, Vol. I, p. 6.

76 Victor Murdock, interview, September, 1938.

77 Butt, *op. cit.*, Vol. I, p. 10.

If I told them how much sympathy I have for them in their fight against Cannon, they might have reason to feel encouraged.

By March 12, three days before the opening of the final struggle on Cannon in the special session, Secretary of the Navy Meyer noted in his diary that the question of the speakership and what the Insurgent-Democratic coalition would be able to accomplish was discussed at a cabinet meeting. " It is very close," he recorded,[78] " but the Administration having taken a hand, Cannon will be re-elected."

On the same day that the cabinet was ratifying Taft's policy, the President assumed the new role of compromiser.[79] Senator Cummins, who had the Iowa delegation fairly well under his thumb, was anxious to have the rules fight postponed until the opening of the regular session in December of 1909, in order that the more vital problem of tariff revision might be attacked comprehensively. Taft, Cummins and the Iowa Representatives very nearly arrived at a compromise which would have averted the bitter fight of March 15, with its resultant schism in the party. The President favored a committee on revision to look into the rules and make its report at the opening of the regular session in December. Taft's gesture failed completely because ". . . neither side would agree to the compromise I suggested . . ."[80] The Insurgents insisted that the proposed committee on revision should also act as the committee on rules for the special session,[81] while the regulars were uncompromising.

Despite Taft's position, it remained apparent that more than twenty-four of the Republicans would nevertheless bolt upon the question of revision of the rules. There was but one course for Cannon to follow and that was to attempt to win over some of the Democratic votes to support rules that would keep power in his own hands.

78 M. A. De Wolfe Howe, *George von Lengerke Meyer*, p. 427.
79 William Howard Taft to George W. Norris, January 11, 1910.
80 William Howard Taft to George W. Norris, January 11, 1910.
81 *Washington Times*, March 13, 1909.

On Saturday noon, March 13, Vice-President Sherman, an old crony of Cannon's when he had been in the House, conferred for an hour with Cannon and Taft, and that evening caught the ten o'clock train for New York. When he returned he brought with him ex-Representative Lucius N. Littauer, a wealthy glove manufacturer of Gloversville, New York, who had achieved considerable personal influence with House Republicans and New York City Democrats. When in the House, Littauer had sponsored a bill raising the salaries of Congressmen, which enhanced his popularity with them. According to an account that Congressman Murdock released a year later, the light burned in Cannon's office all Sunday night. Murdock, patiently spying from a nearby cubbyhole, saw Littauer and Cannon use the telephone frequently.[82]

Patrick McCarren, Democratic boss of Brooklyn, and a Standard Oil attorney in odd moments, entered the picture. It was obvious that the Standard Oil Company would not disapprove of a higher duty upon petroleum and petroleum products in the impending tariff bill, and no one appreciated this more than did Speaker Cannon himself. Cannon got in touch with the chief of Tammany Hall, and immediately the swift machinery of the Wigwam was set in motion. Fitzgerald, acknowledged leader of the Brooklyn and Tammany delegation in Congress, drew up a resolution changing the rules to provide greater freedom for the individual member, but like the Dalzell compromise of March 1, 1909,[83] the Fitzgerald proposals would not hamper the Speaker's control of the committee on rules, or his power to appoint the standing committees of the House. The measure was, however, a genuine improvement over the existing arrangement. It provided for a unanimous consent calendar which obviated the necessity of the daily trek to the Speaker's office on bills meeting with general approval; it strengthened the Calendar Wednesday rule by raising the requirement for setting it aside from a majority to a two-thirds

82 *Philadelphia Record*, July 20, 1910.
83 *Supra*, p. 47.

vote; and it permitted one recommittal motion after the previous question had been moved on any bill.[84]

On Sunday afternoon, the day before the vote on the speakership and adoption of the rules, William Sulzer, an independently minded Tammany Democratic Congressman, strode up to Representative Nelson, a Wisconsin Insurgent Republican. Sulzer was visibly agitated.

"There's going to be an awful fight tomorrow," said Sulzer breathlessly. "Murphy had me on the 'phone for a couple of hours today. The old man is really putting the pressure on me, and he's trying to make me vote with Cannon."[85]

"But how could Uncle Joe Cannon get ahold of Boss Murphy to put pressure upon *you?*" Nelson asked.

Sulzer replied:

Well, this Standard Oil magnate, H. H. Rogers, is a great friend of Murphy's, and Uncle Joe asked Rogers to see if he could get Murphy to bring the Tammany delegation over to support the House rules. Murphy is doing everything he can to bring me into line, and he has threatened me with political ruin if I didn't vote with Fitzgerald.[86] But I'm going to stand fast.[87]

In the morning of the Republican caucus, March 14, Watson and Littauer joined a last-minute conference with the Speaker and his leaders, at the Speaker's home on Vermont Avenue, and there the details of the alliance with Tammany were probably perfected.[88] There were thirty-two absentees from the full caucus of the Republican Party, twenty-one of whom were rules Insurgents.[89] The vote for Speaker in the caucus was as follows:

---

84 *Congressional Record*, 61 : 1 : 22.

85 Sulzer and Willett were the only members of the Tammany delegation who voted against Cannon on the question of fundamental rules revision.

86 Sulzer was later impeached while Governor of New York, largely through Tammany influence. But this cannot be the "political ruin" of which Sulzer spoke, inasmuch as Tammany secured his election to the governorship in the first place.

87 John M. Nelson, authorized interview, February, 1939.

88 *Ibid.*

89 *New York World*, March 14, 1909.

Cannon, Illinois 162
Smith, Iowa 10
Tawney, Minnesota 7
Kiefer, Ohio 7
Crumpacker, Indiana 1
Maguire, Oklahoma 1

The votes registered against Cannon cannot all be classified as Insurgent votes, inasmuch as all of the men supported for Speaker were allies of the Cannon machine. Walter Smith of Iowa alone drew Insurgent support, mostly from the delegation of Iowa Insurgents who decided to attend the caucus, and who had previously announced their support of Smith. The Insurgents attending the caucus refused to be bound by anything but the decision to support Cannon.

In the morning of the final showdown on the floor of the House, the Democrats held a caucus and passed overwhelmingly a resolution pledging the party to support reform rules sponsored by the Insurgents and the Democrats. At the caucus, Fitzgerald was silent on his own proposal. Queried on the floor as to why he had not brought up his proposal in the Democratic caucus, he lamely said " I had only three minutes to state my position on the rules," [90] and he declined to elaborate further.

It was a tense gathering of the House which assembled on March 15. Only five members were absent. On the vote for Speaker, Cannon was victorious by a comfortable margin.

The following votes were tabulated on the ballot for the Speaker:

Cannon 204
Clark 166
Scattered 12

The extreme Insurgents who refused to vote for Cannon distributed their votes as follows:

For Cooper (8) .... Cary, Davis, Hubbard, Lenroot, Morse, Murdock, Nelson, Poindexter
For Norris (2) .... Cooper, Hinshaw.
For Hepburn .... Lindbergh.
For Esch .... Kopp.[91]

90 *Congressional Record*, 61 : 1 : 33.   91 *Ibid.*, 61 : 1 : 18.

The group of Democrats with whom Cannon had made his deal voted solidly for Champ Clark as Speaker, but they drifted gradually to the Republican side as the votes on the rules began.

Dalzell's motion to readopt the old rules was defeated [92] and the door was left wide open for the amendment of the rules. Champ Clark promptly offered a resolution that would deprive the Speaker of the power to appoint committees and would set up an expanded committee on rules. The Clark resolution specifically named the members of the new committee on rules, to consist of six Democrats, five regular Republicans, and four Insurgent Republicans (Hayes, Nelson, Norris, and Gardner.) [93]

When Clark moved the previous question on the adoption of his resolution, the combine started to take form. Sixteen Democrats bolted their party, and the previous question on Clark's motion was defeated, 203-180.

Thus the stage was set for the presentation of the Fitzgerald resolution amending the rules, which has been described above.[94] A spirited debate followed, during the course of which Fitzgerald yielded ten minutes of his time to Dalzell, a significant fact. On the final vote on the Fitzgerald resolution, twenty-three Democrats voted with the regular Republicans.

Copious tears streamed down Clark's face as he came up to Nelson, the leading Insurgent negotiator, after the fiasco.

" You kept your word," said the minority leader with his voice shaking, " you gave me one more vote than you promised, but I lost twenty-three Democrats." [95]

Although these twenty-three Democratic bolters have been loosely termed " Tammany " or " Fitzgerald " Democrats, only eight of them actually came from New York. Some clues exist as to how the other fifteen were induced to bolt the Clark Democratic leadership, but the evidence is far from conclusive.

92 *Ibid.*, 61 : 1 : 21.

93 *Ibid.*, 61 : 1 : 22.

94 *Supra*, p. 54.

95 John M. Nelson, interview, February, 1939.

McDermott of Illinois, who resigned from Congress under fire in 1914, may have been reached through Representative Mann and the Chicago packing interests, according to several contemporary Congressmen. O'Connell, a Democratic Congressman from Massachusetts who voted with Cannon, was given a favorable decision by the committee on privileges and elections on his contested seat.[96] It was generally felt that Broussard and Estopinal of Louisiana had deserted the Democratic Party in exchange for sugar duties in the new tariff bill, while hopes of a tariff on lumber were held out to the group of Georgia Democrats.

Herbert Parsons of New York charged that still another element helped bring about the deal: the Tammany Democrats had been prevailed upon to support the Cannon rules, in return for an agreement upon the part of the Republicans in the New York legislature both to abstain from initiating a prosecution for election frauds and to hold up the passage of certain pieces of legislation considered inimical to Tammany. The Parsons charge was freely bandied about, yet there does not appear to be a scrap of evidence supporting it.

The aftermath of the Fitzgerald defection is interesting and significant in tracing the reasons for the bolt which defeated the Insurgents in 1909. Wrangling and bitterness immediately broke out in the Democratic caucus, where Fitzgerald and his group were bitterly denounced as traitors.[97] The Democrats agreed that none of their number should accept a committee assignment without the sanction of Clark.[98]

Fitzgerald was subsequently appointed by Cannon to membership in the committee on rules, while Broussard and Griggs

---

96 Henry Cabot Lodge to Theodore Roosevelt, July 20, 1910; *New York World*, March 8, 1909.

97 Although he was deeply incensed at the time, Clark harbored no permanent ill-will against Fitzgerald, and does not even mention in his memoirs the details of the Fitzgerald bolt, beyond a vague reference to "bad blood" engendered. Clark, *My Quarter Century of American Politics*, Vol. II, p. 271.

98 The conservative Democrats bolted the caucus on this vote, *Washington Times*, March 16, 1909.

received appointments to the ways and means committee without Clark's approval.

Among the Insurgents, it was generally believed, both in the House and Senate, that a deal had been made.[99] Miles Poindexter wrote:[100]

As to the means by which the Tammany Hall Pat McCarren support was obtained for the Cannon rules, Congressmen Fowler of New Jersey and Cooper of Wisconsin can give you particular information.

Appeal was made to him for support for Cannon by Littauer of Gloversville, N. Y., millionaire glove manufacturer . . . who was here on the ground exerting himself to save the power of the system. Men can be found who heard the conversation.

Even the regulars in both Houses spoke of the deal as if it were a fact.[101]

Subsequent developments during the consideration of the Payne-Aldrich tariff bill show how well Cannon kept his word to those interests that had won support for him. The Payne bill in the House carried a duty on gloves which exceeded that in force under the existing Dingley tariff. This higher duty on gloves was eliminated in the Senate, but Cannon fought strenuously for its retention in the conference committee.

Fuller details of the Cannon-Littauer machinations were brought to light when President Taft entered the picture. Before he had gotten wind of the deal, Taft had steadfastly opposed a rise in the duty on gloves.[102] When the tariff bill went to the conference committee, the President began to hear rumors of what Cannon was trying to do for Littauer.[103] Ten

99 Joseph L. Bristow to A. C. Mitchell, October 18, 1909; Charles A. Lindbergh to *Little Falls Daily Transcript*, March 22, 1909.

100 Miles Poindexter to Charles H. Braden, January 6, 1910.

101 Henry Cabot Lodge to Theodore Roosevelt, July 20, 1910; Charles F. Scott to Joseph L. Bristow, October 9, 1909.

102 William Howard Taft to E. E. Colston, June 24, 1909; William Howard Taft to Samuel A. Harper, July 13, 1909.

103 William Howard Taft to Mrs. H. H. Taft, July 13, 1909.

days later the full facts of the bargain were brought out at the White House when Payne and Aldrich revealed the true reason why Cannon was so solicitous for the glove duty.

It is nothing but the pound of flesh that Littauer is demanding, and I should think that Littauer would be ashamed to use such an argument, and I should think that Littauer would be more ashamed to hold the Speaker to such a bargain,

the President expostulated to his confidential aide Archie Butt.[104] After the Cabinet meeting on July 27, Taft promised his Secretary of the Navy that he would not give in to Cannon's efforts to raise the duty on gloves.[105] Cannon enlisted the support of the leader of the Senate in a desperate attempt to fulfill his end of the bargain, and when Aldrich insisted that the duty be raised, Taft's true mettle was revealed and he politely but firmly informed Aldrich [106] that he was " opposed to any increase in the duty on gloves for the purpose of establishing a new industry and the making of women's gloves at Gloversville or anywhere else."

The conduct of Cannon in seeking to fasten a $4.00 duty on ladies' gloves in order to accommodate Littauer, who had helped him to be elected Speaker, is and ought to be sharply condemned,

said the President to his brother.[107]
Interestingly enough, the individuals who were striving for a higher duty on petroleum were also eventually disappointed, although through no remissness on the part of the Speaker.

Norris presented an amendment which called for the reduction of the duty of 25% on petroleum and its products to a nominal 1%. Dalzell's point of order against the Norris attempt was sustained by Chairman Olmsted of the committee of the

104 Archie Butt, *Taft and Roosevelt: The Intimate Letters of Archie Butt*, Vol. I, p. 154.

105 M. A. DeWolfe Howe, *George von Lengerke Meyer*, p. 443.

106 William Howard Taft to Nelson Aldrich, July 29, 1909.

107 William Howard Taft to Charles P. Taft, August 1, 1909.

whole; but Olmsted allowed an appeal from his decision to get on the floor and he was overruled by 168-136 on a teller vote.[108] Then the Norris amendment passed even after Cannon had made a vigorous plea on the floor for the adoption of the Vreeland amendment.[109]

Behind the scenes even more sinister intrigue took form. Again Cannon bent every sinew of his lithe body to repay the men who had helped him to retain his prerogatives. The details of the backstage machinations were brought into the open when Judge Crumpacker of Indiana became sickened by the brazen attempts of the regulars to raise the oil duty. Crumpacker told one of the Insurgents exactly what had occurred.[110]

While the tariff bill was being considered, Crumpacker revealed, the Republican members of the ways and means committee had formed a sub-committee for the strategic political purpose of presenting a united front to override the Democrats when the committee met in full. This group of potent Republicans unanimously agreed to put petroleum and its products on the free list. But the day before they were to call in the Democrats and run the steam-roller over them on all the items of the projected tariff bill, Payne summoned the sub-committee to a secret meeting. This was attended by Speaker Cannon, who demanded that they reconsider their vote and place a tax upon

108 *Congressional Record*, 61 : 1 : 1168.

109 Joseph L. Bristow to William J. Tod, April 14, 1909, describes vividly Cannon's antics during this speech. In considering what part Fitzgerald had in the deal, a speech which he made on the floor upon the presentation of the Norris amendment should not be overlooked. In urging the adoption of the amendment, Fitzgerald said he would do so to " fling back the foul calumnies and insinuations that have been thrown at me through discreditable prints in this country by men who have not had the courage to make those statements to my face." *Congressional Record*, 61 : 1 : 1170. The writer makes no pretense at reconciling this statement or vote with the rest of the story; nor does he view it as a conclusive refutation of the fact that Fitzgerald played a role in the deal.

110 George W. Norris to William Allen White, September 21, 1929.

petroleum.[111] Cannon told them frankly that he had made an agreement, and the members of the ways and means committee would have to do this in order to make good the promise of the party.[112] A heated debate followed and a great amount of feeling was shown on all sides. When a vote was taken, however, Cannon's power over the group was demonstrated by a majority of only one, and with the Norris amendment the bill was reported on the floor.

Even after the Norris amendment was carried against Cannon's wishes, the Speaker had one more trump to play. Subsequent to the passage of the Norris amendment the House machine moved to amend the bill by placing petroleum on the free list, claiming that a 1% duty would be next to useless.[113] This was apparently a capitulation to the Insurgents, and was easily adopted. But the amendment as framed by the House regulars included only petroleum, and did not cover the products of petroleum. Obviously, this was an intentional oversight designed to recapture some of the losses. While petroleum itself went on the free list, the entire series of petroleum products became automatically taxable at 25% along with the other items not specifically mentioned in the bill. The following colloquy occurred between Cannon and Cooper on the floor after the vote to adopt the " concession " of the regulars:

MR. COOPER: Mr. Speaker, I do not understand that the words " and its products " are in any of the amendments we have voted on in the House.

THE SPEAKER: The amendments are disposed of that were reported to the House.[114]

111 A sketchy outline of these occurrences, not mentioning names, was reported in an article which Norris asked leave to print. *Congressional Record*, 61 : 2 : 6279.

112 Norris frankly says he does not remember the details of the deal of which Crumpacker told him, but guesses that it involved campaign contributions; it is apparent, however, which deal Cannon and Crumpacker were talking about. George Norris to William Allen White, September 21, 1929.

113 *Congressional Record*, 61 : 1 : 1266.

114 *Ibid.*, 61 : 1 : 1266.

With this statement, Cannon's gavel fell, and it seemed likely that he would attempt to defy the majority of the House by the trickery of a phrase. But the press reaction was so immediate and insistent that the bill was recalled after it had been sent to the Senate, and the words " and the products thereof " were inserted by Payne.

The Speaker's allies in the Democratic Party succeeded in suppressing the Insurgents in 1909, but these strange bedfellows did not sleep together long. It was Fitzgerald himself who, by raising a point of order against a Cannon ruling a year later, set the wheels in motion for an ultimate Insurgent victory.[115]

8. THE LULL BEFORE THE STORM

It is amazing how suddenly Cannonism became, temporarily at least, a dead issue within the halls of Congress. After a few days of recriminations over the Fitzgerald bolt, all the Insurgents settled down to a serious consideration of the details of the new tariff bill, which occupied them steadily for another month.

Even during the three months when the tariff battle was being waged in the Senate, the House Insurgents held their peace. They continued to study the question carefully; but a majority of them abandoned any hope of revising the rules during the remainder of the Sixty-first Congress. It was too much to hope that the canny leaders of the regular organization would be foolish enough to leave an opening whereby the question could again be brought to the floor of the House.

Throughout the country, however, especially in the press and in the pulpit, denunciations of Cannon and his system were frequent. These built up such a strong sentiment that many of the regulars began to wonder whether it would not be more expedient to support the Insurgent fight against Cannon than to continue to vote with the organization." [116]

115 *Infra*, p. 66.
116 Charles F. Scott to Joseph L. Bristow, October 9, 1909.

During the fall and winter of 1909-1910, a movement got under way within the regular organization to ditch Cannon as a step in " liberalizing " the Republican party. It was thought that the Insurgents could be thus appeased and that a more solid front against the Democrats could be presented in the 1910 elections. In November Lodge wrote to ex-President Roosevelt in emphatic terms that re-election of Cannon to the speakership would be disastrous to the Republican Party.[117] President Taft had begun to consider this idea in October,[118] and by December, he was casting around for a new candidate.[119]

The Insurgents engaged in one minor skirmish with Speaker Cannon before the final struggle in March, 1910. On January 7, 1910, a resolution to investigate the Forest Service and the Department of the Interior was up in the House, because of the squabble that arose between Chief Forrester Pinchot and Secretary of the Interior Ballinger.[120] Norris offered an amendment [121] vesting in the House instead of in the Speaker the power to elect the Ballinger-Pinchot investigating committee. The amendment carried by a vote of 149-146,[122] twenty-six Insurgents combining with the Democrats to overthrow the regulars.

Heartened by their victory over Cannon, the Insurgents, at a meeting in Hubbard's office, decided that when the election came they would insist upon the appointment of Madison of Kansas to the committee, and would refuse to countenance the appointment of either Payne or Dalzell.[123] At this point, the breach between the regulars and the Insurgents temporarily

117 *Selections from the Correspondence of Theodore Roosevelt and Henry Cabot Lodge*, Vol. II, p. 354. (November 30, 1909).

118 William Howard Taft to Mrs. H. H. Taft, October 28, 1909.

119 William Howard Taft to Otto Bannard, December 20, 1909.

120 *Infra*, chap VII.

121 *Congressional Record*, 61 : 2 : 390.

122 *Ibid.*, 61 : 2 : 404.

123 George W. Norris, interview, December, 1938; Victor Murdock to Kenneth W. Hechler, October 6, 1939.

closed when President Taft concluded with Hayes of the Insurgents and Dwight of the regulars an agreement which assured the Insurgents that their views would receive full consideration in the Republican caucus.[124]

In the caucus, the Insurgents succeeded in having Madison placed on the investigating committee. But old sores were reopened when the regulars decided to reject Rainey and James, the nominees of the Democratic caucus. Because of his vitriolic denunciations of the Roosevelt-Taft policies in Panama, Rainey was anathema to the regulars. Immediately, Cooper of Wisconsin led a group of radical Insurgents from Minnesota and Wisconsin out of the caucus. Order was finally restored only when the remaining Insurents and regulars agreed to accept James, but to reject Rainey. This was ratified on the floor of the House, and harmony reappeared at least on the surface.[125]

After the fight over the appointment of the Ballinger-Pinchot investigating committee, Representative Nelson was able to report from the front:

We have balm in Gilead nowadays, and to spare. The dove of peace is hovering over the Republican Party. Regular and Insurgent walk arm in arm. The jolt we gave Uncle Joe has had wonderful results ... [126]

9. The Fall of the Czar

As the day of Cannon's doom approached, the Insurgents were clearly fencing for an opening, while administering as many small pin-pricks as possible. A few minutes after five o'clock on March 15, 1910, the Insurgents, by a prearranged agreement,[127] caught the regulars napping. Suddenly combining with the Democrats, they struck out an appropriation for auto-

---

124 *New York Tribune*, January 15, 1910.

125 *The New York Times*, January 21, 1910; Poindexter was the only Insurgent voting on the floor to support the Democratic claims that Rainey should have a place on the Committee. *Congressional Record*, 61:2:840.

126 John M. Nelson to E. M. Keyes, January 25, 1910.

127 *Washington Times*, March 4, 1910.

mobiles for the Speaker and the Vice-President. Alarms were sounded in the cloakrooms, but dinner engagements had already taken many regulars away from the Capitol. Fourteen Insurgents with the Democrats were enough to defeat the Cannonites, 113-94.[128] This was a petty thing for the Insurgents to do, as it set them up as cheap obstructionists who were interested more in embarrassing the Speaker than in attacking his power directly.

Fortunately for their cause, this phase of the onslaught was lost in the great conflict that shook the House to its foundation a few days later. On Calendar Wednesday, March 6, 1910, Crumpacker called up an amendment to the census bill. Against this Fitzgerald immediately raised a point of order, claiming that Calendar Wednesday should be preserved for its original purpose—that of providing a day when neglected committees could report in alphabetical order. " We immediately felt that the Cannon machine was trying to cheapen the Calendar Wednesday rule which it had conceded," said one of the Democrats some years later.[129]

Crumpacker saw the trouble he had caused, and moved to postpone consideration of the whole question until the morrow so that he would not violate the sacred integrity of " Holy Wednesday." The House was determined to administer its rebuke, however, and 34 Insurgents voted with the Democrats against a postponement, 121-153.[130] The Speaker waved aside the point of order raised against the resolution, ruling that since the Constitution provides for the taking of a census, the resolution was constitutionally privileged and entitled to consideration, despite the " sacredness " of the day. Cannon felt in his bones that there would be an appeal from his ruling.[131] Fitzgerald, the Democratic traitor of the 1909 session, immediately appealed and the census resolution was thrown out by an overwhelming

128 *Congressional Record,* 61 : 2 : 3221.
129 Finis J. Garrett, interview, December, 1938.
130 *Congressional Record,* 61 : 2 : 3247-8.
131 L. White Busbey, *Uncle Joe Cannon,* p. 251.

vote, 163-112. The same 34 Insurgents voted to overrule Cannon.

The persistent Crumpacker again called up his resolution on the following day. This time the House decided that the resolution was in order, by a vote of 201-72.[182] The Insurgent vote split on illogical lines, with 24 Insurgents—including Norris—still insisting that the amendment of the census was not a constitutionally privileged resolution.

For some time Norris had been carrying around in his pocket a resolution to amend the rules, hoping that an opportunity would arise to present it on the floor. The resolution was somewhat like the one introduced by him in the Sixtieth Congress and smothered by the committee on rules.[133] It called for an expanded committee on rules to consist of fifteen members elected by the House according to geographical considerations. Nine of the members were to come from the majority party and six from the minority, and the Speaker was not to be a member.

Norris did not seek to create this opportunity by his own connivance, for he honestly believed that it was foolish to call a census resolution privileged by the constitution,[134] and he so voted on both March 16 and March 17. But when the House put itself in the position of claiming privilege for the Crumpacker resolution, Norris hastened to point out that similar logic would give privileged status to his own resolution, since the rules were mentioned in the constitution also. The Speaker afterward agreed that Norris was wholly justified in taking this position.[135] Deep in his own heart, Norris regarded his motion as unprivileged,[136] but he was quick to seize the opportunity offered by the rulings on the Crumpacker resolutions. Indeed, Norris would have been willing even to violate the sanctity of Calendar

132 *Congressional Record*, 61 : 2 : 3293.
133 *Supra*, p. 47.
134 *Congressional Record*, 61 : 2 : 3293.
135 L. White Busbey, *Uncle Joe Cannon*, p. 254.
136 George W. Norris, interview, December, 1938.

Wednesday with his resolution had the House decided that the census amendment was privileged on that day. He explained:[187]

> If on the day before the House had decided that the Crumpacker resolution was in order I would then have offered my resolution, but on that day they decided the other way.

Does this statement indicate that Norris already sensed the opportunity to present his resolution on March 16? He definitely had it in mind during the debate on March 17.[138] This is clearly evident from the remarks that he exchanged with Olmsted, in an attempt to extract an admission from the Pennsylvania Representative that a constitutionally privileged resolution need not have the sanction of a committee behind it in order to attain its privileged status.[139]

Even while Norris was debating with Olmsted, the real object of his questions was lost on the average member. None of the Insurgents had any inkling of the brilliant coup which Norris was planning.[140] Twice he rose after the Crumpacker resolution had been declared in order:

> MR. NORRIS: Mr. Speaker, I have a privileged resolution—
>
> .   .   .   .
>
> MR. NORRIS: Mr. Speaker, I have a matter of privilege—
> MR. BENNET: Mr. Speaker, I have a matter of privilege—
> THE SPEAKER: The chair is notified that there are many matters of privilege.
> MR. BENNET: But mine is a conference report.[141]

Finally the break came, and Norris was recognized by the Speaker:

> MR. NORRIS: Mr. Speaker, I present a resolution made privileged by the Constitution.

137 George W. Norris to George Rothwell Brown, March 7, 1923.
138 *Ibid.*
139 *Congressional Record*, 61 : 2 : 3285.
140 Irvine Lenroot, interview, November, 1938.
141 *Congressional Record*, 61 : 2 : 3291.

With surprising equanimity, Cannon replied:

THE SPEAKER: If it is a resolution made privileged by the Constitution the gentleman will present it. (Laughter).[142]

Dalzell immediately raised a point of order against the Norris resolution, and the extended struggle started.[143] In the brisk debate that followed, Norris defended his position ably; it was almost unassailable, indeed, for he himself had voted against giving the Crumpacker resolutions constitutional privilege at any time. This threw the blame upon the majority of the House for raising the whole question by expanding the meaning of "privilege" beyond what Norris actually believed it to be.

Cooper called upon Murdock, Norris and Fowler to explain what treatment they had received from Cannon in committee demotions, in punishment for their Insurgency. The Speaker thereupon interrupted to ask Gardner why he was not reappointed to his committee chairmanship. Gardner explained that he had specifically requested Cannon not to reappoint him lest the Insurgents should accuse him of selling out if he ever wanted to vote with the Speaker.[144] The explanation seems to have satisfied Cannon.

The Insurgents' course was now charted for them. After Cannon sustained the point of order against the Norris resolution, an appeal from the decision of the chair would follow. If the chair were overruled, the Norris resolution then would be up for a vote. It soon became apparent that the regulars did not have the votes to defeat the Insurgent-Democratic coali-

---

142 *Ibid.*, 61 : 2 : 3292. The *Record* stenographer's notation " laughter " might indicate that others suspected the nature of the resolution. On this point, Norris writes that "... the laughter was probably laughter directed at me." George W. Norris to Alfred Lief, February 25, 1939.

143 Excerpts of the outstanding comments during the debate are detailed in C. A. Atkinson, *The Committee on Rules and the Overthrow of Speaker Cannon.*

144 *Congressional Record*, 61 : 2 : 3320; L. White Busbey, *Uncle Joe Cannon,* p. 259.

tion; so Speaker Cannon and his lieutenants launched into a filibuster to give themselves time to round up regulars from every part of the country. Telegrams were dispatched by both sides, but the midnight train found only seven Cannon Republicans and six of the Insurgent-Democratic allies arriving in Washington.[145] The Cannon men unsuccessfully attempted to adjourn the House while they sought reinforcements.

All night long and until 2 p. m. on March 18, the House remained in session while frantic efforts were made to reach absentees. That Cannon regarded the situation as serious was indicated by another hurry call which he dispatched to Rushville, Indiana, to bring Watson to Washington to be the Speaker's personal whip.[146] Throughout the night, most of the Insurgents remained at their posts, indulging in strenuous efforts to force the Sergeant-at-Arms to bring to the bar of the House those regulars who were sleeping comfortably in nearby hotels. The pathetic regulars' pleas for a recess evoked catcalls from the Insurgents, who were determined to hold out and force the presence of a quorum despite the low level to which debate had descended by 4 a. m.

At 11 :30 a. m. on the 18th, the regulars requested a conference, and the leaders of the three factions met in Gardner's committee-room. Norris was " worn and haggard, his unshaven face drawn and pale and his eyes red and swollen from sleeplessness and hours of intense application." [147] At the conference, the regulars proposed a ten-man committee on rules, with the Speaker a member.[148] When the Insurgents refused to compromise, the regulars grudgingly offered to make a gentlemen's agreement that the Speaker would not seek membership on the new committee on rules. After extended argument, however, the Insurgents rejected this proposal also. Half an hour later the regulars offered to report a resolution from the committee

145 Champ Clark, *My Quarter Century of American Politics*, Vol. II, p. 276.
146 James E. Watson, *As I Knew Them*, p. 119.
147 *Nebraska State Journal*, March 19, 1910.
148 *Washington Times*, March 18, 1910.

on rules providing for a new committee on rules of fifteen members. Democrats and Insurgents alike again objected to the fact that the Speaker was not excluded from membership on this committee. At this juncture the conference broke up and all parties returned to the floor.[149]

By 2 p. m. of March 18, the Insurgent resistance to recess or adjournment had dwindled to 20, and a motion to recess for two hours was carried by a vote of 160-152.[150] The milder Insurgents, including the Iowa bloc, voted for the recess motion in the hope that a compromise might still be possible. At the next conference, the regulars promised to back the entire Norris resolution on condition that the sentence banning the Speaker from membership on the committee on rules be stricken out. Once again the compromise was wrecked on this issue. Reconvening at 4 p. m., the House heard the Speaker announce that he was finally prepared to rule on the validity of the point of order against the Norris resolution. Gaines moved to postpone the ruling until 12:05 p. m. on the 19th. His motion was carried, 163-151, the radical Insurgent resistance reaching a new low of 17.

On the morning of the 19th, Gardner, Hayes, Norris and Lenroot for the Insurgents conferred with Clark and Underwood of the Democratic forces, and Dalzell, Payne, Mann and Tawney of the regulars, but their deliberations hit the same stumbling block. The regulars were in an embarrassing situation, because Cannon had directed them under no circumstances to yield on the vital point of membership in the committee on rules. When they had pleaded with him to yield, the Speaker's oaths reverberated down the corridors of the Capitol.[151]

By 11 o'clock the final conference had broken up, with Lenroot and Norris expressing confidence that the outcome would be in favor of the Insurgents. " They didn't offer us any-

---

149 *Ibid.*, March 18, 1910.
150 *Congressional Record*, 61:2:3415.
151 James E. Watson, interview, December, 1938.

thing," lamented Mann when emerging; "I think we'll be beaten, at least that is the way it looks to me now." [152]

At one of these many conferences between the Insurgents and the Democrats, Clark and Underwood persuaded Norris that it would be impossible to solidify Democratic support behind his resolution unless it were altered in certain details.[153] The Democratic leaders then persuaded the Representative from Nebraska to abandon the principle of geographical selection of the committee on rules, and to reduce the number of members from fifteen to ten, six to be chosen from the majority and four from the minority party. This new resolution also excluded the Speaker from membership in the committee on rules, and provided that the committee itself elect its chairman from among its own members. The power of the Speaker to select the personnel of the other committees of the House was not touched. " I still think my original resolution was better," says Norris today.[154]

When the House convened on March 19, Cannon upheld Dalzell's point of order, as expected, and was overruled, 182-163.[155]

The final vote on the Norris resolution as amended was carried by 191-156.[156] For opportunistic reasons there was a wild scramble among some of the regulars to line up with the Insurgents on the last roll-call. Therefore, although forty-two Republicans united with the Democrats on the final roll-call, it cannot be claimed that all of them were dyed-in-the-wool Insurgents.

On the other hand, many of the Congressmen who steadfastly supported Cannon and the regular organization, were basically in sympathy with the principles for which the Insurgents were contending. A number of regulars furtively congratulated Victor Murdock for his fight to reform the rules, yet confessed an

152 *Washington Times*, March 19, 1910.

153 Confidential memorandum.

154 George W. Norris, interview, December, 1938.

155 *Congressional Record*, 61 : 2 : 3428.

156 *Ibid.*, 61 :2 : 3436.

unwillingness to break their party bonds and vote with the Insurgents.[157] Charles F. Scott, a Kansas regular and supporter of Cannon, showed that he chafed under what he regarded as his political duty. He wrote to Senator Bristow:[158]

I will say to you confidentially that I am more nearly agreeing with you on Cannon now that I ever was before. I thought that his make-up of the conference committee on the tariff bill was wholly unjustifiable and I resented deeply his attempt to have the glove schedule boosted for Littauer's special benefit. Furthermore, if the charges Parsons makes about the Tammany deal are sustained no decent American citizen can defend it. I believe I was right in voting for Cannon last time for the reason that the choice lay between him and Champ Clark and I did not see how a Republican could vote for Clark any more honorably than a Taft elector could have voted for Bryan. I shall have to radically change my present sentiment, however, if I vote for him again, although as a matter of fact I never expect to see him a candidate for another term . . .

Even such a confirmed regular as Nicholas Longworth, whose regularity aided in his eventual accession to the speakership, revealed to his illustrious father-in-law that he was surfeited with Cannon's dictatorship.[159] Longworth said that the only reason why he had consistently supported Cannon was to hold the party together and secure the passage of legislation pledged in the platform, but he warned that he would bolt if the issue arose again.

The final overthrow of Cannon's power provided one of the most dramatic scenes in the history of the House. The old Speaker's bearing through this adversity was admired even by his bitterest opponents. As Oscar W. Underwood, one of the Democratic leaders, strode triumphantly up the aisle to receive the approving glance which his wife always accorded him after a notable victory, he looked up to the gallery and saw Mrs.

157 Victor Murdock, interview, September, 1938.
158 Charles F. Scott to Joseph L. Bristow, October 9, 1909.
159 Nicholas Longworth to Theodore Roosevelt, April 27, 1910.

Underwood and the Speaker's daughter, Miss Helen Cannon, bathed in tears of genuine sympathy for the Iron Duke of Danville.[160]

Considerable difference of opinion has arisen as to the real authorship of the resolution which Norris presented on March 19, 1910. Champ Clark in his memoirs records that the Norris resolution was one which Underwood had prepared, " and which I had been lugging around in my pocket for three days."[161]

When presented with Clark's contention written in the Democratic leader's memoirs, Norris replied, " I did not consult anybody in connection with the resolution I introduced on March 17, 1910 . . . I did not talk to Champ Clark about it." [162]

This apparent contradiction can easily be explained. Norris himself presented the *original* resolution, with its geographical selection of the committee on rules, without previous consultation with anyone. Then, when Clark and Underwood entered the picture, they took a hand in reframing the resolution. In fact, great consternation appeared in the Democratic camp when it became known that Norris was to offer the revised resolution, Clayton swearing profanely because the Insurgents wanted to monopolize the limelight. Clayton called it a case of " the tail wagging the dog." [163]

A moment after the Norris resolution was adopted one of the most dramatic events in the entire battle occurred. Norris moved to adjourn,[164] but Cannon asked leave of the House to make a brief statement. The old Speaker then brilliantly defended the principle of government by parties. He concluded by insisting that since the effect of the passage of Norris' resolution was to

160 Mrs. Oscar Underwood, interview, November, 1938.

161 Champ Clark, *My Quarter Century of American Politics*, Vol. II, p. 277.

162 George W. Norris to Alfred Lief, April 27, 1938; George W. Norris, interview, December, 1938.

163 Clark, *op. cit.*, Vol. II, p. 277.

164 *Congressional Record*, 61 : 2 : 3436.

put the House in the hands of a bipartisan coalition, he would now entertain a motion to declare the speakership vacant.

Cannon's speech was written by his personal aide, James Watson, on the evening of March 17, in the library of the Speaker's Vermont Avenue home.[165] After three days of fumbling and bungling during the party crisis, this was a most astute piece of political strategy. Cannon and Watson knew that it would provide a sure means of dividing the Insurgent ranks between the Murdock radicals, who wanted to depose the Speaker, and the Norris conservatives who were concentrating their fire upon the rules.

Now frenzied discord arose within the Democratic Party. Burleson of Texas was adamant in his determination to present a resolution declaring the speakership vacant.[166] As soon as Garrett of Tennessee heard of this, he went to Burleson and pleaded with him not to offer the resolution because if it resulted in the election of a Democratic Speaker, it would place him in an impossible position in trying to control a minority House. " Wait and see if some Insurgent won't take the lead, and thus the responsibility, for such a resolution," Garrett urged, but Burleson stood firm.[167] Some of the Democrats also realized that to allow the Burleson resolution to be presented meant an almost certain triumph for the regulars.[168]

That Burleson communicated his intentions to the Insurgents in advance is evident. Murdock, the dynamic leader of the radical Insurgents, immediately went out to round up votes to support it; Norris did the same for the other side, with considerably more success.

165 *Washington Times*, March 21, 1910; James E. Watson, interview, December, 1938.

166 *Nebraska State Journal*, March 19, 1910, claims that Hardwick, Shackleford, Kitchin and Garner assisted Burleson in drawing this resolution. It is Garner's recollection today that after the Speaker had ruled on the Norris resolution, Burleson sat down and drafted the resolution declaring the speakership vacant, without consultation with anyone; Louis Friday, Clerk to Vice-President John N. Garner, to Kenneth W. Hechler, March 2, 1939.

167 Finis J. Garrett, interview, November, 1938.

168 Swagar Sherley, interview, November, 1938.

After the Speaker had concluded his statement, wild turmoil prevailed. The conservative Insurgents and the Clark-Underwood Democrats pressed for an immediate adjournment when the victory was theirs. The Burleson Democrats and the radical Insurgents were eager to push on and make the kill. Brandishing his resolution above his head, Burleson roared for recognition, while Swagar Sherley tried to persuade Burleson to desist. Sherley limped down to Burleson and tried to force him back to his seat, shook his finger under the Texan's nose, and punched him in the ribs without avail.

" You damn coward, why don't you go through with it? " shouted a Burleson supporter from North Carolina, shaking his fist in Sherley's face. In reply, Sherley waved his arm over to the Republican side of the chamber, where the regulars were joyously grinning and back-slapping each other. " Vote on it, show your colors, what's the matter with you? " Rodenberg, an Illinois regular taunted.[169]

The Congressional Record stenographer's repeated notations, " Great confusion in the hall," were mild characterizations of the scenes that followed. Most of the Insurgents stood up speechless by their chairs. Hinshaw alone approached Burleson, tugging at his arm, and pleading: " It is untimely. It is suicidal. Don't offer it now. Don't do it this evening. Wait till we have had time to think it over." [170]

" Start up the music; let the dance go on! " cried Chairman Tawney of the committee on appropriations, while the white-lipped Sherley advanced to the well of the House and thundered that Norris' motion to adjourn had precedence over any other motion. Burleson continued to bawl for recognition, and it was a foregone conclusion that Speaker Cannon, who thoroughly enjoyed the situation, would recognize him. The vote followed, and as expected, only the more radical Insurgents joined with the Democrats to defeat the Burleson resolution, 192-155.[171]

169 *Nebraska State Journal*, March 20, 1910.
170 *Nebraska State Journal*, March 20, 1910.
171 *Congressional Record*, 61 : 2 : 3438.

Nine radical Insurgents—Cary, Cooper, Lenroot, and Nelson of Wisconsin, Davis and Lindbergh of Minnesota, Murdock of Kansas, Gronna [172] of North Dakota, and Poindexter of Washington—voted for the deposition of Cannon.

Davis and Murdock of the radicals were unsparing in their condemnation of their conservative associates. Davis warned the conservatives that they would have to answer to their constituents for abandoning the cause on the crucial vote. Murdock still maintains that the conservative action in refusing to depose Cannon was "political pussy-footing." [173]

The position of the conservative Insurgents has been admirably expressed by Norris: [174]

We would probably have been justified in deposing the Speaker, but, if we had taken such action, we would never have been able to justify our contention that we were not against the man, but against the system, and against the power the rules gave to the man.

The regulars made a great show of victory, unfurling American flags and throwing their hats in the air after the vote on the Burleson resolution; but they were not sanguine about the future. Representative Currier of New Hampshire narrates: [175]

The result of the contest in the House is in a way a great personal triumph for the Speaker, but I doubt if it has left the party

172 At the conclusion of the poll, but before the vote was announced, the following appears in the *Congressional Record*, 61:2:3439:

Mr. Gronna. Mr. Speaker, I wish to change my vote. I voted "no," and I wish to change it to "aye".

The Clerk called the name of Mr. Gronna, and he voted "aye," as re-recorded.

Many years later Victor Murdock was told that Mrs. Gronna had been in the gallery at the time and had heard her husband vote against the deposition of Cannon; she immediately descended to the floor, summoned him, and directed that he vote with Murdock and the radical Insurgents to depose Cannon. Victor Murdock, interview, September, 1938. Perhaps this could be termed "petticoat Insurgency."

173 Victor Murdock to Alfred Lief, October 26, 1937.

174 George W. Norris to Alfred Lief, April 27, 1938.

175 Frank B. Currier to William E. Chandler, March 20, 1910.

in any better condition than it was before. The Insurgents were placed in a very embarrassing position when they had to vote on the question of removing the Speaker, and the trouble is that it was the better class of Insurgents who were hurt the most.

At this time Taft was on a northern trip which included settlement of some of the details of his projected scheme of reciprocity with Canada. A series of telegrams was exchanged in code between Knox, Carpenter, and Wickersham and their chief, but Taft remained undisturbed.[176] At breakfast on the morning of the 19th, the President looked up from his morning papers, laughed rather roguishly, and said to his aide, " Well, Archie, I think they have got the old fox this time." [177]

10. Aftermath and Results

Personally, Cannon was unshaken by the terrific legislative battle. He still claimed that the Insurgents constituted but five per cent of the party and that it was better to " fight and fail standing by Republican policies than to fight and win and have victory like Dead Sea fruit, turn to ashes on our lips." [178] He unleashed a vitriolic attack upon the Insurgents at a dinner of the Illinois Republican Association on March 20, and spared no slander against the personal character of all who by " cowardice " refused to follow out their position logically by voting for the Burleson resolution.[179]

The general disposition among the regulars was to let the " erring sisters " depart in peace. Evidently some of the more sensible regulars circulated word among the Insurgents that they should not take Cannon's rantings too seriously, although all of the Insurgents were intensely angry at the tone and temper of the Speaker's diatribe.[180]

176 William Howard Taft to Fred Carpenter, March 18, 1910.

177 Butt, *op. cit.*, Vol. I, p. 307.

178 Joseph G. Cannon to George Perkins, March 22, 1910.

179 *New York Times*, March 21, 1910.

180 Frank B. Currier to James O. Lyford, March 24, 1910.

There was a strange letdown of Insurgent activity after they had achieved their victory. Even the most radical refused to fight for adequate representation on the committee on rules. Murdock accepted the six nominees of the Republican caucus, since the Insurgents had been fighting for enlargement of rather than representation on the committee.[181] Probably they were also thinking of how the populace would view the results of the fight, and concluded that a struggle for representation on the committee would make it appear that they were motivated by personal ambitions. Kopp, Miller, Murdock, and Davis, representing all shades of Insurgent thought, all expressed this general viewpoint.[182]

With harmony advocated by everybody except Cannon, the Republican caucus of March 23 was all sweetness and light. The lieutenants of the Republican machine kept the more reactionary regulars in the background, and Representative Currier reports: [183]

Not a single unkind word was said by anyone. No man attempted to crowd any proposition to which there was objection, and the result was as good-tempered and harmonious a political gathering as I have ever attended.

When Tawney laid down his slate of six men for the committee on rules with an indication of what was expected of the caucus, a chorus of protests led him to withdraw the list hastily, and more than thirty nominations were made from the floor. Gardner, Cooper, Murdock, Martin, and Davidson of the Insurgents were nominated, but the six that Tawney had originally proposed, all organization men, were eventually named to the committee on rules.[184]

181 *New York Sun*, March 21, 1910; *Philadelphia Press*, March 24, 1910. The Insurgents met on the evening of the 23rd, and expressed opposition to giving Dalzell and Fassett places on the committee on rules, but indicated willingness to go along with the outcome of the Republican caucus.

182 *Washington Times*, March 21, 1910.

183 Frank B. Currier to James O. Lyford, March 24, 1910.

184 *New York Times*, March 24, 1910.

How did the actual results of the fight on Cannon and Cannonism compare with the objectives for which the Insurgents
were striving?

Many of the Insurgents felt that the immediate results were
slight, since the new members of the committee on rules represented everything for which Cannon himself stood; however,
they felt that they had established a great principle of representative government and they had hopes of eventually restoring the House to conformity with that principle. " I agree with
you," wrote Poindexter to a constituent, " that Cannonism has
not been killed by a long shot. It is scotched, however." [185]

Specifically, the Speaker was excluded from membership in
the committee on rules, and the committee was expanded
and made elective. The 1910 rebellion did not touch the
Speaker's power to appoint committees, which was not taken
away until the Democrats put through this reform in the Sixty-
second Congress. Even after the Democratic change of 1911,
the Speaker retained the power to appoint the House managers
of conference committees and of other select committees, and
the chairman of the committee of the whole. Recognition still
remained a potent and often arbitrary force in the hands of the
Speaker, along with the power to rule upon points of order.

The domination of the committee on rules by the Speaker
was smashed, yet the results failed to dissipate the charges of
despotism. As a result of the rebellion, a group of individuals
inherited some of the former power of the Speaker, and often
used it in an arbitrary fashion. The chairmen of the key standing committees, of the steering committee, and the floor leader
now share with the committee on rules the control over the
timetable of the House, and the shifting of legislative proposals
to be reported upon the floor of the House.

It is inevitable that if complete chaos is to be avoided, there
must be some prior selection of the legislation to be considered
by the House. Writers like Luce have argued that the over-

185 Miles Poindexter to F. O. Rex, March 26, 1910.

throw of the Speaker's personal power has obscured and divided responsibility which was once concentrated.[186] " The Insurgents wanted to beat the czar, and what did they do but immediately pave the way for eighteen czars instead of one," is the conclusion of one of the Democrats who fought with the Insurgents against Cannonism.[187]

One of the Insurgents, viewing the battle in retrospect, appraises the results of the activities of March 19, 1910, in terms of

moving a few chairs around so that instead of having the power centred in the Speaker alone, it was necessary for the Speaker to lean over and whisper with the majority leader and the chairmen of the important committees. To ever secure a thorough-going reform of the rules of the House, you have to reform human nature itself.[188]

Other Insurgents, viewing the subsequent development of events in the House, are more disposed to see a realization of the ideals for which they were fighting. They regard it as a distinct victory for representative government over the autocracy of a political closed shop.[189] " The change we have made in the organization of the House is extremely important and has already created a different spirit in the conduct of its affairs," wrote one of the Insurgents at the time.[190]

It is this spirit more than any concrete results that characterized the aftermath of the revolt against Cannon. It was still possible to point to abuses in the rules and in their administration; but never again was the House presented with the spectacle of one arrogant individual with pronounced social and economic views, who could hold at bay some four hundred

---

186 Robert Luce, *Legislative Procedure*, pp. 472-489.

187 Swagar Sherley, interview, November, 1938.

188 John M. Nelson, interview, February, 1939.

189 Irvine Lenroot, Miles Poindexter, Victor Murdock, George M. Norris, miscellaneous interviews.

190 Miles Poindexter to C. M. Miller, March 24, 1910.

associates and bend them to his personal will. It became harder
for special economic interests to exert control over Congress
when they had to deal with the " eighteen czars instead of the
one." Seekers after additional economic privileges were forced
into the open in their efforts, or they transferred their battles
from the floor of Congress to the committee rooms, the courts,
and the governmental agencies administering the law.

But most significant of all was the tremendous impetus
that the Insurgent victory gave to the entire progressive
movement, an impetus that can never be measured by a studious analysis of legislative procedure within the House of
Representatives. Cannonism was a great symbol of reactionary
tyranny, and when the blasts of Norris' trumpet felled its walls
the Insurgents were spurred to press forward with the balance
of their progressive program.

CHAPTER IV

THE GLADIATORS OF THE SENATE

1. ROBERT M. LA FOLLETTE

WHEN Robert M. La Follette came to the Senate in 1906 after having spent more than a decade of constructive work in making Wisconsin the most progressive commonwealth in the nation, he found himself alone among a body of fairly staid conservatives. For three years he labored to extend upon a broader national scale the work that he had accomplished in Wisconsin, but he made few dents upon the rigid Republican organization. Not until the arrival of Bristow, Borah, Cummins, Bourne and Dixon, and the regeneration of Dolliver, Clapp, and Beveridge, did La Follette come into his own as the leader of the Insurgent bloc of the Senate.

After a generally regular career in the House in the 1880's, La Follette was retired in the Democratic reaction against the McKinley tariff bill in 1890. Perhaps he would have remained a regular had he not been shocked severely by the attempt of Senator Philetus Sawyer of Wisconsin to bribe him to influence his brother-in-law, Judge Siebecker, to swing a case in favor of Sawyer. Shunned by his former allies for denouncing Sawyer, La Follette had plenty of spare time to think and talk with University of Wisconsin professors and other liberal thinkers during the early 1890's, and eventually he resolved to free the state from the corrupt influence of men like Sawyer and the corporate interests that they represented. He wrote later: [1]

I felt that I had few friends; I knew I had no money—could command the support of no newspaper. And yet I grew strong in the conviction that in the end Wisconsin would be free.

La Follette's conviction carried him to victory. Starting in 1894, when he backed Nils Haugen in an unsuccessful cam-

---

1 Robert M. La Follette, *Autobiography*, pp. 164-165.

paign for the governorship, "Fighting Bob" struggled in an uphill fight against corruption until he himself reached the State House in 1900. In three terms as governor, he accomplished phenomenal results in railroad taxation and regulation, direct primary, and child labor legislation.

In the Senate, La Follette was immediately recognized as the outstanding member of the Insurgent group. "La Follette is the crusader, the pioneer. He has blazed the way and opened up the road for the rest of us to follow him . . ." said one of his close colleagues before Insurgency had fairly gotten under way.[2] He was the outstanding figure in the debates upon the Payne-Aldrich tariff and Canadian reciprocity, and he played a leading rôle in espousing the other principles for which the Insurgents stood.

La Follette's intellect and constructive genius approached that of Alexander Hamilton and it was coupled with the broad sympathy of Thomas Jefferson for the people. He possessed intense zeal for research which was motivated by a moving passion for championing the cause of the underdog. As a dramatic orator and sound debater, he possessed no equal among the Insurgents. Beveridge could deliver a mellifluous oration which held his listeners spellbound, but he could not compete with La Follette in hammering home the facts in an inspired fashion.

Sheer devotion to ideals made La Follette spurn compromises. This caused Bristow to call him "the ablest of all the progressive Senators; a tireless worker, bold and fearless and reckless as a fighter, giving nor asking favor or quarter. . . ."[3] Because of this trait, he was not as effective a leader as would have been a man who could handle clashing personalities and issues and give them their proper weight. But as a protagonist of the causes for which the Insurgents were fighting, he was pre-eminent.

2 Joseph L. Bristow to Harold Chase, March 27, 1909.
3 Joseph L. Bristow to C. B. Kirtland. March 20, 1909.

2. Moses E. Clapp

Whereas most of the Insurgents had hair-trigger personalities, Senator Moses E. Clapp of Minnesota was an easygoing, genial, and tolerant man. He was very nearly a contemporary prototype of Falstaff in nature and temperament. These traits he used to smooth over many rough and tempestuous wrangles which the fiery Insurgents had among themselves.

Clapp's Minnesota constituency made him a progressive, and he came to the Senate after a distinguished career as Attorney-General of the state. But there was more than constituency behind Clapp's Insurgency. Beneath his hearty exterior there was a layer of steel which would not yield to the pressure of party regularity when it clashed with conviction. He had fought with Dolliver against Aldrich in the latter's effort to bury the Hepburn bill in the committee on interstate and foreign commerce.[4] He was by no means an outstanding progressive in the latter years of the Roosevelt administration, nor was there any sudden transformation in his character as was the case with Dolliver. But when the Insurgent battle started, Clapp fell in line and fought with unwavering loyalty.

Clapp's greatest role in the Insurgent fight was his cooperation with Cummins on the committee on interstate and foreign commerce in the Iowa Senator's efforts to secure an equitable railroad regulation bill in 1910. Clapp and Cummins both signed the minority report attacking the administration bill, although Cummins bore the brunt of the battle on the floor.

As Clapp was probably the least industrious of the Insurgents, he took no extended part in most of the debates. He was ready and sharp-witted in short speeches and interjections on the floor, but he was not capable of the lengthy analyses of La Follette, or the patient three-hour dissertations of Cummins. Yet unlike many of the " cold-feet " Insurgents, Clapp could always be counted upon to vote for his convictions despite presidential or party influence, and this made him one of the most valuable of the Insurgent group.

4 Jonathan P. Dolliver to Shelby M. Cullom, February 28, 1906.

3. Albert B. Cummins

As governor of Iowa, Albert B. Cummins had transformed that state in much the same manner that La Follette had reconstructed Wisconsin. He constantly fought monopoly and railroad domination in the 1880's when he was the farmers' attorney against the barbed wire trust. Later as state legislator he strongly supported a measure to establish the liability of railroads for the injury of their employees. Like La Follette, Cummins early became a political pariah because of his independence, and the corporate interests unceasingly fought his efforts to attain the governorship or a seat in the Senate. In 1894 and again in 1900 he made an unsuccessful bid for the Senate, and after bitter opposition was elected governor in 1901 by a coalition of independent Republicans and Democrats.

Almost immediately, Cummins moved against the forces that had dominated Iowa's political and economic scene for a generation. He extended the power of the railroad commission as had La Follette, and carried out the same general program of reform: direct primary and political campaign contribution laws, abolition of railroad passes, prohibition of discrimination in intrastate rates, and establishment of higher corporation fees. Cummins was the popularizer of the " Iowa Idea " which called for a regulation of corporations, and tariff reductions in rates that afforded a " shelter to monopoly."

Early in 1908 Cummins in his third attempt to reach the Senate was defeated by the aged Senator Allison, but when Allison died in the summer of 1908, Cummins finally achieved his goal. It was preordained that he should join with the Insurgents when he came to Washington, and for some time he was regarded as the potential leader of the Insurgent group.

When Bristow first came to the Senate he wrote: [5]

Am very much taken with Cummins. From my brief association with him he impresses me as a man of unusual strength, possessing striking elements of leadership. He is thoroughly aggressive and

5 Joseph L. Bristow to Harold Chase, March 27, 1909.

systematic in his work, and I think he has abundance of courage. He will be far more successful in managing a fight in the Senate than La Follette, but will never impress the country like La Follette has . . .

But Cummins lacked the driving and passionate persistence La Follette possessed. He was a little too professorial for the rough and tumble of Insurgent combat. Humorless to the extreme, Cummins was nevertheless one of the most influential of the Insurgents socially. He had a knack for handling men. With his erect and graceful bearing and graying handle-bar moustache, he presented a strikingly handsome appearance.

In debate Cummins did not possess the power of La Follette or the eloquence of Beveridge, but instead tended to be long-winded and prosaic. He could, however, analyze a subject with depth and mastery. There was in the Senate no greater authority upon railroad problems than Cummins. He very naturally took the lead in the fight for railroad legislation with teeth in it. Likewise, he was the leader in the efforts to add an income tax amendment to the Payne-Aldrich tariff bill, and to modify the postal savings bank bill so as to distribute funds among the local communities. Moreover, he was a tower of strength during the battles against the tariff and reciprocity. Nevertheless, one occasionally had the feeling that in view of his extraordinarily brilliant career as governor of Iowa, he should have overshadowed La Follette in pressing these two issues.

Perhaps it is the subsequent career of Cummins that causes one to wonder about his early Insurgency. In 1920 he attached his name to a railroad bill that none of his earlier Insurgent colleagues would have sanctioned. In his later years, like the Newton Bakers and the Mark Sullivans, he forgot his rash youth, while the world moved on ahead of him. But during the Taft administration, there never was a shadow of a doubt as to where he stood on public questions. He gave the Insurgent movement substance, backbone, and dignity.

4. JOSEPH L. BRISTOW

Before entering the Senate in 1909, Joseph L. Bristow of Kansas had made a notable record in the federal service under McKinley and Roosevelt. As Fourth Assistant Postmaster-General he had done an outstanding job of cleansing the Post Office Department of frauds, and as a result was sent to Cuba to perform a similar task. Under Theodore Roosevelt he became special commissioner of the Panama Railroad. During his purging operations, Bristow displayed a dogged persistence and unimpeachable honesty in probing to the roots of the issues at hand.

Like the rest of the Mississippi Valley, Kansas had been in a political ferment for some years prior to 1909, but her regeneration came slightly later than Wisconsin's and Iowa's, because she possessed no outstanding leader like La Follette or Cummins. Rather, the burden was shared among Bristow, William Allen White, Walter R. Stubbs, Henry J. Allen and a score of others.

Bristow carried the banner of progressivism and reform of railroad abuses in his newspaper, the *Salina Journal,* during the early 1900's. He defeated conservative Senator Long in the Republican primaries in 1908, largely because he brought home to the farmers the fact that the railroads were charging them exorbitant and discriminatory rates for the transportation of their products.

Tall, awkward and bespectacled, Bristow was unusually self-effacing in manner. He fell in naturally with the Insurgent group whose social and economic views approximated his own. He was a galley slave for work, and made one of the most brilliant speeches, during the debate on the Payne-Aldrich tariff, in analyzing the sugar schedule. He also participated whole-heartedly in the fight for a genuine long and short haul clause in the railroad bill, for the income tax, and in the struggle against reciprocity.

Because of his modesty, Bristow never made the headlines, or received the wide publicity that La Follette and Cummins commanded. In comparing him with one of his Insurgent colleagues, William Allen White writes: [6]

Beveridge was a trotting horse. Joe Bristow was a Clydesdale with whiskers on his feet, built for draft and general purposes. Or to change the figure, Beveridge was a geared up speedster, a show car. Joe was a truck, but he always brought it home full of bacon.

Beveridge himself wrote to Bristow in 1910: [7]

Your industry, your intense earnestness, your careful and studious investigations have made you one of the most effective men on the American political platform . . .

Quietly, uneffusively, Bristow plodded onward, fighting for his ideals. He wrote in 1909: [8]

It is not always comfortable to be hooted at as an ' Insurgent,' but I know I am contending for the things that are just to the people of this country, and I intend to keep it up.

When the full history of the progressive era is written Bristow will loom large as one of its key figures.

5. JONATHAN P. DOLLIVER

Jonathan P. Dolliver of Iowa unlike La Follette or Cummins had no background of Insurgency. Rather, he was steeped in the traditions of standpat conservatism. Early in his political career, he fell under the benevolent tutelage of Senator Allison, who kept him on the straight and narrow path of party regularity.

But progressivism was latent in Dolliver. It cropped up first when the Hepburn bill was slumbering in the committee on interstate and foreign commerce, in 1906. " Brother Aldrich and the fellows with him have claimed that the bill was not worth

6 William Allen White to Kenneth W. Hechler, November 26, 1938.

7 Albert J. Beveridge to Joseph L. Bristow, August 9, 1910.

8 Joseph L. Bristow to M. L. Stockton, June 18, 1909.

a cuss for any purpose . . ." he indignantly wrote to Senator Cullom.[9] When Aldrich gave the measure to Tillman to report lest Dolliver have his name attached to any railroad legislation, the latter was incensed, but bided his time within the regular organization for three more years before bursting his bonds.

Dolliver was by nature somewhat indolent. For years in the House and Senate he pursued an undistinguished course. He had a giant intellect, and was one of the most powerful Insurgent orators—in fact Beveridge described him as " beyond any possible doubt the greatest orator in the contemporaneous English-speaking world." [10] But he did not use his intellect to the fullest advantage until Aldrich peremptorily excluded him from membership in the Senate committee on finance in March, 1909. This shock brought his full powers to the surface.

Free from the Allisonian strings, which had been holding him in line, Dolliver now sprang into prominence as a leading Insurgent. He sweated and labored over the intricacies of the cotton and woolen schedules and mastered them completely. He showed them in such a light that the exposure discredited the standpatters. He continued as a strong Insurgent throughout the session of 1910 by aiding Cummins in the latter's fight for an effective railroad bill. A lesion of the heart was Dolliver's heritage from the strain of the tariff session of 1909, and his sudden death occurred in October of 1910. His loss was felt deeply by the Insurgents, and he was generally regarded as a martyr to the cause.

6. ALBERT J. BEVERIDGE

William Allen White's description of Albert J. Beveridge of Indiana as " a geared up speedster, a show car " [11] is very apt. The Hoosier Senator had few superiors in the sheer brilliance of his oratory, which flowed smoothly and tirelessly, and he made a very presentable window-dressing for the Insurgents.

9 Jonathan P. Dolliver to Shelby M. Cullom, February 28, 1906.
10 Claude Bowers, *Beveridge and the Progressive Era*, p. 328.
11 William Allen White to Kenneth W. Hechler, November 26, 1938.

As a progressive, Beveridge was somewhat handicapped by the fact that the political temperature of his Indiana constituents was not so high as was that of the other mid-western progressive states. Upon returning from a campaign trip for Beveridge in 1910, Bristow wrote to Mrs. La Follette:

I could not get hold of the Indiana people as I did in Wisconsin. It was a delight for me to speak to your people as it is to my own constituents, but in these other states they have not got the same atmosphere that we have.[12]

The Democrats had swept Indiana in the 1908 election, and Beveridge himself was to go down to defeat in 1910, which caused him to put the brakes upon the extent of his Insurgency.

Beveridge was an incurable egotist, and as such was given an interesting rôle by his fellow Insurgents. In order to rivet him to the Insurgent group he was thrust forward again and again as the spearhead of the debate. And by pursuing these tactics the Insurgents retained for themselves the valuable services of one of the most scintillating debaters the Senate has ever seen. Hot-tempered and easily aroused, Beveridge engaged in many personal clashes with Aldrich, especially during the debate over the Payne-Aldrich tariff of 1909. Usually he acquitted himself exceedingly well, however, and proved one of the best propagandists for the Insurgent cause.

La Follette was one of the few Insurgents able to adjust his original Insurgency to changing times. In his old age, La Follette was as militantly progressive as during the Taft days. Beveridge, like Cummins, however, remained static after his early Insurgency. In his unsuccessful campaign for the Senate in 1922, Beveridge's speeches sounded like those of a lifelong standpatter. During the latter days of his life he concentrated his energies upon his magnificent biography of Marshall.

12 Joseph L. Bristow to Mrs. Belle C. La Follette, October 10, 1910.

CHAPTER V
ON TO ALDRICH

No single issue looms so large in the story of Insurgency as the revision of the tariff during the special session of 1909. The conservation question rallied more sympathetic adherents throughout the country, and the struggle for an equitable railroad rate bill struck deeper toward economic fundamentals, but the Payne-Aldrich tariff debate cut the first gaping groove into Republican solidarity. Other issues followed naturally along the lines of this schism.

From the death of President McKinley until the opening of the special session of 1909, faint rumblings beneath the surface of political calm revealed that opposition to brazen protectionism within the Republican Party was coming to a boil. Economically, the opposition to excessively high tariffs arose in conjunction with the gradually increasing power of trusts and monopolies. In many cases these huge industrial combinations were protected from foreign competition while they maintained high prices for their products, and the general feeling prevailed that a lower tariff would result in more equitable prices.

McKinley, in the last speech of his life at Buffalo, had advocated reciprocity. Nevertheless, Senator Aldrich and his conservative cabal stood solidly against the Kasson reciprocity treaties, both during McKinley's term, and during the reign of Roosevelt.[1]

Sentiment for tariff revision spread rapidly in Iowa. George Roberts, Director of the Mint, framed a plank for the 1901 Republican state platform which favored a modification of those tariffs schedules that afforded a " shelter to monopoly." [2] Governor Cummins of Iowa quickly took up the suggestion of the 1901 platform, added a leaven of trust regulation and railroad control, and popularized the combination as the " Iowa Idea."

1 Nathaniel W. Stephenson, *Aldrich*, pp. 168, 178.
2 *Iowa Journal of History and Politics*, Vol. II, pp. 69-82.

From Iowa, the influence of Cummins spread to Wisconsin and throughout the Mississippi Valley. Representative Tawney, one of the bulwarks of conservative Republican strength in Minnesota, anxiously inquired: [3]

Don't you think, for the good of the party in the west, some of the eastern Republicans prominent in the councils of the party should say less against a limited revision of the tariff?

Indiana and Kansas inserted tariff revision planks in their state platforms in 1902, and the rising sentiment even permeated New England, with Connecticut and Massachusetts adopting similar recommendations.

One of the proofs of the consummate political genius of Theodore Roosevelt was his refusal to tamper with the tariff. With astute touches, he whirled the oil and water of standpatters and revisionists into an emulsoid solution and kept both elements together until his departure for Africa in 1909. Roosevelt refused to be drawn irretrievably into either camp, although the pressure became tremendous as the split widened.

In 1906, Senator Beveridge began to advocate tariff revision, and Taft at Bath, Maine, began a long series of similar declarations.[4] Despite the fence-sitting of the sage of Oyster Bay, the issue began to take definite form prior to the election of 1908. The high protectionists clamored for a candidate who would be true to the principles of an "adequate tariff," and even opposed Taft upon the grounds that he was not "sound" enough upon this vital issue. The American Protective Tariff League came out against Taft, and the *American Economist* [5] editorially supported this attitude. This opposition seems amusing in view of the subsequent position of Taft in his quarrels with the Insurgents.

3 James A. Tawney to William B. Allison, September 2, 1902.

4 Claude G. Bowers, *Beveridge and the Progressive Era*, p. 239; Henry F. Pringle, *The Life and Times of William Howard Taft*, Vol. I, p. 289.

5 *American Economist*, May 31, 1907.

The Republican platform of 1908 declared "unequivocally for the revision of the tariff by a special session of Congress immediately following the inauguration of the next president." [6] The tariff plank did not specifically pledge that the revision would be downward, and this caused numerous diehards to deny that the party was bound to any clear covenant. To this false contention, Frank B. Kellogg of Minnesota replied: [7]

The claim that the Republican National Convention made no pledges to revise the tariff downward, as Senator Aldrich is reputed to have said, is entirely without foundation. I was a member, as you know, of the Subcommittee on Resolutions and no one of the apostles of protection thought of making any claim that the tariff should be revised upwards.

During the campaign, Taft made it even more clear that the party was committed to tariff revision downward.

A volley of warnings rolled in from the Middle West, demanding that Taft fulfill his pledge for a downward revision. If the rigid protectionists saw fit to caution the President-elect to go slow on revision, they did it furtively, for in Taft's papers there is a notable absence of letters importuning him to disregard the pleas of the revisionists. Rather, the standpatters adopted the technique of assuring Taft that a "fair and genuine" revision would result, if the whole matter were left in their hands. [8]

Assured of a Republican majority in Congress, Chairman Payne called the committee on ways and means on November 10, 1908 for hearings. The general feeling of the public toward the hearings was expressed as follows: [9]

6 Henry F. Pringle, *The Life and Times of William Howard Taft*, Vol. I, p. 421.

7 Frank B. Kellogg to Knute Nelson, May 29, 1909; also, Frank B. Kellogg to William Howard Taft, May 5, 1909.

8 James A. Tawney to William Howard Taft, November 25, 1908; J. C. Needham to William Howard Taft, November 28, 1908.

9 Amasa Thornton to William Howard Taft, November 20, 1908.

The impression among the importers and consumers here is that it is no use whatever to appear before Congress at all as the cards are stacked against fair tariff revision, and that the cold deck will be played by Payne and his friends at the finish.

At first, Taft adopted the course so successfully followed by Roosevelt—that of clubbing both sides toward the center. He warned Representative Needham of the committee on ways and means that revision should be a fact rather than a form.[10] On the other hand, he flatly told H. E. Miles not to "make faces at the committee," and finally expressed his disbelief that there was anything prejudicial to revision in the efforts of the committee.[11]

Originally scheduled to close December 5, the hearings droned on through eight volumes of testimony until Christmas Eve. "Public opinion" soon settled down to its historic role of representing those who knew what they wanted and had set aside a part of the company's payroll to make those wants vocal. Infant industries paraded before the committee asking for protection, and full-grown giants tried to convince it that they were still in diapers.

As the opening of the special session approached, the lines became more closely drawn, and any competent observer could tell that it would take keen political strategy to restrain the two wings of the Republican Party from a terrific battle over the pending revision. All of the pent-up passion of eight years of tariff agitation and fruitless Congressional shadow-boxing made the revisionists determined to strike a knock-out blow, while the standpatters resolved to maintain their control over the party machinery in the interests of a very gentle revision, if any.

The fight on the House rules had widened the gap between regulars and Insurgents. In the Senate a similar dress rehearsal occurred when Senator La Follette led an attack on the slip-

10 William Howard Taft to J. C. Needham, November 21, 1908.
11 William Howard Taft to H. E. Miles, January 22, 1909.

shod manner in which Hale sought to rush through the naval appropriation bill in the closing days of the sixtieth Congress. Cummins, Borah, and Dixon came to La Follette's support, and in the ensuing debate La Follette extended the issue to the oligarchical control of Senate committees and chairmanships. Only an open declaration was needed to transform this tense situation into actual war.

THE TARIFF IN THE HOUSE

Representative Payne introduced his tariff bill in the House on March 17, 1909, and it was generally received with praise throughout the country. New rates appeared upon tea and crude cocoa; increased protection was accorded mercerized fabrics, women's gloves, hosiery, plate glass, and many fruits; wood pulp, hides, iron ore, and raw flax were put on the free list; the duties upon lumber, iron and steel, and a few manufactured products were cut in half; Philippine products were admitted duty-free up to a limit. Standpat Senator Gallinger of New Hampshire moaned at the reduction; [12] the Insurgent *Philadelphia North American* characterized the bill as " thoroughly satisfactory; " [13] while Insurgent Senator Cummins, that prince of tariff revision, admitted that the bill provided a good many more reductions than he had expected. [14]

A general grumbling was heard throughout the corridors, however, on March 18, the day after the bill was taken up in committee of the whole, with some sectional resentment against New England for the maintenance of free hides along with highly protected boots and shoes. Among the Insurgents there was no organized opposition to the Payne Bill before it passed the House on April 9. Individual attacks, however, were numerous, concentrating upon schedules that interested particular constituencies.

12 Jacob H. Gallinger to James O. Lyford, March 19, 1909.
13 *Philadelphia North American*, March 19, 1909.
14 *Des Moines Register and Leader*, March 18, 1909.

On March 31, James Mann of Illinois, who had steadfastly defended Cannonism, announced he would go off the reservation unless the wood pulp and print paper schedule was lowered. Mann was aroused by the insertion of a $4.00 rate into the Payne tariff bill, repeatedly denouncing the duty as outrageously high and asserting that it was solely for the benefit of the spruce producers of Maine and New Hampshire. When the framers of the tariff bill refused to yield, Mann asserted that if two New England states were to be permitted to fix a duty inimical to the interests of the consumers and manufacturers of paper, he would swallow his desire to prove that the Republicans were capable of writing a tariff bill, and vote against it.[15] Mann carried out his threat, but refused to cooperate with any of the more liberal Insurgents opposing the bill.

After fifteen days of consideration of the Payne bill, on April 5 the committee on rules reported a rigid special order which permitted separate votes on amendments to the following schedules: hides, lumber, oil, barley, malt, tea, and coffee.[16] The Insurgents took no part in the debate over this special order, but in the press they damned it right and left. Although the special order carried, 195-176, twenty bolters dared the ire of the Republican leaders.[17]

At this point a new face appeared in the Insurgent line-up, that of James A. Tawney of Minnesota. Over the strenuous objections of Fordney of Michigan, who characterized Tawney as "neither a Republican nor a protectionist,"[18] Tawney pressed for free rough lumber and drastically reduced duties on planed lumber.[19]

Three of Tawney's amendments were defeated by majorities varying from fourteen to twenty.[20] However, his proposals

15 *Chicago Tribune*, July 6, 1909.
16 *Congressional Record*, 61 : 1 : 1112.
17 *Ibid.*, 61 : 1 : 1118-9.
18 *Ibid.*, 61 : 1 : 1130.
19 James A. Tawney to Dunn & Carlson, April 3, 1909.
20 *Congressional Record*, 61 : 1 : 1293-6.

drew all the rules Insurgents and an equal number of western regulars away from the Republican majority. This is Tawney's own explanation of why his lumber amendments were defeated:[21]

The fight on lumber was exceedingly close and had it not been for thirty-seven Democrats repudiating their national platform, which declared in favor of free lumber, and the Massachusetts delegation trading free lumber for free hides and the Ohio delegation changing front on the proposition I would have won easily.

On April 9, after the committee on ways and means had acceded to President Taft's wishes by putting coffee and tea on the free list, the Payne bill passed the House with the approval of every Republican except Austin of Tennessee.[22] Yet though the Insurgents voted against Minority Leader Clark's motion to recommit the Payne bill, they still felt that the bill did not comply with the platform pledges. Lenroot, Nelson and Poindexter all wrote privately that the Payne bill was not satisfactory to the Insurgents in the form in which it originally passed the House.[23]

Why, then, did the Insurgents go along with the regulars in defeating Champ Clark's efforts to have the bill sent back to the committee on ways and means? The answer is that Clark, with poor political tact, framed his resolution of recommittal so that it coincided with the tariff declaration in the Democratic platform of 1908, without considering that the Insurgents desired a downward revision along protectionist lines. The immediate consequence was a clear-cut partisan line-up of protectionists against free traders, and the Insurgents proved their loyalty to the protectionist system by voting against Clark's motion.

21 James A. Tawney to Dunn & Carlson, April 10, 1909.

22 *Congressional Record*, 61 : 1 : 1301.

23 Irvine L. Lenroot to Nils Haugen, April 12, 1909; John M. Nelson to E. M. Keyes, May 6, 1909; Miles Poindexter to A. Baldwin, June 22, 1909.

It may be argued that the Insurgents would have accomplished far more had not the House accepted an iron-clad rule relative to amendments. Yet, although they gave full vent to their personal opposition to the bill in private correspondence, they were not particularly vehement in the defense of their views on the floor of the House itself. Part of this was due to the superiority of the Payne bill over the Aldrich bill, and part to the overpowering interest of most of the Insurgents in reform of the rules of the House. The Insurgents in the House made but a small contribution to the wave of resentment that greeted the passage of the Payne-Aldrich tariff. The press was absorbed with the more violent and personal denunciations that reverberated through the Senate chamber, by contrast with which the opposition in the House appeared weak and ineffective.

THE TARIFF IN THE SENATE

The debate in the Senate over the Payne-Aldrich tariff bill during the summer of 1909 deserves to rank with the League of Nations debate of 1919 and the Supreme Court debate of 1937. Perhaps the immediate issue involved in the tariff debate was not so great as those in the League or Court discussions; but the far-reaching consequences equalled those of the latter struggles. All three debates were studded with powerful speeches; all three presented the unusual spectacle of soul-stirring convictions taking precedence over ties of partisanship; and all three led to a lowering of the prestige of the President in power.

While the Payne bill was being rushed through the House, the Republican members of the Senate committee on finance held extended closed sessions in Aldrich's committee rooms, examining witnesses, communications, and statistics. Half a dozen experts of the Treasury Department assisted the committee on finance in their work, which was characterized by a hostile source as " addition, multiplication, and silence." [24] A

24 *La Follette's Magazine*, May 1, 1909.

hurry call from the White House summoned two members of the Board of General Appraisers of the customs service in New York to aid Aldrich and " to stay such length of time as will enable him to use your knowledge to the best advantage." [25]

This procedure smacked of star-chamber tactics to Senators with progressive leanings, however much Aldrich may have been justified by the situation. But the Senate leader, like the President, never deviated from his course in order to raise his standing with press or public. This was a tariff, and to him tariffs meant dogged work rather than histrionic showmanship. And so the experts sifted the testimony while the cotton, woolen, and iron manufacturers paraded before the committee on finance with their pleas for higher protection.

The spectacle of the House proceedings, the secret sessions of the committee on finance, and the constant pressure of private interests shook Senator Bristow severely, and he well represented the attitude of his progressive colleagues when he wrote : [26]

If you had been here the last six weeks that I have been and observed the insatiable greed with which men pursue Senators and committees in behalf of a tariff, sometimes for protection, but usually for as much profit as can be extracted, you would conclude, as I sometimes do, that the policy of protection, which has done so much for the American people and which is sacred to old-line Republicans, like you and I, is being contorted into a synonym for graft and plunder.

Although the Insurgents looked upon the Payne bill with some small degree of tolerance at first, after a study of its provisions they gradually became hostile. Even before the Senate committee on finance had completed its deliberations, Bristow decided he would vote against the bill unless the duties on gloves, hosiery, and linoleums were materially reduced, and

25 William Howard Taft to Marion deVries, March 17, 1909.
26 Joseph L. Bristow to C. N. Sheldon, April 21, 1909.

steel, lumber, and leather were placed on the free list.[27] Anything short of this, the Kansan regarded as a failure to achieve downward revision.

While the House steamroller was performing its duty, little knots of western Senators began to meet and compare notes.[28] Apprehension arose about the effect which the contemplated provision might have upon the price for consumers' goods.[29]

Dolliver was evidently planning his attack early, for during the consideration of the Payne bill he was seen spending a considerable amount of time in the House wing of the Capitol listening intently to the debates.[30] During this period, La Follette was spending every spare moment in his office, working feverishly to store up statistical ammunition for the ensuing battle.[31] Beveridge, recovering from a serious operation, had gotten wind of the impending battle while still in Johns Hopkins Hospital,[32] and was husbanding his strength for the effort.[33] And Cummins was ready to take the lead,[34] and seize the chance to make his famed " Iowa Idea " a reality.

Considerable controversy has arisen as to whether Taft directly asked any of the Insurgents to conduct their fight in the Senate for reductions in rates. At the outset, the Insurgents felt they were breaking a lance for Taft against the party leaders, to achieve his campaign pledge for downward revision. According to La Follette, after the Payne bill had passed the House, Taft told him to go ahead and criticize and amend the bill in the interests of reduced duties.[35] Beveridge relates that

27 Joseph L. Bristow to Fred C. Trigg, April 7, 1909.
28 Joseph L. Bristow to Walter Pierce, March 30, 1909.
29 Albert J. Beveridge to A. L. Bodurtha, March 18, 1910; Bowers, *op. cit.*, p. 340.
30 *Washington Times*, April 4, 1909.
31 Joseph L. Bristow to Walter Pierce, March 30, 1909.
32 Claude G. Bowers, *Beveridge and the Progressive Era*, p. 309.
33 *Washington Times*, April 5, 1909.
34 Joseph L. Bristow to W. R. Stubbs, March 24, 1909.
35 Robert M. La Follette, *La Follette's Autobiography*, p. 440.

Dolliver was called to the White House and asked to convey the news to the other progressives that a fight for downward revision would be in order.[36]

No corroborating evidence of these talks exists in the Taft papers, and Senator Bristow doubts that Taft made any promises to the other Insurgents that a veto would be his answer to a high tariff bill.[37] Yet in view of Taft's state of mind when the Senate battle opened, it seems plausible that he did make such statements to La Follette and Dolliver. He was apprehensive lest Aldrich fail to carry out the party pledges, and specifically told Secretary Meyer that he would not permit Aldrich to sacrifice the party on this score.[38] What Taft was attempting to do was to use the Insurgents and the press to enforce the promise of adequate revision which Aldrich and the regulars had given him.

Thus the whole tariff battle resolved itself into a guessing game. The high protectionists tried to figure out how high they could boost the rates without encountering presidential displeasure and risking a veto; the President wondered how far he could threaten the regulars without alienating them and how far he could encourage the Insurgents without making them uncontrollable firebrands; and the Insurgents meanwhile tried to guess how sincere Taft really was in his campaign utterances and subsequent personal exhortations to them. Out of this welter of political maneuvering came the decision of the Insurgents to cut straight ahead in line with their ideals. Their determination was based upon the original supposition that the President was sympathetic, and the subsequent realization that they were fighting a battle that the President was afraid to make.

36 Albert J. Beveridge to Ida M. Tarbell, September 13, 1910; Claude G. Bowers, *Beveridge and the Progressive Era*, p. 337.

37 Joseph L. Bristow, interview, September, 1938.

38 Archie Butt, *Taft and Roosevelt: The Intimate Letters of Archie Butt*, Vol. I, p. 41.

The bill that Aldrich introduced in the Senate in mid-April was riddled with 600-odd amendments, some of which seemed to the Insurgents to be unusually odd. It is true that the notoriously high glove and hosiery duties were cut by the committee on finance. But these reductions were more than offset when iron ore, raw flax, and coal were replaced on the dutiable list; the tariff on print paper was doubled; and duties on lumber, lead , fruits, silks, scrap iron and steel were generally raised. But the two schedules of the bill that did most to goad the Insurgents and the country into opposition were Schedule I (cotton) and Schedule K (wool). It was not so much the outright increases of these schedules that irked the Insurgents, as the subtle methods by which the increases were effected. Court decisions, Senator Aldrich claimed, necessitated alterations in the Dingley bill; but when the alterations took the form of applying the duty on colored cloth to goods into which a single colored thread had been woven, and of providing that a few mercerized threads granted a much higher classification, there was rebellion in the air.

Early in the session, one of the Insurgents commented: [39]

There are some pretty smart fellows here. They are as smart as men ever get, and it is very interesting to watch them operate.

But when they started to operate, they struck snags that their party colleagues in the House had not encountered.

Dolliver and Beveridge started their cautious criticism by asking that certain amendments be passed over for further consideration. Aldrich was serene and self-confident as he benignly assured Dolliver: " I am perfectly certain that the Senator from Iowa, when he gets the facts before him, will accept the action of the Committee." [40] What Dolliver may have replied under his breath was lost to the Senate reporter and to history.

On April 22, La Follette launched a blasting attack upon the tariff bill. Gas retorts became the innocent subject of the first

39 Joseph L. Bristow to Cyrus Leland, Jr., March 20, 1909.
40 *Congressional Record*, 61 : 1 : 1433.

direct challenge to Aldrich's authority,[41] and set off the fire-
works of Insurgency. What was the cost of production? How
did Aldrich assess reasonable profit? Did he swallow the statements of interested parties as to the difference in cost of production here and abroad? Was no further investigation made
to discover the facts? These and other questions La Follette
presented, and the battle was on.

Knute Nelson of Minnesota attacked the tribute levied upon
the American consumer through higher duties on cotton,
woolens, glass and earthenware. Thereupon Dolliver threw
aside his caution and denounced the textile schedules as bad
advertisements for the Republican Party. Then Beveridge also
became bold, and he and Dolliver criticized Aldrich for allowing tariff revision by manufacturers. As Dolliver persisted in
making biting comments about the principles that dictated
the formation of the tariff bill, Aldrich could answer only by
the counter-charge that the Iowa Senator was indulging in
Democratic propaganda and departing from the tried and true
course of party regularity set by his late colleague, Senator
Allison.[42]

Coe Crawford of South Dakota also strayed from the
reservation by making numerous objections and requests that
certain schedules be passed over for future consideration. When
the Senate finally called a halt at 6 p. m. on April 22, no
doubt remained that the hitherto unchallenged leadership of
Aldrich and his lieutenants would be subjected to severe attack
in the coming weeks.[43] A profound impression on the country
was created by this opening attack, and almost immediately
the Insurgents were deluged with approving letters from their
constituents. An excited Iowan wrote to Dolliver:[44]

41 *Ibid.*, 61 : 1 : 1451.
42 *Ibid.*, 61 : 1 : 1464.
43 *Washington Times*, April 23, 1909.
44 C. W. Goddard to Jonathan P. Dolliver, April 26, 1909.

I am very much pleased to see you stirring up " Dr." Aldrich on the tariff question. I think you can make the Rhode Islander believe that his state ain't the only one in the nation that produces good fighters.

Of the 733 paragraphs of the bill covered in its first reading, 217 were passed over for further consideration.[45] A majority of these demands for additional debate were made by Republican Insurgents rather than by Democrats.

As the bill unfolded, Insurgent discontent crystallized. The opponents of the measure were unanimous in their support of the protectionist system, agreeing that protection was necessary to foster undeveloped American resources, and to protect American wages against destructive competition from abroad. Their main objections to the bill were three: use of the protective principle to guarantee excessive profits on manufactured goods, raising of the tariff upon raw materials that were also natural resources, and lowering of the tariff upon raw materials that aided trusts in gaining greater profits. The Insurgents wished oil, coal, lumber, iron, lead and lead ore placed on the free list, so that the influx of these natural resources from foreign countries might contribute to the preservation of American mines and forests.

45	Schedule	Paragraphs Agreed To	Passed Over
	A—Chemicals, oils, paints ...	56	23
	B—Earthenware, glass	14	20
	C—Metals	54	28
	D—Wood	7	10
	E—Sugar	3	1
	F—Tobacco	5	0
	G—Agricultural products ...	48	25
	H—Spirits, wines, etc.	12	1
	I—Cotton	12	9
	J—Flax, hemp, jute	18	9
	K—Wool	13	24
	L—Silks	8	2
	M—Pulp, paper, books	9	6
	N—Sundries	44	20
	Free List	213	39
	Total	516	217

One could argue *ad infinitum* that the protection of industries in certain localities is not a sectional program, but one designed to foster prosperity throughout the nation. Aldrich and his followers sincerely believed this doctrine, and felt that the Insurgents were really nothing more than sectional snipers.

The Aldrich system was to fashion a tariff that would benefit the manufacturers of New England, the owners of timber lands on the Pacific Coast, the mine-owners and cattle-herders of the Great Plains and mountain states, the fruit-growers and lumber interests of the South, and the steel, iron and coal men of Pennsylvania, West Virginia, and Ohio. It was beautifully symmetrical, but failed utterly in its comprehension of that vast, inarticulate group scattered throughout the country—the consumers of the finished product of these gigantic protected interests.

By practically refusing to recognize the existence of the consumer, Aldrich dismissed the claims of the group that the Insurgents were trying to defend: [46]

I ask who are the consumers? Is there any class except a very limited one that consumes and does not produce? And why are they entitled to greater consideration?

The Insurgents were not fighting for greater consideration for any one group, but for a better balance in the entire protective system, an ending of the excessive favors to specific classes, and a guarantee that prices of finished products would be within the reach of more people. As their congressional speeches and private correspondence testify, in almost every case, the Insurgents were pressing for reasonable prices for consumers all over the country. When we consider these things, the truly national scope of their program becomes clear.

Comparative calm settled upon the Senate after the spectacular outburst that greeted the first reading of the bill on April 22. Nelson continued to prance up and down the floor with his

46 *Congressional Record*, 61:1:1846.

uncompromising demands for free lumber, but Insurgency lapsed into relative silence for almost a fortnight. On Thursday the 23rd Aldrich moved an adjournment until Monday, and the air cleared somewhat. The Senate leader was still definitely worried about the initial greeting the measure had received, however. He conferred with Nelson and Cummins after the Senate finished its session on the 29th, and hinted that he was willing to meet them halfway in their demands.

A veiled warning was sent to Senator Dolliver that if he persisted in his attacks on the textile schedules, the committee on finance would overwhelm and confound him with such a barrage of facts and figures that he would be cheapened in the eyes of his constituents.[47] After this warning, Dolliver was seldom seen in public or even on the Senate floor; for three days he locked himself in his room. Aided by personally hired expert assistants, he pored over every paragraph of Schedule I and Schedule K, and singled out the jokers that would result in higher duties. The conservative *New York Tribune* looked forward with awe to what would happen when Dolliver opened fire.[48]

Dolliver's intellectual sledgehammer finally descended on the tariff bill in a devastating analysis of the cotton and woolen schedules on May 4 and 5.[49] Instead of the old orator who had painted the glories of sound Republican doctrines, and had championed protectionism in all its forms, the Senate saw a new Dolliver who rested his argument on coldly factual statistics. There was little emotional appeal in his two-day speech on the woolen and cotton schedules, and very little evidence of resentment toward the regular faction of the Republican Party with which he had been associated for so many years.

Dolliver began by pointing out the new responsibilities of Congress to public opinion, and showed how it had neglected them in the new tariff bill. He pointed out that the duty on

47 *New York World*, April 29, 1909.
48 *New York Tribune*, May 2, 1909.
49 *Congressional Record*, 61 : 1 : 1706-23 ; 1734-42.

wool "tops," the raw material of the yarn maker, was singled out for a prohibitive duty which caused greatly increased prices in many woolen products. He showed how the maintenance of the Dingley rates discriminated against the importation of cheap blankets and flannels, and how rubber boots or automobile tires with slight amounts of cotton or woolen linings were protected not under the rubber schedule, but by the excessive rates of Schedules I and K.

As dart after dart was driven beneath Aldrich's cuticle, the Senate leader squirmed and protested. He was not completely routed, and Dolliver could not controvert a few of his rebuttals. But the honors of the conflict were clearly with Dolliver, for Aldrich fell back upon his usual method of reply—an attack upon those who dared to depart from regular Republicanism.

Aldrich tried to explain in the decisive terms of one who had assisted in the framing of many tariff bills just how distorted were Dolliver's conclusions. He said in an insinuating tone that he knew the cause of Dolliver's irritation, and hoped he would not have to allude to it further—obviously a charge that the Iowan had donned feathers and paint because he had been excluded from membership in the committee on finance. When Dolliver refused to be non-plussed at this, the Senate leader dodged around a direct answer in this fashion: [50]

MR. DOLLIVER: Do you dispute the truth of what I say about these things?

MR. ALDRICH: I do not.

MR. DOLLIVER: Then you ought not to attack men of character who have been sitting up nights with me.

. . . .

MR. ALDRICH: When the Senator gets through, I will put in the Record statements made in the debate upon the Act of 1897 by the late Senator from Missouri, Mr. Vest, precisely along the lines of the statements the Senator is now making. They could be taken word for word and read by the Senator from Iowa and would produce the same effect.

50 *Ibid.*, 61 : 1 : 1715.

When Aldrich accused Dolliver of peddling Democratic propaganda, he admitted in effect that he had no specific answer to Dolliver's charges. Thereupon, the Iowa Senator quickly resumed his attack on the cotton schedule. He referred to the fact that Henry Lippitt—later Aldrich's successor in the Senate —had requested on behalf of the cotton manufacturers that no increases be made in the cotton schedule.

"Do I not speak the truth?" Dolliver quietly asked.[51]

Once again Aldrich squirmed. He protested:

Mr. President, I have no knowledge whatever of anything that transpired before the Committee on Ways and Means. I have never read the hearings before that body. I have no knowledge or idea about any statement that was made before that committee.

Certainly a damning admission from the framer of a tariff bill!

Then Dolliver proceeded to point out the myriad changes in classification of grades of cotton which had resulted in raising tariff rates in almost every category. Mercerization, dyeing, bleaching, shrinking, thread-counting—Dolliver paraded them all out to support his thesis on the second day of his speech. Lodge and Smoot then vainly tried to defend the committee on finance, after a fumbling effort by Aldrich. The leader of the Senate was shaken, and he could defend the bill only by saying that the attack on the cotton and woolen schedules was an assault upon "the very citadel of protection."

The first test of Insurgent strength came, colorfully enough, on the duty on red paint. Bristow, thinking of the barns his Kansas constituents had to keep painted, moved the substitution of the House rate of 2⅞ cents per pound for the 3⅜ cent rate backed by the committee on finance. When Aldrich tried to pass off the increase in rate as simply a restoration of the Dingley duty, Burkett demanded that he give a fuller explanation for the change. Annoyed, Aldrich replied vaguely that

51 *Ibid.*, 61 : 1 : 1719.

protection was necessary for the lead industry. Then the machine moved on irresistibly to a victory which threw out the Bristow amendment, 41-35.[52]

Among the thirty-five votes in the minority were those of ten Republicans. Of these Insurgents, Beveridge alone refused to back Bristow, claiming rather feebly that he did not know enough about the subject.[53] Beveridge apparently was still undecided as to which group he would join, for on May 3 the press listed him as willing to stand with Aldrich right or wrong.[54]

In the short period of intense feeling that followed Dolliver's speech, Bristow appears to have taken the initiative among the Insurgents. He devoted himself exclusively to mastering the lead schedule: [55]

I conducted the three days' fight with meager preparation, being in the Senate chamber all day and having to make my investigations during the night, and having made no preparation whatever on that schedule, I was at a great disadvantage. But nevertheless I seemed to acquire more information during the period between the daily sessions than the members of the Finance Committee had, and so persistent and dogged was the contest during the first day that I interested some of my good friends like Senator Nelson of Minnesota, Cummins and Dolliver and others, and they began to join in and help along.

To cut off this insistent chatter of opposition, strong-arm tactics became the next order of the day. On May 6, Bristow continued his attack on the lead paragraphs in the chemical schedule. Aldrich, who like Abou Ben Adhem always headed the list in a roll-call, kept demanding a vote during Bristow's attempts to make himself heard. The Kansan burst out with an impassioned arraignment of the senatorial procedure adopted

52 *Ibid.*, 61 : 1 : 1759.
53 *Ibid.*, 61 : 1 : 1758.
54 *New York World*, May 3, 1909.
55 Joseph L. Bristow to Harold Chase, May 22, 1909.

by the standpatters, flailing the air with his doubled fists, and demanding his constitutional rights.[56]

There was no reason why I should not be heard. I simply rose to ask some questions in order to get information which I didn't have, and my inquiries were met with sneers upon the faces of Aldrich, Hale, Keane, Penrose and a few others and a cry for a vote; and then was when it appeared to me that I either had to sit down and keep still and never undertake to say anything, or give them to understand that I knew what my rights were and intended to maintain them.[57]

" I guess I did it with a good deal of vigor—at least that is what the fellows tell me," Bristow added to another admirer.[58]

Cummins on May 6 delivered his first analysis of the defects in the report of the committee on finance. The Cummins speech did not create so much of a stir as had Dolliver's because Cummins had been preaching the same gospel in Iowa for eight years, while Dolliver's new position was a sudden break with the past. But Cummins pulled few punches in his keen criticisms of the high duties upon linoleum and oilcloth, and in his arraignment of the steel trust. The junior Senator from Iowa presented figures to support his contention that the United States Steel Corporation could have sold its products for $9 per ton less than the price received, and still have paid more than 6% on its capital.[59]

Scott, Smoot, Depew, and Aldrich ganged up on Cummins, but the suave and debonair sponsor of the Iowa Idea maintained the upper hand. He wound up with the suggestion that the rates on pig iron, structural steel, steel rails, and ingots should be cut in half, and iron ore placed on the free list.

Then Clapp, who had confined himself to brief interjected remarks, entered the fray with a sweeping review of the manner

56 *New York Sun*, May 7, 1909; *Congressional Record*, 61 : 1 : 1797.

57 Joseph L. Bristow to Cyrus Leland, Jr., May 11, 1909.

58 Joseph L. Bristow to T. D. Fitzpatrick, May 11, 1909.

59 *Congressional Record*, 61 : 1 : 1775-89.

in which the party leaders were living up to their platform and campaign pledges on the tariff.[60] Clapp's speech on May 7, like his subsequent speeches on the tariff, did not deal searchingly with specific schedules, but rather gave an overall picture of the methods that had been used in framing the measure.

Much tension and nervousness appeared among the regular leaders on May 8, when Bristow continued his assault upon heavy protective duties on pig lead and lead bullion.[61] Burkett lectured Aldrich upon the lack of information and candor shown by the committee on finance.[62] Clearly the lines had to be re-formed somehow, especially with criticisms of the arbitrary treatment accorded to Bristow now reaching the regular leaders. Finally, the organization men decided to let the Insurgents expostulate as much as they pleased, and to allow full criticism of the paragraphs of the bill before forcing a vote.[63] This was a notable concession; but if Aldrich and his cohorts hoped to stem the flow of oratory by this means they were sadly mistaken, because it acted only as an invitation for unrestricted use of the sounding board.

Returning to the attack on May 10, Cummins and Beveridge offered amendments to the lead bullion and pig lead paragraphs,[64] but they were still eight votes short of a successful alliance with the Democrats which would overthrow the regular Republicans. By this time, the Insurgents had mustered a fairly dependable bloc of eleven Republicans who refused to accept the dictates of the machine. These eleven were Dolliver and Cummins of Iowa, Clapp and Nelson of Minnesota, La Follette of Wisconsin, Bristow of Kansas, Beveridge of Indiana, Crawford and Gamble of South Dakota, and Brown and Burkett of Nebraska. Through a long series of votes during the summer

60 *Ibid.*, 61 : 1 : 1810-13.
61 *Ibid.*, 61 : 1 : 1840-44.
62 *Ibid.*, 61 : 1 : 1844-46.
63 *New York Tribune*, May 9, 1909.
64 *Congressional Record*, 61 : 1 : 1868-91.

of 1909 these Senators voted fairly consistently in combination with the Democrats against the regular Republicans.

An open clash between Beveridge and Aldrich on May 10 widened the breach between the two groups, and placed Beveridge definitely with the Insurgents. It all started when Beveridge had the clerk repeat the confession of Aldrich that the latter had failed to read the hearings of the committee on ways and means.[65] The clash was a purely personal one, and had no effect upon any definite schedule. But Beveridge's feathers were ruffled considerably when Aldrich reminded the " boy orator " that he was hardly in a position to charge lack of diligence to a man who had been engaged in making tariffs for thirty years.[66]

On May 11 and May 12 a rapprochement occurred between the warring Insurgents and their regular Republican colleagues. To emphasize that he still remained a protectionist, Dolliver made a typical high-tariff speech advocating the retention of the duty on earth and stone ware, arguing that such a duty was necessary for the preservation of a handicraft industry.[67] With the aid of Dolliver, the Republican Party became reunited for a day. During the presentation of three amendments relating to glass and china, Bristow, Crawford, and La Follette were the only Insurgents who dared to vote with the Democrats.[68] A genuine spirit of harmony was evidenced, and it looked for a moment as if the tide were turning back. The good humor of both factions reached its high point after Cummins had offered an amendment reducing the rates on all sizes of common window glass. Root, a hide-bound regular, asked Aldrich why the Cummins amendment should not be adopted. Gasps of amazement greeted this query, for it seemed that the Insurgents were about to gain another ally. Aldrich in flustered tones indicated that it was time to move the steamroller ahead a bit

65 *Supra*, p. 109.
66 *Congressional Record*, 61 : 1 : 1869.
67 *Ibid.*, 61 : 1 : 1907-08.
68 *Ibid.*, 61 : 1 : 1911.

and announced that he would give an explanation to Root in a few days.[69] The session of May 12 ended with all parties in good spirits.

The next day Coe Crawford of South Dakota delivered his maiden speech, asking for a low duty on iron ore and free trade in oil, lumber, coke and natural resources, along with income and inheritance taxes; but the typical Insurgent note of serious determination was lacking, and Crawford kept the assemblage in laughter by his constant unparliamentary references to "My Fellow Citizens," which he each time amended to "My Fellow Senators." [70]

In order to hasten the evident movement toward party harmony, Aldrich seriously considered a series of compromises with the downward revisionists, including a reduction in the duties on window glass, scrap iron, iron ore, hides, lumber, and argicultural implements.[71] He told Bristow and Cummins that he would knock ⅛ cent per pound off the duty on white lead as a concession. Bristow vehemently protested that ⅛ cent could hardly be termed a substantial concession, and urged Aldrich to offer one that would amount to something. Aldrich strode away from the pair without a word. When the paragraph was later taken up, Bristow's colleague, Charles Curtis, offered an amendment reducing the duty on white lead from 2⅞ cents to 2¾ cents to carry out the Aldrich program. Bristow was unyielding: [72]

I suppose they thought I'd hesitate to get into a controversy with Mr. Curtis under the circumstances. But I didn't hesitate a minute and we fought it out all afternoon.

On May 15 and 18 a new set of amendments emerged from Aldrich's mahogany-paneled committee room. These included a 5% reduction in the duty on forks and knives; the restoration

69 *Ibid.*, 61 : 1 : 1929.
70 *Ibid.*, 61 : 1 : 1953-62.
71 *Washington Times*, May 13, 1909.
72 Joseph L. Bristow to Harold Chase, May 22, 1909.

of the lower House rates on knitting and sewing needles; the reduction of the tariff on bronze powder and brocades from 12 to 10 cents a pound; and the lowering of the duties on Christmas tree decorations—all on Aldrich's edict.

But appeasement had come too late in the game to bring the Insurgents back into the fold. They had tasted blood, and it seemed logical for them to conclude that further saber-rattling would bring further concessions from the regulars. Insurgency was ingrained too deeply to be bought off by a few sops thrown backhandedly while the regular leaders were holding their noses. Bristow challenged: [73]

I am going to fight it out along the line I have started in. We get licked on every roll call and every vote, but still that doesn't discourage us, because we know we are right and the people are with us; and those who are on the other side will find that out later.

The events of the next few days sealed the doom of the standpat policy.

On May 20 Bristow and Cummins engaged Penrose in a bitter wrangle over the paint trust.[74] To Aldrich's protest that the debate was dragging out too long, Clapp showed his teeth and, waving his finger directly under Aldrich's nose, stated that the debate was prolonged because Aldrich himself could not furnish the requisite data on production costs.[75]

If there was any hope left for harmonizing the differences between the two factions, it was dashed completely on May 21. La Follette opened an attack on the duty upon carbons for electric lighting, charging that the rate unduly benefited the National Carbon Company. When the carbon schedule came to a vote, eleven Insurgents backed the Democrats.[76]

Now Hale of Maine, a dignified standpat elder statesman of retiring disposition, engaged in a heated argument with Bev-

---

73 Joseph L. Bristow to D. A. Valentine, May 14, 1909.
74 *Congressional Record*, 61 : 1 : 2231-33.
75 *Ibid.*, 61 : 1 : 223.
76 *Ibid.*, 61 : 1 : 2261.

eridge. He accused the Hoosier Senator of keeping a debit and credit account with the committee on finance, by distributing his votes equally for and against its proposals.[77]

Beveridge bellowed a criticism of Hale's conservatism, but it did not take Hale long to get his revenge. He introduced and had referred to the committee on finance an order for night sessions of the Senate, to begin within two weeks.[78] This was a direct blow to the Insurgents, for they counted upon having their evenings free to dig out statistical ammunition for their assault upon the schedules. Being forced now to spread their terrific labors over a sixteen-hour day, the Insurgents were hit at a vital spot. Their reaction to the demand for night sessions was typical; their determination to stick together and fight was redoubled.

It was late in May, when the tariff bill had been before the Senate a month, that the Insurgents began to lose their original faith in Taft. Dolliver, trembling with excitement and anger, reported to Beveridge that the President had turned against the Insurgents and had refused to have anything to do " with such an irresponsible set of fellows." [79] Beveridge immediately assembled the downward revision pledges that Taft had made during the campaign, and delivered an appeal to the record in justification of the position that the Insurgents were taking. But the next day when he called at the White House his reception was chilly; "a refrigerator was a bake-oven in comparison." [80]

About this time Bristow, who had placed a great deal of trust in the President at first, now began to wonder whether Taft really meant his campaign pledges seriously: [81]

77 *Ibid.*, 61 : 1 : 2269.

78 *Ibid.*, 61 : 1 : 2269.

79 Claude G. Bowers, *Beveridge and The Progressive Era*, p. 343.

80 Albert J. Beveridge to Nathaniel W. Stephenson, April 5, 1927, Nathaniel W. Stephenson notes.

81 Joseph L. Bristow to Harold Chase, May 27, 1909.

Confidentially, we have received no support whatever in this tremendous fight we have made, from the White House. We can't understand it. This is Taft's special session of Congress for the purpose of revising the tariff, reducing the rates and adjusting it to modern conditions; and instead of that we get a bill probably with no improvements over the Dingley Act, and some features that are very much worse. . . .

Undaunted by the necessity for superhuman labors in night sessions, or by presidential treachery, the Insurgents continued their battle. The first high point of the attack was Dolliver's masterful analysis of the cotton and woolen schedules on May 4 and 5. Bristow equalled this effort on May 26 and May 27 with a thorough and logical presentation of the iniquities of the sugar schedule.[82] The main object of Bristow's attack was the so-called Dutch Standard, or color test for the importation of sugar. He showed that the effect of this color test and the high import duty resulting from it, was to bar light brown sugars. He pointed out that the differential between the duty upon refined sugar and raw sugar was great enough to insure a handsome profit for the American Sugar Refining Company. Aside from the cotton and woolen schedules, this was the most complicated and intricately-phrased schedule in the Payne-Aldrich tariff. Few Senators understood its meaning, and Bristow conducted them on a thorough exploration through its maze of details and jokers. His first step was to secure a vast number of samples from Theodore Roosevelt's former secretary, William Loeb, at that time Collector of the Port of New York.[83] He placed these on exhibit during his seminar, and the Senators crowded around the show-case eagerly during the explanation. Bristow advocated the abandonment of the out-moded Dutch Standard test, and the substitution of the new polariscope test which measured the actual saccharine purity of sugar and which he demonstrated was in use in 110

82 *Congressional Record*, 61 : 1 : 2394-2408; 2427-2445.
83 William Loeb to Joseph L. Bristow, May 26, 1909.

out of 117 nations, most of which had abandoned the Dutch Standard. Bristow wrote indignantly: [84]

It is simply infamous to say to the American people that they should not produce a good, pure light brown sugar which pays the United States Government a duty of $1.80 per hundred pounds, because it has not passed through the hands of the American Sugar Refining Company before it reaches the consumer, and that is what this Dutch Standard means. . . . And the amazing thing is that Senators of the United States, who know this, will still vote to keep it there.

" It is like fighting against a stone wall," the Kansan admitted resignedly.[85]

No one answered Bristow's riddling of the sugar schedule, although Smoot made a half-hearted attempt; eventually the Dutch Standard was eliminated from the tariff law entirely. But since this was a question of party regularity, it seemed essential to the committee on finance to preserve the Dutch Standard against all assaults of its Insurgent enemies. The word went down the line, and Bristow's amendment was defeated, 47-36, with eleven Republicans taking their stand against iniquity.[86]

Little publicity attended the efforts of Bristow and the Insurgents on this schedule, because the whole thing was too complex and unspectacular for a rousing newspaper article. The shy Kansan who led the fight did not have the aptitude for publicity possessed by the dynamic La Follette or the mercurial Beveridge. But something greater than publicity emerged. That was a conviction among the Insurgents that they were fighting for truth. " We were beaten, but I don't mind being beaten when I feel that I have been fighting for the right thing," their leader wrote. [87]

84 Joseph L. Bristow to A. L. Miller, June 1, 1909.
85 Joseph L. Bristow to Harold Chase, May 27, 1909.
86 *Ibid.*, 61 : 1 : 2443.
87 Joseph L. Bristow to J. B. Trinder, May 31, 1909.

And that is the reward after all—namely, realizing in your own mind that you have done what you thought was right and have made the best effort you could, and that the people whom you are trying to serve believe that you have done that and are satisfied with your course.[88]

With the advent of June came night sessions to attempt to break the Insurgent phalanx. With it also came a struggle that Aldrich had long dreaded—the final disposition of the cotton and woolen schedules. Before a week passed, the Republican split had been rendered irreparable.

Up to this juncture La Follette had been relatively quiet on the floor of the Senate. He had asked some embarrassing questions, presented a few amendments, made some brief and caustic remarks, and always voted with the Insurgents, but he allowed his colleagues to take the lead in speech-making. Judging from the peerless quality of his efforts in the ensuing three days, he had been using his absence from debate to full advantage. Not in the entire course of the Payne-Aldrich tariff struggle did the Senate hear such a magnificent display of oratory as La Follette's speeches of June 2, 3 and 4.[89]

He opened by tracing the development of the theory of protection from Hamilton to McKinley. He stressed that the outstanding exponents of protectionism had adhered to the principles that the tariff should measure the difference in the cost of production at home and abroad, and that domestic competition should not be destroyed as a result of the tariff. La Follette described at some length how a revision of certain tariff schedules would aid in checking corporate monopoly. He pointed to the storm of disapproval that had arisen from consumers as a result of excessive duties placed upon trust-controlled products.

After three hours of emphatic gesticulating, intense effort, and constant striding from one side of the chamber to the

88 Joseph L. Bristow to Harold Chase, May 27, 1909.
89 *Congressional Record*, 61 : 2658-2664; 2686-96; 2727-52.

other, La Follette's voice started to weaken and the fire to dim. By the end of four hours the oppressive humidity and heat left him gasping and with great reluctance he yielded to the urging of his colleagues that the Senate take a thirty-minute recess. Returning, he continued his speech in measured tones.

Oil for the lamps of Insurgency was furnished in the evening session of June 3. When Beveridge asked that La Follette be excused until morning because of illness, Penrose sneeringly commented that if La Follette were indisposed he should not be openly abroad on the streets consorting with the editors of yellow journals and uplift magazines. Aldrich refused to hold up the Senate business for the " personal whims " of a single Senator, but the sense of fairness of the other regular leaders forced Aldrich to grant La Follette's request.

The third day of the Wisconsin Senator's speech was considerably tempered, but no less devastating. He was in good humor, with none of the chips that had been on his shoulder the previous day. Beveridge reported to his wife: [90]

> It was murder and sudden death today. La Follette tore the cotton schedule to pieces. I told Dillingham that even if La Follette were the devil himself, his statements were unanswerable. Aldrich has utterly lost his composure.

While his secretary brought milk and bouillon to him, La Follette pressed on with what a friendly newspaper correspondent termed a " brief for the American housewife." [91] When LaFollette concluded his three-day stand, there were few men in the Senate who would deny that the split between the regular and Insurgent factions had become so serious that it would be almost impossible to mend.

If there had been any doubt about the width of the chasm, Dolliver removed the doubt on the following day with one of the greatest oratorical efforts of his career. Dolliver's June 5

90 Albert J. Beveridge to Mrs. Catherine E. Beveridge, June 4, 1909; Claude G. Bowers, *Beveridge and the Progressive Era*, p. 345.

91 *New York World*, June 5, 1909.

speech did not reach the heights of La Follette, but it was far from being an anti-climax. It ripped to shreds the bleeding remains of the cotton schedule. Calmly he started by describing how thirty years before he had made his Republican tariff speeches with the aid of statistics furnished by Aldrich, " with a certain confidence which I confess, without any fault of my own, has gradually slipped from my mind." [92]

Then followed what one Senator present describes as one of the most dramatic moments in his senatorial career.[93] Aldrich arose hastily to leave the chamber, and Dolliver bellowed in loud tones:

" I hope the Senator from Rhode Island will remain here for a few minutes."

" I am engaged elsewhere," protested the Senate leader.

" I want to engage you here," insisted Dolliver.

" All right," said Aldrich, remaining to brave the fire of the aroused Hawkeye.

The Senator will not turn his back upon what I have to say here without taking the moral consequences which would naturally arise in the mind of a man anxious to get at the facts in this case,[94]

warned Dolliver, and hastened on with his criticisms.

He read extracts from letters protesting against increases in the cotton schedule. He cautioned the Senate that the people might tolerate a defense of higher rates, but they would never submit to a claim that the rates had been lowered when in reality there were noticeable increases.

Do adverse court decisions, as Aldrich has claimed, necessitate increases in the rates, Dolliver asked? Then why did the manufacturers during the hearings say definitely that the court decisions had cleared up all the questionable aspects of the customs law?

92 *Congressional Record*, 61 : 1 : 2845.
93 Joseph L. Bristow, interview, November, 1938.
94 *Congressional Record*, 61 : 1 : 2845.

While Dolliver's back was turned, Aldrich sneaked out of the chamber; but he certainly must have overheard the Iowan, whose tones were so stentorian that they drifted clear to the other wing of the Capitol and through the doors of a committee room.[95] This speech was the supreme effort of Dolliver's life, and he later told Senator Flint that it had caused a lesion of the heart, a condition that undoubtedly hastened his death.

Dolliver attacked Aldrich's assertion that millions of dollars had been lost by the government in duties, because of court decisions emasculating the Dingley law. He described in detail how he had approached the Treasury Department on this subject, and how the Acting Secretary of the Treasury had called the assistant collector of customs in the New York customs-house on the long-distance telephone to ask the amount refunded to importers on account of the etamine decisions.

These imaginary millions, wandering like ghosts through the aisles of the Capitol of the United States, filling the great statistical speeches of the Senator from Utah and the Senator from Massachusetts, and even the Senator from Rhode Island; these raids on our Treasury; these perversions of our laws; these nullifications of the intent and purpose of Congress—how much was involved in all of them; how much did you have to give back? Fifty-five thousand dollars! There it is (exhibiting) in the handwriting of the man who took the report over the long distance telephone from the custom-house in New York.[96]

In recalling Dolliver's June 5 speech, Cummins reflected in the words of Webster, " I only had to reach out my hand and grasp the thunderbolts as they went smoking by." [97]

As usual, Beveridge was around to provide the finishing touches for this week of turmoil by engaging in a hand-to-hand conflict with Aldrich. Beveridge was the type of man who never allowed sarcasm to be used against him without

95 Judge Marion deVries, interview, March, 1927 (Nathaniel W. Stephenson notes).

96 *Congressional Record*, 61 : 1 : 2854.

97 Claude G. Bowers, *Beveridge and The Progressive Era*, p. 344.

going his antagonist two better; and his boiling point was the
lowest of any of the generally hot-headed Insurgents. He suggested on June 7 that the tariff increases would be unbearable
to the poor. When Aldrich hotly retorted: " I have heard remarks of that kind before, rarely from Republicans, never from
protectionists," [98] it was the signal for a two-hour altercation
between Beveridge and Aldrich in which brickbats of all sizes
hurtled through the air. Angered, Aldrich began to read the
Insurgents out of the party, an act which played into the hands
of the rebels.

The handsome and polished Senator Cummins then raised
his voice to say that no man, no matter how powerful or influential, could read him out of the Republican Party.[99] He
added that he had no fears that his expulsion would be ratified
by his constituents. Aldrich continued to storm that the Insurgents' self-imposed mission of saving the Republican Party
" will not be accomplished in that manner." Cummins, who
unlike Beveridge always possessed the frigidity of an under-
ripe cucumber, pointedly remarked to Aldrich that party loyalty
consisted of loyalty to principles rather than to the will of certain leaders.

Now Dolliver offered an amendment removing from the cotton schedule the large number of rubber goods dutiable because
small bits of their compound were cotton—rubber boots, automobile tires, etc. Curiously enough, Aldrich arose and announced his acceptance of this amendment.[100] In view of the
vitriolic attacks which Dolliver and La Follette had made on
the regular leaders, and the personal clashes Beveridge and
Cummins had had with Aldrich during the day, it seems hardly
likely that the Senator from Rhode Island did this to revive
the old scheme of appeasement. Rather, he was coming to the
realization that certain portions of the cotton schedule were not
so sacrosanct as he had originally maintained, and he was

98 *Congressional Record*, 61 : 1 : 2887.

99 *Ibid.*, 61 : 1 : 2897.

100 *Ibid.*, 61 : 1 : 2901.

merely starting to give it a little better window-dressing before
the Republican party had to go to its defense at the polls.

Dolliver declined to be diverted from his course by this concession. The following day he took the floor for a five-hour
arraignment of the duties in Schedule K, the woolen schedule.
He insisted that the existing duties would ruin the carded
woolen manufacturing business and that the rates were fixed
solely in the interest of the worsted manufacturers. He showed
the injustice of increasing the duties on woolen waste, since the
carded woolen manufacturers made a uniformly cheaper
grade of goods. Dolliver also pointed out the existence of a
federation between the wool-growers of the West and the
woolen manufacturers of the East, back-scratching and pulling
together for high tariffs on wool and woolen goods.

With the conclusion of Dolliver's speech on June 9 came the
end of another phase of the Insurgent opposition to the tariff
bill. The first nine days of June had borne the most terror for
the regular machine of any during the entire three months when
the bill was before the Senate. In these nine days the Insurgents
rose to their greatest oratorical and analytical heights, and did
their most effective work in exposing the bad features of the
measure. In the four weeks remaining before the final vote
was taken, the Insurgents did not abate their work. But they
raised few new issues and merely rehashed old arguments—
still fighting fiercely, but marking time in comparison with
their earlier efforts.

On June 17 commenced a crusade led by Norris Brown of
Nebraska to place wood pulp and print paper on the free list.
Young, energetic, and keen-witted in debate, Brown made a
sizable dent in the armor of the standpatters by his demonstra-
tion that American mills were able to produce print paper
cheaper than Canada could. Brown urged the necessity of placing wood pulp on the free list in order to conserve American
natural resources, and held his ground well against the heated
questioning of Aldrich, Hale, and Frye.[101]

101 *Ibid.*, 61 : 1 : 3391-3407 ; 3416-3424.

Conviction and party loyalty were contradictory considerations in Brown's mind, and Aldrich knew well that Brown was
not as rabid in his Insurgency as were the other middle-west-
erners. So the Senate leaders adopted the familiar technique of
trying to recapture Brown by warning him that he was a bolter.
Gallinger taunted Brown with being an Insurgent, and Aldrich
joined in the catcalls at the wavering Republicanism of the
Nebraskan. To complicate the situation, or possibly to clarify
it for Brown, Bailey of Texas extended a cordial invitation
to the Nebraskan to come over and join the Democratic Party.
But Brown was fully equal to the occasion: " I simply rose to
say that I cannot consent either to be disinherited by the Senator
from Rhode Island or adopted by the Senator from Texas." [102]

Brown held the floor for more than three hours, and made a
good impression; his argument induced nine Insurgents to oppose the committee on finance proposal to levy a $4 per ton
duty on print paper.[103]

Considered as a whole, the Insurgent efforts in behalf of
revision of Schedule M, the wood pulp and print paper schedule,
seem rather tame in comparison with the magnificent struggle
conducted on Schedules I and K. Yet if Brown's stand for
lower duties in Schedule M had occurred earlier in the session,
it no doubt would have created more of a stir and would have
acted as a great rallying point for the opponents of Aldrich. As
it was, the enervating heat of mid-June and the fact that Insurgency had become a common phenomenon reduced the importance of Brown's two-day stand to a level that the effort in
itself did not merit.

The aftermath of the argument over Schedule M fitted well
into the pattern of Insurgency. Once again Beveridge engaged
in a personal controversy—on this occasion with Burton of
Ohio. On June 19, Beveridge led off with an attack on the cash
register trust. Burton, since the seat of the trust was in Ohio,
was roused to a sharp reply: [104]

102 *Ibid.*, 61 : 1 : 3439. 103 *Ibid.*, 61 : 1 : 3483.
104 *Ibid.*, 61 : 1 : 3496.

I think, Mr. President, we have had a little too much of this style of argument when duties are under consideration here. If anyone desires to lower a duty or raise a duty or advance any wish of his, he can come in here and shout with clenched fists: "Trust! Monopoly! Octopus!" Perhaps he might go on with all the rest of the animals and very likely they have as little to do with the business under consideration as any of the animals that might be mentioned.

Burton's criticism carried a great deal of truth, for the Insurgents indulged in a rather indiscriminate use of symbols in their battle for righteousness. They attached horns and a tail to every individual who was reluctant to move at their pace; they tossed terms around with reckless abandon, solely to conjure up images of evil; but their technique was a howling success both from the publicity and the political angle.

The last extended analysis of a single aspect of the tariff bill was a speech by Beveridge on June 24 supporting his amendment to restore certain taxes on tobacco.[105] A month before, Beveridge had explained in Congress briefly and clearly how the Government had lost close to $200,000,000 in taxes since 1902 because of the repeal of the 1898 tax. Yet he showed that before the repeal of the tax, the tobacco manufacturers had reduced the size of their packages. Thus when the tax was lifted it meant in effect that the consumers paid the difference —which went into the coffers of the tobacco combine. Having laid the ground work, Beveridge now moved forward in June with a proposal to reinstitute the tobacco taxes, and also to place licorice and its extracts on the free list, since licorice had been monopolized by the American Tobacco Company. He also moved to restore the anti-coupon provision of the Dingley Act, this provision having been repealed in 1902 along with the war revenue taxes. The use of the coupon system since 1902 had, he explained, been instrumental in aiding the American Tobacco Company to crush out its independent competitors.

105 *Ibid.*, 61 : 1 : 3728-43.

For four and a half hours on June 24, Beveridge unfolded his tale of pillage and plunder. Besides crushing competition, the tobacco trust maintained a set of paid lobbyists who did not hesitate at bribery to influence legislation directly, Beveridge asserted. The standpatters were silent, just as they had been after Bristow's exposé of the notorious Dutch Standard test used in the sugar schedule. Root congratulated Beveridge privately,[106] and no attempt was made by the regulars to controvert Beveridge's charges. This would not be such a striking thing had not Aldrich a month before, when Beveridge first posed his indictment of the tobacco trust, furiously declared: " You are wrong about this and you will find it out." [107] Now Aldrich ignored Beveridge entirely. Perhaps the Senate leader did not wish to aid in publicizing the Insurgents by engaging in another personal quarrel with Beveridge; perhaps he feared him as a superior antagonist, although Aldrich seldom took this attitude toward any man. In any event, Aldrich's failure to reply created the distinct impression that some truth was contained in Beveridge's charges, and this left the Insurgents in a better strategic position.

Gradually the tariff fight neared its close, with the Insurgents still banded together on amendments in futile opposition to the smooth-functioning Aldrich machine. Time and again the Insurgents were whipped, and Aldrich was serene and unworried as to the ultimate outcome. Four days before the final vote, the Rhode Islander was the object of a bitter verbal attack by La Follette, in the middle of which he left the Senate chamber. As La Follette's diatribe increased in intensity, Smoot and Flint held a hurried consultation and decided that Aldrich should be brought into the chamber to reply. Smoot opened the office door of the committee on finance, and was greeted by a healthy snore; Aldrich was stretched out on his sumptuous leather couch. When Smoot suggested the propriety of respond-

106 Albert J. Beveridge to Mrs. Catherine E. Beveridge, June 25, 1909; Claude G. Bowers, *Beveridge and the Progressive Era*, p. 356.
107 *Ibid.*

ing to La Follette, Aldrich rubbed his eyes, rolled over, and announced that he would take another nap.[108] He was supremely satisfied that the trumps were in his hand, and that oratory would change no votes.

Throughout the tariff struggle, the Insurgents gravely considered how their cause would be affected by an adverse vote on the final roll-call. When the fight had progressed a month, Bristow mused:[109]

I am thinking of voting against it. La Follette feels the same way and so does Dolliver. What the others will decide on doing I do not know.

There was scarcely any doubt about this trio, the three men who had carried most of the Insurgent burden throughout the summer. They were pre-ordained to vote against the bill. With Cummins, the case was slightly different. He was already being outstripped by Dolliver in his ardor for Insurgency, an easily explicable phenomenon because a convert is almost always a more fearless battler than one who has grown up with a cause Yet Cummins was still part and parcel of the old " Iowa Idea ," and his experiences with the metals and glass schedules of the tariff left little doubt that he would vote against the bill.

Clapp was an enigma, because he had been rather quiet in comparison with the others; but he had voted so often with the Insurgents and had been such a pillar of strength in the private conferences that he could be counted among Aldrich's opponents. Clapp's Minnesota colleague, Nelson, indicated that he would be true to his constituency, which was rampantly for downward revision.

The *New York World* of May 3 probably represented Beveridge's attitude correctly when it reported him as willing to stand for the bill and with Aldrich right or wrong.[110] But in the

108 *Washington Times*, July 3, 1909.
109 Joseph L. Bristow to Harold Chase, May 27, 1909.
110 *New York World*, May 3, 1909.

ensuing weeks Beveridge crossed the Rubicon by engaging Aldrich and many of the leading regulars in a series of bitter personal debates. It was almost too late for him to turn back and save face. Brilliant, scintillating, cocksure—he was striving for his place in the sun, and concluded that it could best be attained by casting his vote against the Senate bill.

The position of the four Senators from South Dakota and Nebraska was uncertain as July 8, the day of the final Senate vote, approached. Robert Gamble, the senior Senator from South Dakota, had gone along with the Insurgents in many of their sallies in the early days of the session, but later he faltered and soon was securely ensconced in the regular ranks. Gamble's colleague, Coe Crawford, had a direct mandate from his constituents to throw all his strength to the Insurgents, for in 1908 he had personally defeated the machine of standpat Senator Kittredge. Crawford took an active part in the attack on the tariff, made numerous speeches and criticisms of the schedules, and seemed to be leaning toward the opponents of the bill.

Norris Brown, who had conducted the able criticism of Schedule M, the wood pulp and print paper schedule, was the more progressive of the two Nebraska Senators. He frequently came to the aid of the other Insurgents both in votes and by timely remarks on the floor. He was inclined to oppose the final bill because Nebraska had no great interests or industries to protect—no mines, no lumber industry, no cotton mills.[111] Burkett only occasionally spoke out in favor of the Insurgents, and he tended to cast his votes a little less frequently with the opponents of Aldrich. Yet he appreciated the depth of feeling in Nebraska for a genuine revision of the tariff, as he explained to former Vice-President Fairbanks after the session.[112]

On July 8, La Follette began the Insurgent denunciation of the bill by characterizing it as a revision upward. He topped

111 Norris Brown, interview, September, 1938.
112 Elmer Burkett to Charles Fairbanks, August 31, 1909.

off his two-hour speech with a brilliant peroration calling upon the Insurgents to vote against it.[113]

After La Follette had concluded, Beveridge rose to make his position clear:[114]

Mr. President, when a protective tariff rate is beyond the requirements of honest protection, it represents a moral instead of an economic question. Mr. President, our votes shall be cast in harmony with our party's pledge as voiced by our party leader—the Nation's President.

Beveridge's catechism roused Aldrich to anger, and the Senate leader replied:[115]

Mr. President, I have been in the public service long enough to have seen several occasions when individual members of this body, or individuals outside of the body, have thought that they were wiser than their party associates, and that their views should control the action of the party, notwithstanding the vote of majorities. . . . I say to the Senator from Indiana and his friends that the Republican Party is a party of majorities, and the views of the majority in matters of legislation control party policies and control governmental policies. The Senator from Indiana does not speak for the Republican Party. . . .

The sounding of the tocsin of party regularity by Senator Aldrich was a last attempt to draw the near-Insurgents back into the party fold and force them to vote for the tariff. It was a grievous mistake on Aldrich's part, because it called forth indignant explanations from the other Insurgents.

Coe Crawford was one of those stung by the tone of Aldrich's remarks. The question of regularity worried him, and he lashed back with the fury of a wounded lion. " Yelling as loud as a tornado," [116] he defied Aldrich to read him out of the Republican Party:

113 *Congressional Record*, 61 : 1 : 4308-10.
114 *Ibid.*, 61 : 1 : 4314.
115 *Ibid.*, 61 : 1 : 4314.
116 *New York World*, July 9, 1909.

I do not think the Chairman of the Finance Committee has any more authority to say to me that I have no right to speak as a Republican, or express my sentiments as a Republican Senator, than I have to say the same to him . . . . Does the Senator from Rhode Island say to me that because I propose to exercise my judgment and my conscience in a matter of this kind I am not a good and loyal member of my party? I maintain that it is the duty of every member of this body to stand here and represent his judgment and his conscience in regard to the bill as it is here in any form for consideration.[117]

Clapp arose and announced that the criticism of Aldrich "neither has stung to silence nor entombed at least one Senator." [118] Nelson gave his confession of faith as follows: [119]

I simply wish to say on this occasion that it takes more than the state of Rhode Island to read the state of Minnesota out of the Republican Party.

The Republican ranks were being shattered. The Democrats rejoiced as one Insurgent after another arose to give his reasons for bolting, and the linen of the Republican Party never received a more thorough or a more public ablution. Blind Senator Gore ruminated on the consequences with the comment that " it may not be so wild a prophecy to say that the next President will be an African." [120] This adroit reference to Roosevelt brought down the house.

Up to almost the last minute, claimed one newspaper of the time, it was expected and predicted that the only Republican votes cast against the bill would be those of Senators Nelson, Clapp, La Follette, Bristow and Dolliver, with the possible addition of Cummins.[121] This was but wishful thinking on the

117 *Congressional Record*, 61 : 1 : 4315.
118 *Ibid.*, 61 : 1 : 4315.
119 *Ibid.*, 61 : 1 : 4315.
120 *Ibid.*, 61 : 1 : 4316.
121 *New York World*, July 9, 1909.

part of some old guardsmen, for Cummins, Beveridge, Crawford and the Nebraskans all voted against the bill. It carried by 45-34, but the following ten Insurgents refused to vote with the regulars: [122]

Beveridge, Indiana	Crawford, South Dakota
Bristow, Kansas	Cummins, Iowa
Brown, Nebraska	Dolliver, Iowa
Burkett, Nebraska	La Follette, Wisconsin
Clapp, Minnesota	Nelson, Minnesota

In the House, the Insurgents united behind Norris' resolution instructing the conference committee to accept only those Senate amendments that constituted a lowering of the duties contained in the Payne bill.[123] However, they mustered a strength of only fifteen for this end, and the regular leaders dictated a simple resolution disagreeing with the Senate amendments and asking for a conference.[124]

The tariff bill now started its rocky progress through the conference committee. During the four weeks between the passage of the bill and the consideration of the conference report, most of the Insurgents spent their time recuperating from their arduous labors of the preceding months. They had been running on nervous energy through sweltering heat, pushing themselves to the limit of their endurance. Cummins during this session worked an average of sixteen hours a day, according to his sister who acted as his secretary.[125] Beveridge plunged ahead in spite of his recent operation, and wrote his wife during the battle:

" I'm tired of work—so tired—you can't imagine how tired." [126]

122 *Congressional Record*, 61:1: 4316.

123 *Ibid.*, 61 : 1 : 4374-4376.

124 *Ibid.*, 61 : 1 : 4384-4385.

125 Miss Anna B. Cummins, interview, September, 1938.

126 Albert J. Beveridge to Mrs. Catherine E. Beveridge, June 1, 1909, Claude G. Bowers, *Beveridge and the Progressive Era*, p. 347.

" I must work hard tonight. I am lonely and weary and disgusted and worn out." [127]

" Worked and worried all last night . . . I am very tired and almost at the limit of endurance." [128]

Dolliver, who had relied theretofore upon his oratorical ability, was roused to fury and labored long past midnight throughout the special session in his supreme effort to fashion new arrows to aim at Aldrich and his crowd. Bristow worked like a truck-horse. " I could write a volume about my experiences here, but I am driven to death with work," he wrote to his friend Chase,[129] and yearned for the institution of a longer working day so he could jam in enough time to digest the many intricate details of the tariff bill.

La Follette more than the others applied himself with redoubled vigor while speaking on the floor of the Senate—hence his proximity to collapse during the peerless oration on the cotton schedule. Early in the session one of his colleagues noted that La Follette spent every free moment in his office at work, and that while most of the other Senators were congregating in the cloak rooms or lunch room discussing different angles of national questions, the Wisconsin Insurgent was always " down in his committee room digging out the details of some questions of legislation." [130]

And when the bill finally passed, rest was in order. Beveridge left the bloody scene behind, and retired to Dublin, New Hampshire. He announced :[131]

I shall return when the bill comes out of conference, remain here until its final passage, and then go to Dublin and do nothing but sleep for two months.

127 *Ibid.*, June 28, 1909, p. 347.
128 *Ibid.*, July 8, 1909, p. 347.
129 Joseph L. Bristow to Harold Chase, May 22, 1909.
130 Joseph L. Bristow to D. B. Kirtland, March 20, 1909.
131 Albert J. Beveridge to John C. Shaffer, July 9, 1909; Claude G. Bowers, *Beveridge and the Progressive Era*, p. 360.

La Follette entrained for Wisconsin, and delayed his departure only long enough to submit a memorandum to Taft outlining his view of the changes that should be effected in the conference report in order to make it fulfill the pledges of the party platform.[132]

Immediately the question arose as to how the Insurgents would stand on the conference report. An accurate prediction was made by one of the leading Insurgents as soon as the vote in the Senate had been taken. Thus even before the conference had started its work, it was clear which way the wind was blowing. This party rebel wrote to his wife that Cummins, Dolliver, Clapp, Nelson, La Follette, Bristow and Beveridge would, he was " very sure," be against the conference report. " Possibly but not probably the other three," he added.[133] This indicates that the seven Insurgents who eventually voted against the conference report were already apprehensive that they would lose the votes of Brown, Burkett, and Crawford, who had opposed the bill in July.

Bristow at first hoped that the conference would produce a bill which, although not in strict compliance with the pledges, would be a sufficient improvement over the Dingley law to enable some of the Insurgents to support it.[134] He was far from sanguine, however, as to what the conference would do.[135]

I am waiting to see what it is to determine how I shall vote, but of course expect that my vote on the bill shall be consistent with my votes during the session.

The position of Burkett, an Insurgent who rejoined the regulars on the vote on the conference report, was originally firm. Four days after the Senate had balloted, Burkett outlined to President Taft the items that he thought the conference com-

132 Robert M. La Follette, *Autobiography*, p. 449; Robert M. La Follette to William Howard Taft, July 13, 1909.

133 Confidential manuscript source.

134 Joseph L. Bristow to W. W. Sutton, July 10, 1909.

135 Joseph L. Bristow to O. Lonergan, July 22, 1909.

mittee should alter in order to secure his support. He argued that lumber, iron ore and coal should be placed on the free list, and he criticized the fact that the Senate had raised the steel schedules above the level set in the House bill. " The cotton and woolen schedules are ridiculously high," wrote Burkett.[136] " Of this of course Senator Dolliver can give you more of the details than I." Burkett did not threaten to vote against the conference report unless all of these items were secured, but he made clear his emphatic opposition to certain schedules in the Senate bill.

Beveridge lunched with the President on the 13th, and conveyed the impression that in case the bill were changed substantially in the conference, he would vote for it.[137]

But the conference committee emasculated Beveridge's tobacco tax, and fell with relish upon his proposal for a tariff commission. Taft reassured Beveridge on the subject, but clearly favored a weaker body.[138] Striking out the words "information useful to Congress in tariff legislation," and also the authorization " to make thorough investigations and examinations into the production, commerce and trade of the United States and foreign countries and all conditions affecting the same," the conferees left only a hollow shell of the original proposal.[139]

With both of his hobbies cut to ribbons, Beveridge was sorely shaken. "I don't want to vote against the President, yet I don't want to vote for the report," was his position on July 25.[140]

On the same day Taft was writing to his wife:[141]

I don't know what the insurgents are going to do; whether Beveridge and his crowd are going to vote for the bill or to vote

136 Elmer J. Burkett to William Howard Taft, July 13, 1909.

137 William Howard Taft to Mrs. H. H. Taft, July 14, 1909.

138 William Howard Taft to Albert J. Beveridge, July 26, 1909.

139 Claude G. Bowers, *Beveridge and the Progressive Era*, p. 363.

140 Albert J. Beveridge to Mrs. Catherine E. Beveridge, June 28, 1909, Claude G. Bowers, *op. cit.*, p. 363.

141 William Howard Taft to Mrs. H. H. Taft, July 25, 1909.

against it. It would be better for us if they were to vote for the bill, but I don't know how much better.

Taft was still hopeful of winning Beveridge on July 30,[142] but on that day the latter had definitely decided to throw his lot against the conference report and leave the results of his action to the people.[143]

Meanwhile the conference had commenced its laborious duty of trying to compromise two totally different tariff bills, while the neglected presidential " big stick " was at last swinging into action in a belated endeavor to secure a genuine fulfillment of the party pledges. In general, the House conferees operated on the principle that they would accept any lowering of the rates that had been voted by the Senate,[144] but Payne clamored for a high duty on gloves and stockings.[145] The conference was in a turmoil when Taft interposed his demands for the lower Senate rate on gloves and hosiery, for free iron ore, coal, oil, hides, and a lower duty on lumber. Regarding the conference committee, Taft let it be known that " he would like to tell some of the members that they could go to Hell." [146] The trouble in the conference committee had its roots in the bargains and deals effectuated in order to put through the tariff bill. An indignant friend of Secretary of State Philander C. Knox wrote that the border states had lined up solidly for protected raw materials. He added that the members of the House from those states had been promised by House Whip Dwight and other organization leaders, verbally and in writing, that if the Payne bill passed, the Senate would take care of placing sufficient duties upon iron ore, coal and oil. Also, Knox's informant con-

142 William Howard Taft to Mrs. H. H. Taft, July 30, 1909.

143 Albert J. Beveridge to Mrs. Catherine E. Beveridge, July 30, 1909, Claude G. Bowers, op. cit., p. 363.

144 James S. Sherman to L. W. Emerson, July 21, 1909; William Howard Taft to Mrs. H. H. Taft, July 11, 1909.

145 Archie Butt, Taft and Roosevelt: The Intimate Letters of Archie Butt, Vol. I, p. 148.

146 M. A. DeWolfe Howe, George von Lengerke Meyer, p. 442.

tinued, the Representatives from the border states had been assured that Speaker Cannon would appoint members on the conference committee who would see to it that the duties voted by the Senate would be maintained on these articles. However, *mirabile dictu,* if reports were true, the President was carrying to excess his idea of revision downward and was actually insisting upon free raw materials to the detriment of both the iron and steel interests and the future of Republican control in the border states.[147]

The glove bargain between Littauer and Cannon continued to embarrass the conferees when Taft demanded that it be scotched. Even more embarrassing to Aldrich personally was Taft's firm opposition to higher duties upon hides, for the Senate leader's promise to the range Senators was one that he could not honorably break. However, Taft provided a face-saver for Aldrich by allowing him to pass the buck and put the blame for destroying the bargain entirely on the President:[148]

I told him he could use me as he pleases, and that I would threaten him if he wished me to, with a view to making some of these people come over.

Counterbalancing Taft's pressure on the conference committee were the indicated intentions of thirty Senators from mining and forest areas to vote against the bill if it provided for free ore, coal, and reductions in the duty on lumber,[149] and the persistent attempts of the range Senators and Speaker Cannon to see that their own deals were carried out. If Taft had added Schedules I and K to his reform program, the Insurgents would undoubtedly have supported the conference report; but Taft saw the impracticability of this course since the cotton and woolen schedules had not been lowered in either House,[150]

147 Joseph G. Butler, Jr. to Philander C. Knox, July 17, 1909.
148 William Howard Taft to Mrs. H. H. Taft, July 12, 1909.
149 William Howard Taft to Mrs. H. H. Taft, July 11, 1909.
150 William Howard Taft to Marcus Marks, June 29, 1909.

and the union of wool-growers and woolen manufacturers was too strong to buck.[151] Only in an off moment did he consider touching Schedule K, and this was when Warren's refusal to yield a lower duty on hides riled the President. Archie Butt reports the President's reaction:[152]

Then he made this remark, which smacked so much of President Roosevelt that it made my blood tingle: " I have tried persuasion with Warren, and if that does not do he can go to hell with his wool schedule and I will defeat him without compromise."

" Taft insists party shall keep pledge " was the substance of hundreds of newspaper headlines all over the country on July 17. Twenty of the House standpatters had importuned the President to maintain the protection on oil, coal, hides, and iron ore. Langley of Kentucky snorted at downward revision, and remarked, " If we fail to protect our constituents, we will be revised downward into private life." [153] But Taft was adamant. He replied by repeating the Republican platform and his interpretation that it meant downward revision in most instances.

Taft's statement did not bring any of the Insurgents closer to a support of the conference report, however. Bristow was outspoken in his accord with the President's remarks, but he added ruefully that if the Aldrich bill had complied with the tenor of Taft's remarks, the Insurgents would all have voted for it when it passed the Senate on July 8.[154]

Bristow was bitter against Taft, and lamented:[155]

If there was any place where the President should have shown his hand, it was in this tariff revision. It was his measure, his policy, his pledge, his declaration, his special session; and some of us who

151 William Howard Taft to Albert J. Beveridge, July 13, 1909.

152 Butt, op. cit., Vol. I, p. 146; cf. William Howard Taft to Mrs. H. H. Taft, July 22, 1909.

153 Philadelphia Ledger, July 17, 1909.

154 Philadelphia Ledger, July 17, 1909.

155 Joseph L. Bristow to Fred C. Trigg, June 21, 1909.

have never been very ardent revisionists went into this as much
from a sense of duty as we did from any conviction as to the necessity of the work. . . . If we had had one-half the help from the
President in regard to the revision of the tariff that Aldrich had
had in his opposition to the income tax, we would have had a fine
new tariff bill through the Senate, fulfilling every pledge made to
the people in the last campaign, and had it easily.

In the intervening weeks between July 8 and the Senate
vote on the conference report on August 5, Senator Cummins
was weighing his position. Cummins breakfasted with Taft on
the 22nd, and Taft learned that Cummins wanted to vote for
the bill if several changes were made.[156] Cummins stressed
the iniquities of the cotton and woolen schedules, and pleaded
for a few alterations in the duties on structural iron. After
Cummins had left the White House, however, Taft was rather
dubious as to whether he would be able to get a bill that the
Iowa Senator would support.[157] Eight days later Taft was told
that Cummins was still inclined to vote for the bill.[158] But his
informant must have been an incurable optimist.

Norris Brown had opposed most of the recommendations
of the committee on finance and had voted with the Insurgents
on many occasions during the session. As the final vote on the
conference report approached, he warned Taft against increases
in the leather duties, but the President smoothed over this
difficult situation so adroitly [159] that Brown was ready to support the conference report when it came up on August 5. Brown
wrote some thirty years later: [160]

I voted against the passage of the 1909 Senate Tariff Bill when
it was passed in the Senate, but voted for the Conference Report
because I believed it to be an improvement on the existing tariff law.

156 William Howard Taft to Mrs. H. H. Taft, July 22, 1909.
157 *Ibid.*
158 William Howard Taft to Mrs. H. H. Taft, July 30, 1909.
159 William Toward Taft to Norris Brown, August 2, 1909.
160 Norris Brown to Kenneth W. Hechler, December 1, 1939.

Likewise, Coe Crawford, who had voted against the Senate Bill on July 8, felt that the conference committee had improved the measure enough so that he was prepared to vote for it.[161] Crawford's mouthpiece, the *Sioux Falls Daily Press,* which had been singing hymns of praise for Crawford's fearless opposition to the Aldrich machine, now found itself in as embarrassing a position as a Communist newspaper trying to explain the Russo-German non-aggression pact. The *Daily Press* finally concluded that South Dakota was not as interested in the tariff as were other states, that progressive Republicanism had more to do with the regulation of railroads and corporations than with tariffs, and that " the Progressives of South Dakota may be better satisfied with their Senators' votes when the Senate takes up problems related to the principles for which South Dakota Progressives have stood." [162]

Six of the Insurgents held a meeting on the 25th of July to discuss the position that they would take on the conference report. Beveridge indicated a disposition to vote for the conference report, but seemed unwilling to desert his Insurgent colleagues if they all voted against it. La Follette announced that he would do the thing that conscience dictated, which left no doubt of his position. Cummins laid down as the *sine qua non* of his support for the conference report that the bill must be an improvement over the Dingley bill in the woolen, cotton, glass and steel schedules. Dolliver was strongly against many of the features of the bill. Clapp stood like a stone wall with the Insurgents, and told the other five that he counted upon his colleague, Nelson, to be against anything that came out of the conference.

On the 30th, Nelson, lunching with Taft, announced that he felt he must vote against the bill. Yet even at that late date the President expressed hopes that Cummins, Dolliver and Beveridge might come over to the regulars. It was not until

161 *Sioux Falls Daily Press,* August 5, 1909.
162 *Sioux Falls Daily Press,* August 6, 1909.

six of the Senate Insurgents had made their appearance on the floor of the House and pointed out the conference report jokers to numerous Representatives, that the White House finally gave up hope of the redemption of the rebels. The Republican machine in the House defeated a recommittal motion by the narrow margin of 191-186,[163] which to Taft was "uncomfortably close." [164] The President then conceded that the Senate Insurgents "will vote against the bill probably but I don't think they will make bitter speeches on the subject." [165] That night he and Archie Butt, riding together in a motor car, never spoke, ". . . and stranger than all, he never slept, and when I glanced at him to see if he were asleep, he was looking hard into the fleeting darkness ahead." [166]

Now the Insurgents boldly proclaimed the reasons for their position. Taft's prediction was well-founded, however, for most of the oratory during the last few days was moderate.

Speaking in the Senate three days before the vote on the report, Bristow offered unimpassioned statistical proof that the party pledges were not being fulfilled. He challenged any Senator on the floor to show that the increases he cited were based upon calculation of the difference in costs of production at home and abroad. The statement was concise, tempered and effective, and not intended as a blood-stirring warcry. He concluded: [167]

This is a New England bill. I love the President . . . and for one I will never vote to send him a bill for approval that is a violation of his party's pledges. . . .

One by one the Insurgents followed Bristow in setting forth their reasons for bolting the party. The next day, Clapp ex-

163 Congressional Record, 61 : 1 : 4755.

164 William Howard Taft to Charles P. Taft, August 1, 1909.

165 Ibid.

166 Archie Butt, Taft and Roosevelt: The Intimate Letters of Archie Butt, Vol. I, p. 167.

167 Congressional Record, 61 : 1 : 4789.

pounded his theory of protection, and sadly described its abandonment for a new system whose purpose seemed to be to
perpetuate, uphold and intensify profit.[168]

The parade of Insurgent objections was interrupted on the
day before the vote when Beveridge held the floor for an extended discussion of his pride and joy, a tariff commission, and
he showed how thoroughly the regulars had riddled his plan.
But the Indiana Senator, who had wavered so uncertainly
between Insurgency and regularity before arriving at a final
decision, did not clarify the reasons for his position while the
other Insurgents were making their public confessions of faith.

Gamble of South Dakota, one of the early Insurgents who
made a hurried return to the regular fold before the July 8 vote
on the Senate bill, announced it as his considered opinion that
the conference report was the best possible compromise obtain-
able, and that to vote it down would disorganize the party and
cause unexampled chaos.[169] Gamble spoke in forced and uncon-
vincing tones. Significantly, Crawford, Brown, and Burkett
(the three Insurgents who rejoined the regulars on the
August 5 vote) gave no public reasons why they intended to
support the conference report.

Cummins' final speech was a classic example of measured
criticism. Admitting that the bill was a slight improvement
over the Dingley act, he stated tellingly: " This is not a court
of bankruptcy, and I am not willing to accept ten cents on the
dollar in discharge of the obligations of the Republican
Party." [170]

But no tempers were lost as a consequence of the Cummins
statement, and all was sweetness and light when Dolliver arose
for his final speech of the session. Aldrich was reconciled to
the fact that some of the Insurgents would bolt, and he did his
best to make it appear that there was no deep split in the party.
In line with this program he had already juggled the list of

168 *Ibid.*, 61 : 1 : 4848.
169 *Ibid.*, 61 : 1 : 4875.
170 *Ibid.*, 61 : 1 : 4880.

speakers so as to make sure that La Follette would not take the floor in a rabble-rousing peroration before the vote was taken.[171]

It was Dolliver who wrecked the Aldrich strategy. Three nights before, the Iowa Senator had penned a little note to his wife: " This is Monday night, and we are in the midst of the final struggle on the tariff. I cannot on my conscience vote for it." Mrs. Dolliver telegraphed in reply, " Vote against the report if you are the only one."

The new Dolliver was in full bloom when he spoke on August 5. The facts and figures and easy familiarity with the technical phases of the cotton and woolen industries had come to him by long hours of inspired application. His sense of drama, his powerful voice, and his remarkable memory were developed by many years of training. Woven into these were his emotional zeal, his desperate frustration at the ease with which Aldrich waved his wand to defeat all opposition amendments, and the universal acclaim that Iowa was according the new Dolliver. Gone were his indolence and his dependence upon phrase-turning and flag-waving as a means of gaining recognition. At last he had achieved his full stature.

Scorchingly, he denounced the methods by which the tariff had been prepared—the bargains and deals necessary to corral a majority, the hurried disinclination to consider things beneath the surface, the sneers of ridicule that had greeted any attempt of the Insurgents to discover the facts. He blasted the claims of the regulars that no substantial changes had been made in Schedule I. In reply to the latter claims, Dolliver stated movingly:[172]

I have but a few more years in this world. I sometimes have been willing to deceive myself for the sake of the comfort which comes from the society and good will of others; but I do not propose now to become a party to a petty swindle of the American people

171 *Ibid.*, 61 : 1 : 4954.
172 *Ibid.*, 61 : 1 : 4928.

without telling them the truth and without appealing to their good will and their confidence in the integrity of my motives.

He reiterated his charges against Schedule K, and steadfastly refused to acquiesce in the program about to pass the Senate " under the belated pressure of party authority and influence."

Dolliver's peroration rallied the Insurgents while holding aloft the banner of Republicanism:[173]

Mr. President, the Republican Party, if I understand its history, is a great deal larger than the schedules of a tariff law. There is room in it for every man's honest convictions. . . . The Republican Party is face to face, as in the days of its youth, with the elementary questions which concern justice and liberty.

When Dolliver sat down, everyone realized that Insurgency was a living and a vital movement.

With openly confessed weariness, Aldrich arose as the agreed hour of two o'clock approached. Displaying none of the haughty superiority that had characterized his actions in reading the Insurgents out of the party on July 8, he now resignedly expressed his regret that such an important measure should not receive the unanimous approval of Republicans " who believe, as I do, in the policy of the party and in the principles of protection."[174]

Aldrich made his brief statement just strong enough to clarify the fact that he regarded the issue as a test of party fealty. But it was only for the record, for the lines had long since formed. When the roll was called, seven Republicans voted against the conference report, which was adopted by 47-31.[175] The seven were:

173 *Ibid.*, 61 : 1 : 4932.
174 *Ibid.*, 61 : 1 : 4932.
175 *Ibid.*, 61 : 1 : 4949.

Beveridge, Indiana   Cummins, Iowa
Bristow, Kansas   Dolliver, Iowa
Clapp, Minnesota   La Follette, Wisconsin
            Nelson, Minnesota

A brief scuffle over a concurrent resolution amending the hides schedule, and the Payne-Aldrich tariff debate of 1909 passed into history.

CHAPTER VI
TAXATION AND MISREPRESENTATION

ALTHOUGH the Insurgents altered only a few schedules of the tariff bill, they were more successful in striving for income tax legislation. Cummins and Borah, who formed the spearhead of the Insurgent drive for an income tax, threw holy terror into the regular ranks and hastened by several years the adoption of the sixteenth amendment.

Since the Supreme Court in 1894 ruled an income tax unconstitutional there had been considerable agitation for such a levy, whether by constitutional amendment or by simple statute. Not so much of this sentiment had developed within the Republican Party as in the Bryan wing of the Democratic Party; yet President Roosevelt, in his annual message in 1906, recommended it as a desirable type of taxation if the constitutional obstacles could be hurdled.[1] Pioneering Wisconsin had been contemplating it as an accession to its social laboratory since 1903; but by 1909 it had not advanced beyond the test-tube stage. In his speech accepting the presidential nomination, Taft expressed the opinion that a constitutional amendment was unnecessary for the enactment of such legislation, so it was generally conceded that action of some sort would be taken during the special session of 1909.

Early in April when the Payne tariff bill arrived in the Senate, the committee on finance deftly extracted a provision for an inheritance tax. The finance committee feared that the House proposal would raise too much revenue, and thus furnish additional justification for the demands of the downward revisionists.[2]

Cummins had been discussing and planning a graduated income tax with his colleagues for some time,[3] but the first move

1 Edwin R. A. Seligman, *The Income Tax*, p. 591.

2 Henry Cabot Lodge to Theodore Roosevelt, June 21, 1909; *Selections from the Correspondence of Theodore Roosevelt and Henry Cabot Lodge, 1884-1918*, Vol. II, p. 338.

3 Joseph L. Bristow to E. C. Manning, April 23, 1909.

came from the Democrats rather than from the Insurgents. Senator Bailey of Texas introduced an amendment to the tariff bill on April 15, imposing a flat rate of 3% upon individuals and corporations earning over $5000 annually. On the 19th, six of the Insurgents met at Cummins' house to consider plans for an income tax, and presumably ironed out the finer details in his proposal. Two days later, Cummins proposed a rate starting at 2% for incomes of $5000 and gradually stepping up to 6% for incomes of $100,000 or over.[4] His defense of the tax, and his refutation of the charge that it paved the way for abandonment of the protectionist system were so convincing that twenty-one Republicans indicated their support of the Cummins proposal.

Aldrich huffed and puffed at the latest move of the Insurgents. He stressed the size of the surplus that would result from the tariff bill, and " ardently and feelingly " stated that no additional taxes were necessary.[5] But the agitation for an income tax was bearing fruit, nevertheless. Regulars who would not have dared to defy Aldrich on the tariff, now were willing to line up with Cummins and his group. In vain did Aldrich try to stem the rising Insurgency. Three days after Cummins had introduced his bill, he tried a favorite trick to sidetrack the movement when he advocated that a commission be appointed to study the whole problem of an income tax and thoroughly plan its details.[6] Few revolting Republicans were misled by this artful dodge.

Up to May 1 Cummins might fairly be considered the outstanding leader of the income tax drive among the Republican Insurgents; from that date until the close of the special session, he shared that leadership with Borah. The young Senator from Idaho, undoubtedly the keenest constitutional analyst in the Insurgent group, delivered a two-day defense of the Cummins proposal on May 3 and May 4. Like Lincoln in his attitude

4 *Congressional Record*, 61 : 1 : 1420-1421.
5 *Washington Times*, April 20, 1909.
6 *Washington Times*, April 24, 1909.

toward the Dred Scott decision, Borah made a plea for the reconsideration of the Pollock case by the Supreme Court. Logic, dignity, and power were Borah's tools in arguing the constitutional plausibility and the economic necessity for an income tax.[7]

Cummins and Borah now engineered a coup to unify the advocates of any form of statutory income tax. On May 18, these two Insurgents met with Bailey to agree upon a common ground upon which both Insurgents and Democrats could stand.[8] In its final form, the proposal resembled more closely the original Bailey plan: the graduated features of Cummins' tax were abandoned, and the bipartisan conferees agreed to unite behind a uniform 2% rate upon all incomes above $5000.

Aldrich became more desperate as the whirlwind Insurgent publicity campaign developed too much strength to be combated by the ancient methods of senatorial derision. First he threatened the right-wing Insurgents with a scaling down of their pet tariff schedules unless they stopped their agitation for the tax.[9] This, however, was a weak club, because those who were threatened realized that it would take something approximating a calamity to force Aldrich into any serious move for the downward revision of the tariff schedules.

By May 24 it became apparent that the Insurgents were winning. Jubilantly they prepared for their first roughshod victory over the senatorial machine. A hurried check by Aldrich showed that he would be a few votes short if he tried to force a motion to refer the proposal to the committee on judiciary.[10] He must appeal to a higher law than the power of the Senate oligarchy.

Aldrich's capable but oversympathetic biographer hails his next step as " his most brilliant parliamentary *coup*," [11] and

7 *Congressional Record*, 61 : 1 : 1680-1687; 1696-1701.

8 *Washington Times*, May 18, 1909.

9 *Ibid.*, May 21, 1909.

10 *Des Moines Register and Leader*, June 12, 1909.

11 Nathaniel W. Stephenson, *Aldrich*, p. 355.

intimates that it was the Rhode Islander's personally conceived
plan to split the opposition by proposing a tax upon the earn-
ings of corporations. But it was President Taft who really held
the key to subsequent developments. On May 24 Aldrich, Crane
and Lodge trooped up to the White House.[12] There they
figuratively threw themselves at the President's feet. They appealed to him to save them from their intolerable predicament
of facing defeat by a combination of nineteen Republican Insurgents and Democrats.[13] Aldrich recognized a corporation
tax as the only escape from the unendurable position into which
he had been thrown, but he hoped to limit its operation to a two-
year period. Taft insisted upon the removal of the two-year
limitation and hinted that there might not be a tariff bill at all
unless the Senate leaders acceded to his views. " That is why
we came to you," admitted Aldrich, frankly.[14] On the 26th,
Crane bore to the President the capitulation of Aldrich on the
two-year limit. Taft immediately directed Attorney-General
Wickersham to draft a bill in compliance with the outline
that Aldrich had accepted.[15]

Unfortunately for Taft, the Insurgents and their Democratic
allies remained in total ignorance of the developments behind
the scenes. Cummins and Borah did not have definite assurance
of what was to happen until the day before Taft's message to
Congress.[16] Accordingly, it is not at all surprising that they
continued to press for an income tax amendment to the tariff
bill.

Bombshell was indeed a mild word for the reaction that
Taft's corporation tax message of June 16 had upon the Insurgents. A significant description by Senator Bristow reveals

12 *New York Tribune*, May 25, 1909.

13 William Howard Taft to Horace Taft, June 27, 1909; Archie Butt,
Taft and Roosevelt: The Intimate Letters of Archie Butt, Vol. I, p. 131;
cf. Henry F. Pringle, *The Life and Times of William Howard Taft*, Vol. I,
pp. 434-436.

14 Butt, *op. cit.*, Vol. I, p. 31.

15 William Howard Taft to Horace Taft, June 27, 1909.

16 Joseph L. Bristow to Fred C. Trigg, June 21, 1909.

the reaction of the radical Insurgents, and also gives a picture of the power of the White House: [17]

The first movement was for the President to send for certain progressives, and explain to them how impossible it was to get the income tax amendment through, and suggest that they substitute this corporation dividend tax in the place of it. After some two or three weeks of cautious and quiet work, it was learned that three and possibly four of the Senators who had pledged themselves to the income tax had been influenced in this way. They were Bourne of Oregon, Curtis of Kansas, Carter of Montana and Brown of Nebraska. Brown was the real surprise to us. He has been one of the faithful progressives who never wavered. But the great influence of the President, the way it was brought about, being invited to the White House to meet the President socially upon an occasion or two—you can see how he might drop into the arrangement. But fearing to undertake to hold the progressives away from the income tax by personal influence alone, Mr. Aldrich conceived the idea of the message, putting behind the progressives who were to desert the income tax proposition the influence of the President and his great following throughout the country . . .

The radical Insurgents held a hurried conference in Borah's rooms, and decided to stand by their guns. Borah and Bristow prepared a statement signed also by Cummins, La Follette and Clapp, saying that they felt it their duty to try to secure the adoption of the Bailey-Cummins amendment to the tariff bill.[18]

But now a peculiar change came over the Senate leaders. Whereas they had just been forced by the Insurgents to beg at the White House for relief, they now took on an air of gentle amusement at the predicament in which Taft's message had placed the Insurgents. Lodge conceded that the Cummins-Bailey combine had had enough votes to win, but " in order to beat them we have determined to put in a tax on the net receipts of corporations. . . ." [19]

17 Joseph L. Bristow to Fred C. Trigg, June 21, 1909.
18 *Washington Times*, June 16, 1909.
19 Lodge, *op. cit.*, Vol. II, pp. 338-39.

The constituents of the ultra-conservatives reacted to the sudden developments in an interesting fashion. Senator Root was deluged with indignant protests from men of high standing, charging that the American system of free enterprise and private profit was going to be undermined.[20] Representative Fairchild told Vice-President Sherman that Taft's proposition was "one of the most preposterous ever put forward." [21] Patiently and gently, men like Root and Sherman had to bridge the gap in these men's minds between innate convictions and political necessity. Root informed one constituent that the question was between the income tax and the corporation tax, not between the corporation tax and no tax.[22] Likewise Sherman blandly declared that there was little doubt in his mind that the corporation tax would be accepted by the Senate.[23] President Taft had to explain, too, that the time had passed for objection to all forms of taxation, and that now it was a question of the corporation tax or something more radical.[24]

Thus the Insurgents, by their agitation for an out-and-out income tax had pushed backward the ramparts of the conservative defense. Once again social progress moved a step forward to cover the conservative retreat. And like true apostles of social progress, the more radical Insurgents did not invite the conservatives out to shake hands, but they kept on firing until the bitter end of the income tax fight, still unsatisfied with any sort of compromise.

In the interests of consistency, Cummins and Borah came out against the White House proposal. Cummins assailed Aldrich for using the corporation tax as a means to kill the income tax, and criticized Taft's inconsistency in alternately backing the

---

20 Philip C. Jessup, *Elihu Root*, Vol. II, p. 230.

21 George W. Fairchild to James S. Sherman, June 18, 1909.

22 Elihu Root to Charles F. Mathewson, cited in Philip C. Jessup, *Elihu Root*, Vol. II, p. 230.

23 James C. Sherman to George Fairchild, June 19, 1909.

24 William Howard Taft to John A. Sleicher, June 25, 1909; William Howard Taft to Frederick P. Fish, June 28, 1909.

income tax, the inheritance tax and the corporation tax. The
measure, he declared, was unconstitutional on discriminatory
grounds, since it left individuals and copartnerships untaxed.[25]
On July 1 Borah took up and expanded the charges that
Cummins had flung at Aldrich, and showed that the Republicans
then hiding behind the corporation tax had unanimously opposed it in 1898. He denounced the economic basis of the tax as
one that could be easily passed on to the consumer.

The conservatives laughingly admitted the charges; they were
now in the saddle. Aldrich gloated over the misfortunes of the
Insurgents: " I shall vote for the corporation tax as a means
to defeat the income tax." [26]

The House, moved by the stirring speeches of Cummins
and Borah, started pressing for some means of aiding the
radical Insurgents to defeat the Taft proposal. A good-sized
group announced that they would favor an income tax should it
come to a vote.[27] It was a forlorn hope. Not only did the
Senate oligarchy have the situation completely in hand, but it
would have been well-nigh impossible to slip such a proposal
past the watchful eye of " Uncle Joe " Cannon.

The climax in the Senate came on July 2. On the vote to
incorporate the Wickersham-Taft proposal in the tariff bill,
the Insurgents suffered a 59-11 defeat.[28] Borah, Bristow, Clapp,
Cummins, Dolliver and La Follette were faithful to the end.
Bristow, in explaining his vote, said: [29]

I could not consent to be switched about to please Mr. Aldrich,
even by the President. So I not only voted against substituting
the corporation tax for the income tax, but voted against the corporation tax, because I believe it is a mere subterfuge, and unjust
and inequitable.

25 *Congressional Record,* 61 : 1 : 3954-3958.
26 *Ibid.,* 61 : 1 : 3929.
27 *New York Tribune,* July 1, 1909.
28 *Congressional Record,* 61 : 1 : 4066.
29 Joseph L. Bristow to W. H. Pratt, July 5, 1909.

By the latter phrase, Bristow meant that it taxed the stock-holders in a corporation while relieving the bondholders, and inasmuch as a straight income tax would cover partnerships and all net income, he, like the other Insurgents, stuck to their original proposal.[30] The defection of Beveridge from the Insurgent group was fully expected, as he had not lifted a finger for the income tax all session.

The constitutional amendment providing for an income tax was passed by the Senate unanimously, but before the final passage of the tariff bill by the Senate, the regular leaders were forced by Senator Clapp to accept another proposition which wiped out the proposed exemption of holding companies from the operation of the corporation tax. But Aldrich accepted the Clapp amendment with his tongue in his cheek, for, as he anticipated, the amendment was stricken out when the tariff bill was in conference.

While the political storms were swirling around the conference committee, there was some talk that the corporation tax might be removed. Taft wrote his brother that quite a number of the members of the conference committee were against the corporation tax but " I don't think they will dare retreat from it." [31] In any event, there was absolutely no sentiment in the conference committee for appeasing the Insurgents by returning to the income tax.

When the measure emerged from the conference, the fire of the Insurgents was concentrated upon the tariff schedules. In the breathless final days of consideration of the conference report, the income tax issue was but a bitter memory for a majority of the Insurgents.

Just as the conservatives would not concede that they had been defeated by the Insurgents and driven to accept the corporation tax, so the Insurgents refused to admit that they themselves had won a notable victory.

30 Joseph L. Bristow to A. S. Alferman, July 5, 1909.
31 William Howard Taft to Charles P. Taft, August 1, 1909.

CHAPTER VII

THAT NATURAL RESOURCES AND PRIVATE SAVINGS BE CONSERVED

1. THE PINCHOT-BALLINGER CONTROVERSY

RIGHTEOUS public indignation formed the basis for the outstanding Insurgent successes, and conservation stirred up more support than some of the drabber issues which concerned the progressives.

When the countrywide storm of disapproval descended upon Taft's legalistic Secretary of the Interior, Richard A. Ballinger, the Insurgents were quick to capitalize upon the issue and to defend Gifford Pinchot, Chief of the Forest Service, in the latter's adherence to Roosevelt's more liberal conservation methods.

Ballinger was bound to suffer by comparison with his crusading predecessor. The press and the professional conservationists had been solidly behind James R. Garfield, Roosevelt's Secretary of the Interior, and viewed Ballinger's appointment with suspicion. Taft was warned two months before he took office that Pinchot might prove a refractory subordinate, as the editor of the *Outlook* wrote: [1]

> You will smile when I refer to the Secretaryship of the Interior, but I thought you might be interested in a comment made by Gifford Pinchot to me the other day concerning Dick Ballinger: " I couldn't work with him as I have with Jim. Jim and I think alike concerning the matters in which the Forest Service and the Department of Interior are closely related. Ballinger and I might clash."

The first clash occurred when Ballinger restored to private entry vast sections of lands which Garfield had set aside for public water-power sites and reclamation projects. The meticulous legal mind saw in Garfield's action an unwarranted assumption of power without congressional authorization, and could point to the portions of the withdrawn area where water

1 Elbert F. Baldwin to William Howard Taft, January 13, 1909.

could exist only in mirages. Pinchot, whose zeal for conservation overlapped the ordinary confines of the Forest Service, and who as a favorite of Roosevelt had been accustomed to short circuit the usual hierarchical channels, protested to Taft late in April that Ballinger's action constituted a reversal of the Roosevelt policies. The President reassured him, and Pinchot denied the charges that the Taft administration would undo the Rough Rider's work.[2] Ballinger, in his turn, again withdrew a few hundred thousand acres of the precious water sites.

Although this incident was settled satisfactorily, a more bitter conflict arose over the Cunningham coal claims in Alaska. These claims had been pending for some years, when in 1907 Cunningham moved to hasten the formal procedure of patenting them. Thereupon Louis R. Glavis, a fiery young subordinate in the General Land Office who had been investigating the case, branded the claims as fraudulent and as secured in bad faith because a Morgan-Guggenheim syndicate appeared to be interested in these coal lands.

Apparently Glavis and his superiors became mutually suspicious during the summer of 1909, with the higher Interior Department officials suspecting that the young investigator was stalling.[3] But Glavis finally took the bold step of going outside of the Department to appeal to the Forest Service for aid. He justified this move on the ground that the Forest Service had an interest in the matter since, if the Cunningham claims were not validated, the territory that they covered would then become included in the Chugach National Forest.

For the Insurgents, conservation was a relatively unimportant issue at this time. Dolliver and La Follette were preoccupied with their mercerized cotton and wool tops, and Bristow was demonstrating what the Dutch Standard did to the tariff rates on sugar. And the country was talking tariff from morning till night.

2 *Washington Times*, April 21, 1909.

3 Henry F. Pringle, *The Life and Times of William Howard Taft*, Vol. I, p. 489.

But the lid blew off at an opportune time for the Insurgents. They had barely returned to their homes after the heated tariff session when on August 9, 1909, Ballinger and Pinchot appeared at the Irrigation Congress in Spokane. In their speeches before the Congress, the two men displayed a fundamental divergence in their philosophy of conservation. Briefly epitomized, their attitudes revealed complete fealty to a strict construction of the law on the one hand and concern for the interests of the people on the other.

More important than the speeches was the meeting between Glavis and Pinchot at which the former's convictions on the Alaskan coal claims were unbosomed. Thereafter developments were rapid. On August 21, that advance guard of Insurgent public opinion, *La Follette's Magazine,* took editorial cognizance of the controversy and sounded the trumpet call for the Insurgents, and when early in September Taft completely exonerated Ballinger, La Follette and his followers were furious.

Wearied by a new squabble coming on the heels of the tariff fight, the President tried in vain to stem the tide of criticism, and to smooth the ruffled feathers of Pinchot.[4] But he stood loyally behind Ballinger on all questions of legality and policy,[5] and authorized the dismissal of Glavis after the latter had written an article for *Collier's Magazine* entitled " The Whitewashing of Ballinger—Are the Guggenheims in Charge of the Department of Interior?" [6] More and more Taft believed that the accusations against Ballinger were generated by muckrakers; [7] whatever the case, the muckrakers were stirring the country and the country was looking to the Insurgents for leadership.

When Congress convened in December, 1909, the Democrats started pressing for an investigation of the General Land Office, while the regular Republicans immediately moved to head off

4 William Howard Taft to Gifford Pinchot, September 13, 1909.
5 William Howard Taft to Richard A. Ballinger, September 13, 1909.
6 *Collier's Magazine,* November 13, 1909.
7 William Howard Taft to Walter L. Fisher, September 25, 1909.

such an obvious slap at Ballinger by broadening the inquiry to cover the Forest Service. At first the Insurgents were lying low, waiting for a moment to assert themselves. That moment came almost simultaneously in both the House and Senate. In response to a request by Senator Dolliver, chairman of the committee on agriculture, Pinchot wrote to the Iowa Insurgent outlining in detail his charges against Ballinger and defending Glavis' action in protesting the validation of the Cunningham coal claims.[8] Dolliver read Pinchot's letter on the floor of the Senate and the next day the Insurgents had their issue—Taft, after long wrestling with his spirit, dismissed Pinchot.

Meanwhile, the House Insurgents were moving forward toward the citadel of Cannonism, by taking from the Speaker the power to appoint the committee that was to investigate the Interior and Forestry departments.[9]

The effect upon the Insurgents of Pinchot's removal was electric. Miles Poindexter wrote:[10]

The dismissal of Gifford Pinchot by the administration and the attitude of the administration in endorsing and supporting Ballinger against Pinchot and his conservation and forest reserve policies is a great blunder both in statesmanship and in politics, and I am very much afraid that unless the Republican Party shows clearly that it does not endorse this action that it will be a great burden to carry in future campaigns.

The Insurgents were placed in a peculiar position by Taft when he urged Congress to pass conservation legislation that would legalize the withdrawals of land from entry which Roosevelt already had authorized by executive order. Obviously, the Insurgents could not oppose the President's suggestions because such a course would seem to indicate opposition to the entire policy of conservation, so they went along with the regulars and the Democrats in backing the proposals. Toward the close of the regular session of the Sixty-first Congress, the In-

8 Gifford Pinchot to Jonathan P. Dolliver, *Congressional Record*, 61 : 2 : 368.
9 *Supra*, pp. 64-65.
10 Miles Poindexter to J. Van Winkle, January 21, 1910.

surgents pressed for amendments that would broaden the scope of the bills, but all of the amendments failed of passage.[11]

One of the most significant consequences of the whole controversy was the reaction it produced when the news of Pinchot's dismissal reverberated through the jungles of Africa. Wallace Irwin, in his inimitable "Interviews of a Japanese Schoolboy," kept the country laughing by his apt account of how the fortunes of Pinchot and the Insurgents were tied in with Theodore Roosevelt: [12]

"Unless Public Conscience return to America pretty soonly there will be no property for poor folks to camp on." This from Hon. Gifford.

"When are Public Conscience expected back?" This from me.

"Before 1912, I hopes," says he, looking coaxingly in direction of Africa.

Of the public officials who had worked with Roosevelt, Pinchot was one of his favorites.[13] As early as September, 1909, Ambassador Bacon wrote to Roosevelt from the Court of St. James: "Is it possible that Gifford, good old Gifford, has to go too? I do hope the rumor cannot be true." [14] And the head forester had lost no time in excoriating the entire Taft administration in a letter to Roosevelt on December 31, 1909.[15] When the ex-President received a first-hand account at Khartoum of Pinchot's treatment, it could not have failed to confirm Roosevelt's sympathies for the Insurgents.

2. POSTAL SAVINGS BANKS

Speaker Cannon told President Taft in 1910 that postal savings banks represented a decided step toward populism. "Uncle Joe" remonstrated:

11 *Congressional Record*, 61 : 2 : 8169.

12 *Washington Sunday Star*, October 17, 1909.

13 Theodore Roosevelt to Gifford Pinchot, March 2, 1909; Theodore Roosevelt, *Autobiography*, p. 429.

14 Robert L. Bacon to Theodore Roosevelt, September 3, 1909.

15 Gifford Pinchot to Theodore Roosevelt, December 31, 1909.

I am getting so damned tired, Mr. President, of this everlasting yielding to popular outcry against wealth that unless we put a check on it somewhere there is no telling where it will lead.[16]

Judging from the Speaker's remarks, we would expect to find the Insurgents lined up in favor of the establishment of postal savings banks. In fact, most of the House Insurgents were. But in the Senate Insurgency developed a different pattern. A small group of middle western Senators battled for modification of the measure in the interests of their communities, and against the principles of what students are pleased to dub " sound " economics. After pushing through some amendments, the senatorial Insurgents counted upon their House colleagues to support them. However, Taft induced the House Insurgents to join the regulars in withdrawing the radical Senate amendments.

The proposal for the establishment of a system of postal savings banks had been before the country for some time, and the Republican national platform of 1908 embodied a plank advocating their establishment. Aldrich, like Cannon, was dead set against the scheme, and it was not until New Year's Day, 1910, that the President was able to say that " Mr. Aldrich has changed his mind about the postal savings banks, and I am quite sure he is with us now." [17]

This sudden change of heart by Aldrich aroused grave suspicion among the Insurgents in the Senate. In their eyes Aldrich's conversion was explainable because of his solicitous concern for the national banks,[18] as the postal savings bank bill proposed that the funds collected all over the country should be invested in the 2% bonds held by the national banks. " It is the boldest effort yet made in the history of this country to intrench (sic) the control and dominion of the Goverment in

16 Archie Butt, *Taft and Roosevelt: The Intimate Letters of Archie Butt*, Vol. I, p. 303.

17 William Howard Taft to Knute Nelson, January 1, 1910.

18 Jonathan P. Dolliver to Gifford Pinchot, March 25, 1910.

the hands of a few rich men from New York," stormed Bristow.[19]

For five weeks after Senator Carter had reported the measure, no action was taken; but finally the sputtering fire of Insurgent criticism opened. Cummins led a fight to provide that the deposits remain within the locality where they were originally placed, rather than be transferred to large cities or to the East.[20] To Root, the Cummins proposal amounted to debasing the credit of the United States,[21] and the New York Senator offered an amendment stipulating that the funds be invested in government securities which could be sold for cash in times of panic. The Root amendment alarmed Bristow, who gravely reported: [22]

In my judgment this is the preliminary move in behalf of the Aldrich central bank plan, the purpose of which is to subordinate the banking business of the country to a central bank in New York City, which of course would be controlled by J. P. Morgan and Rockefeller; and I am very much opposed to this monopoly of the banking business by these New York financiers.

The bogey of Wall Street was once again conjured up to scare the westerners. Whether Bristow's fears were justified is questionable; one of his fellow Insurgents in the House, Victor Murdock, claims that the senatorial jitters over Aldrich's manipulation of the postal savings bill in the interests of the wicked east were entirely without logical foundation.[23]

On March 5, Borah moved to the fore with an amendment of tremendous significance. This amendment would prohibit the investment of the postal savings funds in bonds bearing a rate of interest less than $2\frac{1}{4}\%$; obviously the passage of the Borah amendment would scotch Aldrich's plans to use the funds for

19 Joseph L. Bristow to Professor H. J. Hoover, March 7, 1910.
20 *Congressional Record*, 61 : 2 : 1433.
21 Philip C. Jessup, *Elihu Root*, Vol. II, p. 233.
22 Joseph L. Bristow to Charles E. Moore, February 4, 1910.
23 Victor Murdock, interview, February, 1939.

investment in the 2% national bank bonds. The vote was a surprise, for a number of regulars joined the Insurgents in adopting the Borah amendment, 49-11.[24] Why the regular support? It is significant that the fatigued Aldrich was in Florida when this vote was taken. Carter, in charge of the bill, was anxious to secure a unified vote on the final passage, and he was worried that the Insurgents would bolt. "To avert this threatening danger," he explained, "I dictated and procured the introduction of what is known as the Borah amendment. . . ."[25] The Insurgents, elated with their slap at Aldrich, lined up solidly for the bill on its passage in the Senate, 50-22.[26]

In the House, the Borah amendment was withdrawn, and the work of the Senate Insurgents was wrecked. President Taft arranged with Weeks, who was piloting the bill through the House, that the Insurgents confer with Secretary Norton, ". . . so as to give a bend to their minds in the right direction."[27] The results were eminently satisfactory, and Secretary Norton wrote:[28]

The House bill is admirably drawn, backed by all the more conservative insurgents, who behaved like trumps in a trying situation by refusing utterly to have anything to do with the Senate bill which was a very bad bill as I wrote you.

The House Insurgents backed the bill to a man when it passed on June 9, 195-102, with the Senate fangs removed.[29] Victor Murdock gave a rousing speech in favor of the bill and Taft's course in sponsoring it, and thus for the time closed the breach in the Republican Party in the House.[30] Back in the

24 *Congressional Record*, 61 : 2 : 2761.
25 Thomas Carter to O. M. Lanstrum, March 9, 1910.
26 *Congressional Record*, 61 : 2 : 2780.
27 Wiilliam Howard Taft to John W. Weeks, May 17, 1910.
28 Charles D. Norton to H. H. Kohlsaat, June 20, 1910.
29 *Congressional Record*, 61 : 2 : 7768.
30 *Ibid.*, 61 : 2 : 7670.

Senate, Bristow, Cummins and La Follette were the only Insurgents opposing the final passage of the bill.

The victory was all Taft's in the postal savings bank battle. He let the radical Insurgents in the Senate run wild, and then cajoled the House Insurgents into framing a bill which he approved. Such triumphs as this were few and far between for the President, but none was more clearly his.

CHAPTER VIII
RAILROADS ON TRIAL

As the tariff issue had dominated the political scene in 1909, so the question of regulation of railroads overshadowed all other issues during the 1910 session of Congress. But there was a tremendous difference between the course that Insurgency pursued in dealing with the Payne-Aldrich tariff and its tactics in connection with the Mann-Elkins railroad rate act. In the case of the tariff, the Insurgents beat vainly against the stone wall of protection, received but a few minor concessions and voted against the final product of the conference. On the railroad bill, however, the Insurgents completely revamped the measure as originally introduced and forced the regulars to modify and abandon whole sections containing objectionable features, with the result that the Insurgents supported it on the final vote.

The Republican platform of 1908—that sacred charter of Insurgent liberties—was as emphatic as such documents can be in its pledge to increase the powers of the Interstate Commerce Commission, and to check stock-watering, excessive rates and other common railroad abuses. During the campaign Taft took his stand firmly on the platform, but declined to make any moves until after the Payne-Aldrich tariff had run the gauntlet of the special session of 1909.

Scarcely had the torrid tariff session adjourned when the indefatigable Insurgents were sounding out the possibilities of a railroad bill in the 1910 session. It was natural that this little group should be keen for additional legislation along these lines. As Governor of Wisconsin, La Follette had been a pioneer in pushing the enactment of legislation regulating the railroads. " Fighting Bob " continued his battle after reaching the Senate, and was thus unusually well primed on the subject. Likewise Cummins in Iowa and Crawford in South Dakota had taken the lead in abolishing unfair railroad practices, and Bristow had won his Senate seat by protesting against the iniquitous effects of railroad rate discriminations in Kansas.

La Follette, Bristow and Dixon did yeoman work on the floor during the 1910 fight for railroad regulation, while Dolliver, Beveridge, Borah and Clapp entered into the debate frequently and nearly always voted with the Insurgents. But Cummins was clearly the Insurgent leader and bore the brunt of the burden. He drew up most of the plans, opened the debate, framed most of the amendments, approached the regulars with compromise plans, and was ever on guard to interpose questions and objections to the remarks of the opposition. La Follette, who with Dolliver had carried off the honors in the tariff debate, was an able right bower during the spring of 1910, and none of the Insurgents was so deeply steeped in the details of capitalization, valuation and consolidation as was the Wisconsin Senator. Bristow and Dixon concentrated upon one important phase of the question—discriminations in rates through the operation of the long and short haul clause. The other Insurgents adopted catch-as-catch-can tactics, with Clapp outstanding because of his work on the committee on interstate commerce. Except for the work of Bristow and Dixon, there was no such division of labor as there had been in the tariff debate.

While Attorney General Wickersham was drafting the administration bill to introduce in the regular session opening in December, 1909,[1] Bristow, Clapp and Cummins were suspicious. " I don't think it is well to let them prepare the bill," Bristow cautioned Cummins, " get the approval of the President, and force us to fight it. Let us get to the country first. . . ."[2] Several weeks later he wrote:[3]

I have no faith whatsoever in getting the President to stand with us against Root, Knox, Wickersham, Aldrich and Company, and from present indications it seems to me that we are confronting the bitterest fight we have yet been in.

1 George W. Wickersham to William Howard Taft, September 2, 1909.
2 Joseph L. Bristow to Albert B. Cummins, September 7, 1909.
3 Joseph L. Bristow to Albert B. Cummins, October 30, 1909.

But despite their lofty objectives, the Insurgents made few moves beyond comparing notes in the fall of 1909. At the request of the President, Cummins went to Washington before the opening of the regular session of the Sixty-first Congress. Expecting to aid in shaping the bill to be presented, Cummins found that Attorney General Wickersham dominated the proceedings, and this discovery was one of the factors in thrusting the Iowan into the lead in the Insurgent fight during the spring of 1910.

To the Insurgents, it seemed sinister that executives of the leading railroads were helping to shape the legislation. In November, the interested parties appointed a committee to meet Taft and see what could be done about influencing the framing of the bill,[4] and a month later they were sanguine about the amenability of the President to their suggestions.[5] In advance of the publication of the bill, private copies were dispatched to the railroad men for perusal and comment,[6] and early in January, six railroad presidents held a three-hour conference with Taft. According to the *New York Sun,* a conservative organ, the railroad executives induced Taft to abandon some of the more stringent regulatory features of the bill and Wickersham was directed to alter those sections.[7] Naturally when news such as this reached the Insurgents, it increased their apprehension. They resolved to fight the bill until they either defeated it, or strengthened its provisions. Senator Elkins introduced the bill on February 24.[8] Clapp and Cummins joined in a stinging minority report, charging that the railroad bill as framed by Wickersham was a " long step backward." [9]

In the middle of March, while the Insurgents in the House were getting ready to crown " Uncle Joe " Cannon with thorns,

4 Frank Trumbull to Grenville Dodge, November 7, 1909.
5 Frank Trumbull to Grenville Dodge, December 3, 1909.
6 George W. Wickersham to Grenville Dodge, December 30, 1909.
7 *New York Sun*, January 3 and 7, 1909.
8 *Congressional Record*, 61 : 2 : 2379.
9 *Ibid.*, 61 : 2 : 2655.

Cummins made a memorable speech which cut a deep gash in the administration defenses.[10] Speaking from two to three hours on each of four days, " Pulchritudinous Albert " ripped and tore the railroad bill to shreds. There was no bitterness in his tone, but there was bitterness in his heart as he described in detail how Attorney General Wickersham, Solicitor General Bowers, Secretary of Commerce and Labor Nagel, and a few members of Congress and the Interstate Commerce Commission had cooked up a smelly mess of pottage, rendered even more odoriferous when the railroad presidents intervened to rid the bill of its stringent provisions. Tellingly, Cummins pointed out that although the transportation tycoons had made a beaten path to the White House to beg for alterations, only one of them deigned to appear publicly before the committee on interstate commerce to present his views.

Cummins directed most of his fire against the Court of Commerce that had been proposed to handle rate disputes. He stressed the danger of isolating railway cases in one tribunal, which would subject it to the concentrated pressure of all the power of the railroads, both in the appointment of judges and in the conduct of cases—a contention borne out in part by the subsequent impeachment of one of the judges of the Commerce Court. Why should not the shipper or the Interstate Commerce Commission be allowed to appeal to the Supreme Court if the Commerce Court enjoined the I. C. C. from putting one of its orders into operation, Cummins demanded. He repeatedly pointed out that the sanctioning of traffic agreements would mean in effect the repeal of the anti-trust laws. The legal defense machinery would be lifted from the Commission and put into the Attorney General's office, he insisted.

Wickersham branded Cummins' four-day effort as a " generally nasty talk," [11] but it made a profound impression upon the Senate. It did not rouse the country, because the newspapers were at this time featuring the dramatic fight of the House

10 *Ibid.*, 61 : 2 : 3341-3385.

11 George W. Wickersham to William Howard Taft, March 19, 1910.

Insurgents against Cannon. Yet it caused considerable worry to the regular Senate leaders. Barely had the magnificent argument of Cummins been concluded when Elkins, Root, Sutherland, Kean, Crane, Hale and Flint—the cream of the standpat crop—sent out a hurry call for Attorney General Wickersham to go over the bill with them. Wickersham, when commenting upon Cummins' speech and the reaction of the Senate, revealed to Taft that " three or four points he dwelt on developed so much support that the gentlemen with whom I met thought it was important that the bill should be amended to meet them." The senatorial leaders singled out from Cummins' attack some items upon which they thought concessions should be made. As reported to Taft, they were:

1st. That there should be a right of appeal to the Supreme Court from an interlocutory order of the Court of Commerce granting an injunction to restrain the operation of an order of the Commission.

2nd. That no interlocutory injunction or temporary restraining order be granted, except on five days' previous notice.

3rd. That it be expressly stated in the bill that the agreements between carriers permitted by the new section in the bill should be " subject to the approval of the Commission."

4th. That there should be some means provided for shippers or individuals affected by an order of the Interstate Commerce Commission attacked by suit in the Commerce Court, to intervention in the proceeding, and to be heard in their own right.[12]

The Attorney General agreed to the first two propositions. As to the third, he rejected the suggestion of the Senators that traffic agreements had to be approved by the Interstate Commerce Commission before filing. As to the fourth, Wickersham struck a compromise that gave the court discretion to permit intervention by a private party; " this being, in effect, the jurisdiction which the court has anyhow," he explained triumphantly to his chief.[13]

12 *Ibid.*
13 *Ibid.*

So the railroad bill was hastily withdrawn from the Senate to repair the damage Cummins had done through his speeches. By April 1, a number cf amendments had been tacked on, embodying the results of the Wickersham conference with the Senate leaders. The Insurgents felt that they were getting their teeth into the bill and really making progress.

Bungling Mr. Wickersham now chose this inopportune time to lay down a challenge to the Insurgents. Speaking at the Hamilton Club in Chicago, Taft's Attorney General, in an apparently inspired address, made support of the railroad bill an issue of loyalty to the Republican Party. La Follette was quick to reply on the floor of the Senate.[14] He used some significant material furnished by a Massachusetts lawyer, Louis D. Brandeis,[15] and arraigned Wickersham for supinely withdrawing a projected suit against the merger of the New York, New Haven & Hartford Railroad with the Boston & Maine Railroad. La Follette's speech was a damning indictment of the laxity of Wickersham in abandoning a case that had every prospect of succeeding. It was designed to discredit that provision of the administration bill which gave the Attorney General power to prosecute railroad cases. It presented a vivid object lesson to the Senate, and Beveridge called La Follette's effort " the ablest thing he has ever done." [16] Shortly after La Follette's speech, the regulars once again gave ground and the Interstate Commerce Commission was allowed to have counsel represent it in prosecuting cases before the Commerce Court.

The Insurgents moved resolutely onward. On April 23, the Republican opponents of the railroad bill opened a ten-day attack which approached in intensity the famous nine-day bombardment that the Insurgents had directed against the tariff bill the previous June. If it did not create as much furore as had the tariff assault, it nevertheless had more concrete results in the modification of the legislation at hand.

14 *Congressional Record*, 61 : 2 : 4549-4564.

15 Alfred Lief, *Brandeis: The Personal History of an American Ideal*, p. 155.

16 Albert J. Beveridge to Albert Shaw, April 14, 1910; Claude G. Bowers, *Beveridge and the Progressive Era*, p. 376.

Borah opened on the 23rd with a further analysis of traffic agreements and their effect upon the existing anti-trust laws.[17] The sparring continued on the next day, and on the 25th, Dolliver, in one of the few extended speeches he made on the railroad bill, considered the same subject that Borah had treated.[18] Dolliver was in a gentle and philosophical mood when he arose to criticize those who would question his Republicanism; the tenor of his speech was restrained and without a touch of bombast. One could almost feel that he had worn himself out the previous summer in fighting Aldrich and the tariff; and indeed within six months he was to start his endless sleep in Iowa's sod. Now he wasted no breath lest he hasten that moment. He ran over the familiar ground that the new act perpetuated pooling agreements under a different name, in violation of the Republican platform. He paid his tribute to the Attorney General deliciously: [19]

The good legal brother who feels warranted by a little brief authority to purge the Republican party of unworthy members, when this bill was written either did not know what the Republican platform was or felt at liberty to treat it with that silent inattention which is the characteristic of really great minds.

Three days later Bristow started a comprehensive description of the evils of the long and short haul discriminations which the act of 1887 had unsuccessfully sought to check.[20] Statistics galore rolled off Bristow's tongue as he demonstrated with the display of huge maps how railroads set excessive rates for short hauls to compensate for low rates charged in long hauls between key cities at competitive points. Using his home town of Salina, Kansas, as an illustration, Bristow demonstrated that the rate on sugar from San Francisco through Salina to Kansas City was 6oc per hundred pounds; yet the rate from San

17 *Congressional Record,* 61 : 2 : 5261-5270.
18 *Ibid.,* 61 : 2 : 5322-5330.
19 *Ibid.,* 61 : 2 : 5328.
20 *Ibid.,* 61 : 2 : 5483-5496.

Francisco to Salina only, a distance of 185 miles less, was
89c per hundred pounds. Likewise he pointed out that discriminations in the transportation of cotton, woolen and canned
goods throughout the country levied tribute upon smaller communities for the benefit of the larger cities.

The Senate was in the right mood for Bristow's penetrating
discussion. Dolliver had laid the groundwork with his philosophical generalities, and now Bristow dug in with hard, cold
figures.

At the end of April came a showdown in the fight that the
Insurgents had been waging against the legalization of traffic
agreements in violation of the Sherman Anti-Trust Act. It will
be recalled that in March Cummins had thrown such a scare
into the regulars by his attack on this section that a hurry
call by the Senate leaders to Wickersham resulted in a compromise proposal making such agreements " subject to the
approval " of the Interstate Commerce Commission. But the
regulars still felt that the wording of the Wickersham draft
did not expand sufficiently the prerogative of the Commission.[21]
So when one of the milder Insurgents, Crawford, amended
the bill to provide for submission of the agreements directly to
the Commission, the regulars decided to yield a step. Cummins
immediately perceived that the Crawford proposal, although
subjecting the initial agreements to the careful eye of the Interstate Commerce Commission, said nothing about having the
Commission review the rates emanating from such agreements.
Accordingly, Cummins offered an amendment giving the Commission power to look over both the original traffic agreements
and the specific rates flowing therefrom. To Lodge, Crawford's
proposal was perfectly sensible and understandable, but the
Cummins idea was just a little too extreme and would render
the whole paragraph nugatory.[22]

The regulars rallied and mustered enough votes to carry
the Crawford amendment and defeat the Cummins substitute

21 Henry Cabot Lodge to Theodore Roosevelt, April 30, 1910.
22 *Ibid.*

by a margin of 35-29.[23] Now Cummins used a little justifiable parliamentary strategy in offering a second proposal which would send the rates resulting from tariff agreement up for the inspection of the Commission if those rates were *higher*. Lodge viewed this new strategy not as an effort to make a good bill, but as a sheer attempt to wreck the Republican Party by breaking down the administration.[24] What good would result from fiddling around with an amendment precisely similar to the one just defeated? Lodge was to discover the answer in a few days.

The persons to blame for the sudden crumbling of the regular defenses within the next forty-eight hours seem to have been Dixon, Cummins and Bristow, with Dolliver hovering in the background. Dolliver had started the trouble on April 25 with his humorous taunts; Bristow then barged in with the gracefulness of a ten-ton steam shovel, and blasted the regular position with his incontrovertible statistics; Cummins kept the flames of revolt alive by his shrewd parliamentary tactics.

Now it was Dixon's turn. The Montana Senator had been one of Aldrich's most trusted supporters on the tariff bill, remaining regular because his state demanded a tariff on wool.[25] But the streak of independence that he had occasionally displayed since his North Carolina boyhood came to the surface. On May 2, Dixon made a memorable speech in support of Bristow's position that the long and short haul clause needed revision in order to remove discriminatory rates.[26] He soon announced that twenty Insurgents were available for a little surgical work on the long and short haul clause.

After Dixon's speech the western Insurgents conducted a caucus and decided that they had enough votes to carry the Cummins amendment on traffic agreements and the long haul and short haul clause then pending in the House. The regulars

23 *Congressional Record*, 61 : 2 : 5567.
24 Henry Cabot Lodge to Theodore Roosevelt, April 30, 1910.
25 Mrs. Virginia Dixon Dean, interview, February, 1939.
26 *Congressional Record*, 61 : 2 : 5653-5663.

were frantic. They did not fully realize their untenable position until the damage was done.

Aldrich, Kean, Elkins and Crane quickly put their heads together for a council of war to determine what terms of surrender they could best obtain. When the Senate had adjourned on May 2, Cummins was approached. He was asked if the Insurgents would not consent to some provisions a little less obnoxious to the regulars. But the debonair Iowan knew that at last he was in the driver's seat, and it was not for the vanquished to dictate the terms. He cautiously replied that he did not think he could persuade his colleagues to consent to any provision that did not compel the railroads to get advance approval from the Commission for both the rates and the nature of the traffic agreements concluded. He glided easily out of Aldrich's committee room, leaving the regulars to stew in their own juice. " We are not compromising," he announced. " We believe we have the votes to adopt my amendment." [27]

Confronted with the possibility of suffering a humiliating defeat by the Insurgents in a roll-call on the floor of the Senate, the regular leaders decided to burn their dirty linen in private. They determined to abandon sections 7 and 12 entirely rather than give Cummins and the Insurgents the satisfaction of winning a straight-out fight on the floor.[28] Section 7 legalized traffic agreements between railroads, while section 12 allowed increased leeway for railway mergers where one road owned 50% of the stock of another.

At last in mid-May the final tussle over the long and short haul clause started. Aldrich was faintly hoping that he might perfect a coalition with the Democrats to defeat this provision which, twenty-three years before, when it was embodied in the original Interstate Commerce Act, he had denounced as " revolutionary in its character " and " made to answer the clamor of the ignorant and unreasoning." [29] Suddenly, an hour

27 *Philadelphia Press*, May 3, 1910.

28 *New York Times*, May 3, 1910; Albert J. Beveridge to William Dudley Foulke, May 4, 1910.

29 Nathaniel W. Stephenson, *Aldrich*, pp. 67-68.

before the vote on Senator Dixon's amendment making the clause effective, Aldrich got wind of the fact that his Democratic friends had deserted him in favor of a more drastic amendment by Senator Overman. Hastening to Dixon, he offered a new compromise. La Follette and Cummins were disgusted when Dixon decided to accept Aldrich's suggestion. When Dixon started to read the substitute amendment, a great uproar arose. The extreme conservatives were angry at Aldrich for even sanctioning a compromise in the first place; the radical Insurgents were bitter at Dixon for conniving with Aldrich; the Democrats were peeved at everybody because they were being crowded out of the picture; and Aldrich was angry at Dixon for making such a mess of things.[30] A short recess was called for a few minutes to cool the senatorial tempers. A few hasty conferences were held in Aldrich's committee room, perhaps in the hope of scotching the plan entirely. But when the regulars returned to the floor it was clear that the jig was up. On the final vote, the long and short haul clause amendment was overwhelmingly adopted, 56-12,[31] with ten die-hard Republicans holding out to the bitter end.

Meanwhile, the House was struggling with the Mann version of the railroad bill. Although the Insurgents were almost victorious on several occasions in their attempts to alter the provisions of the measure, they did not succeed as well as their senatorial brethren. As in the Senate, the House Insurgents attempted to delete the clause providing for a Court of Commerce to try railroad cases. In this effort they succeeded in getting a tie vote, 140-140, in committee of the whole, but could not quite muster enough support to have the provision removed. On May 10, twelve radical Insurgents, Cary, Davis, Fowler, Gronna, Haugen, Hubbard, Lenroot, Lindbergh, Nelson, Norris, Poindexter and Woods voted with the Democrats in support of a motion to recommit the Mann bill with in-

30 George Mowry, *Theodore Roosevelt and the Progressive Movement*, p. 243.

31 *Congressional Record*, 61 : 2 : 6208.

structions. The move was defeated, 157-176.[32] However, this group of twelve immediately thereafter voted with the regulars to pass the bill, and as a result the Republicans had a comfortable 201-126 majority on the question of passage.[33]

The Senate spent three more weeks revising the bill before turning it over to the conference committee. The progressives secured the insertion of an amendment putting telephone, telegraph and cable companies under the jurisdiction of the Interstate Commerce Commission. Bristow reported on June 1:[34]

We got a very good amendment into the bill yesterday putting the burden of proof on the railroads, to show why an increase in rates should be made, and giving the Commission authority to suspend action for ten months. This is so much better than we hoped to get that we feel fairly well satisfied, but I am in absolute accord with your view that the fight has just begun.

When Cummins had started the Insurgent fight on the administration railroad bill some three months before, it seemed that the protests of the middle westerners would fall among thorns and be choked as they sprang up. Early in the battle, the Insurgents were fairly set in their opposition to the bill and considered voting against it. " I will not vote for a bill regulating the railroads which was drawn by the railroad attorneys in New York, any more than I voted for a tariff bill that was written by the manufacturers of New England," snorted Bristow.[35] But as they moved on from victory unto victory, and felt that Satan's host was indeed vanquished, the Insurgents gradually came around to voting for the bill.

In the form in which it passed the Senate, the railroad bill still contained several features that were objectionable to the middle western group. Senator La Follette, in one of the most able speeches of the entire session, detailed the provisions that

32 *Ibid.*, 61 : 2 : 6032.
33 *Ibid.*, 61 : 2 : 6032-6033.
34 Joseph L. Bristow to Hugh A. Holmes, June 1, 1910.
35 Joseph L. Bristow to C. L. Holcomb, April 18, 1910.

remained unpalatable,[36] and listed the accomplishments of the Insurgents. But in view of the many changes secured the Insurgents decided to support the bill, and on June 3 it passed overwhelmingly, 50-12.[37]

The House Insurgents decided that the Senate version was so much more progressive than the House bill in its features that they would move to concur in the Senate amendments. Lenroot made an extended argument in the House on June 7 in support of this position.[38] Although the House bill provided for physical valuation of railroads as a rate base, and extended the jurisdiction of the Commission over water transportation in Hawaii and transportation to Alaska, it fell short of the Senate bill in several ways, Lenroot declared. The Senate version was more acceptable because it placed the burden of proof upon the carriers to show that increases in rates were reasonable. It provided that the Commission could suspend rates for as long as ten months, while the House bill allowed for suspension for only 120 days. The prohibition against the disclosure of information regarding shipments was in the Senate but not in the House bill. No provision in the House was made for an analysis of rates upon the principal commodities, with a subsequent report to Congress. Finally, the House measure did not force the railroads engaged in interstate commerce to maintain an agent in Washington for process-serving purposes.

The House Insurgents lined up behind Lenroot in his proposal to yield to the Senate. The regulars taunted the Insurgents for their supine surrender to the Senate when they had been fighting for rules reform as a means of restoring the prerogatives of the House. But the Insurgents were now fighting for economic principles, and ignored these charges. They succeeded in rounding up twenty-five Republicans to vote with the Democrats in refusing to hold a conference. The regulars barely squeaked through on the strength of a handful of Demo-

36 *Congressional Record*, 61 : 2 : 6882-6908.
37 *Ibid.*, 61 : 2 : 7375.
38 *Ibid.*, 61 : 2 : 7568-7577.

cratic votes. On the Lenroot motion to concur in the Senate amendments, six Democrats voted with the regular Republicans against the coalition of Republican Insurgents and regular Democrats.[39] Four of the six bolting Democrats—Fitzgerald, Harrison, Goulden, and Goldfogle—had backed Speaker Cannon fifteen months before when he had first tottered on the brink of defeat. The vote was so close that the support of four of these six Democrats would have blocked a conference and resulted in the adoption of the more progressive Senate amendments. The final vote on the Lenroot motion was 156-162, with twenty confirmed Insurgents being joined by five men who had never been very noted for their Insurgency— Crow, Foelker, Kustermann, Martin and Murphy.[40]

Just after the Senate, with the belated support of Aldrich, had passed the amendment strengthening the long and short haul clause, Bacon teased the Republican leader and his followers for changing their colors in a moment of defeat and marching on to victory under strange banners. Aldrich's reply was short and direct: " Has the Senator ever heard of the adage that ' he laughs best who laughs last ' ? " [41]

This cryptic comment was taken by the Insurgents to mean that Aldrich's last laugh would resound behind the closed doors of the conference committee when he started to emasculate the progressive provisions of the railroad bill which had been inserted by Insurgent amendments on the floor. Aldrich denied that he meant this, but the intimation was so obvious that the Insurgents decided to insist doggedly upon the gains that they had made during the preceding months.

Bristow relates: [42]

We saved the bill from mutilation by the conference committee by notifying the Senate conferees that if the bill was materially changed we would stay in session all summer before we would per-

39 *Ibid.*, 61 :2 : 7577.
40 *Ibid.*, 61 : 2 : 7577.
41 *Ibid.*, 61 : 2 : 6214.
42 Joseph L. Bristow to M. F. Amrine, June 23, 1910.

mit the conference report to be adopted; and then during the sessions of the conference committee, some of us every day warned Elkins that if the bill was materially changed he and Aldrich could cancel their European trips and spend the summer in Washington. And it was only the determined effort we made, and the grim resolve we had entered into to keep Congress continually in session, if it was necessary, before we would permit the iniquities we had forced out of the bill to be brought back, or the good things we had put into it to be taken out of it, that caused the bill to come out of conference as good as it did.

The Insurgents rallied to the support of the conference report on June 17 after the regulars had heeded their threats, and the long struggle ended when the Mann-Elkins bill was passed by 50-11.[43] Cummins made a final protest against the inclusion of the Court of Commerce, but announced his support of the conference report because it preserved most of the progressive provisions for which the Insurgents had fought. La Follette was keenly disappointed that the physical valuation provision passed by the House had been taken out in the conference. But the bill set up a special investigating commission to survey the necessity for such valuation, and after a favorable report by the Commission in November, 1911, President Taft aided in the realization of La Follette's dream by signing a bill starting the machinery of physical valuation in March, 1913.

All in all, the Insurgents were eminently successful in their conduct of the fight on the objectionable provisions of the Mann-Elkins Act. Time and time again they brought the regulars to their knees begging for mercy and offering compromises. The regulars compromised not because they were motivated by a new philosophy about the proper treatment of the rebels, but rather because they were anxious to get the bill passed in any form.

43 *Congressional Record*, 61 : 2 : 8391.

CHAPTER IX

WHOSE OX WAS GORED?

1. RECIPROCITY

THE last significant legislative battle waged by the Insurgents during Taft's administration was against the Canadian reciprocity scheme proposed by the President. This issue tore the Republican Party asunder during two sessions of Congress and caused the defeat of Sir Wilfrid Laurier's government in Canada.

Politically, the time was ripe for reciprocity, and Taft was anxious to do something to fulfill his pledges of downward revision of the tariff. Had the agreement been framed more deftly, it would have met the support of the Insurgents and possibly reunited the party.

To understand the Insurgent opposition to Canadian reciprocity it is necessary to examine a few of the bill's provisions that militated against agrarian interests. Schedule A, the free list operating for both countries, consisted mainly of agricultural products, with the exception of wool. Livestock, barley, wheat, rye, corn, oats, fruits, butter and eggs, hay, fresh vegetables, and flaxseed were to be placed on the free list, along with fish, unfinished lumber, gypsum, wood pulp and print paper. Taken as a whole, the free list included chiefly those raw materials imported by the United States from Canada. Schedule B provided for equalization of rates between the two countries on secondary products, such as canned vegetables, lard, oatmeal, flour, bran, meats, and products that flowed largely from the United States into Canada. In the latter category also were additional items in Schedule B, including farm machinery, automobiles, and manufactures of iron, glass, stone, wood and leather — articles like clocks and watches, canoes, roofing-slates, plate glass and pocketbooks. Schedule C provided for reduced duties by the United States on planed lumber and shingles, while Schedule D pledged Canada to a reduction on miscellaneous items, the most important of which was bituminous coal.

The United States Tariff Commission, in an analysis of the reciprocity project of 1911, concluded that as estimated on the basis of the trade of 1910, the total free imports from Canada into the United States would have been doubled had the new duties gone into effect.[1] Is it any wonder that the Congressmen from the farming states hit hardest by Schedule A were up in arms?

On January 26, 1911, Taft sent a message to Congress embodying the proposed reciprocity arrangement. After futile efforts to secure its introduction in the House by Payne or Dalzell, the President entrusted it to McCall, who introduced the measure on January 28. It was reported back from the committee on ways and means only three days before passage. The Insurgents reacted slowly to the challenge of the bill for they knew they would be placed in an inconsistent position if they attacked a genuine reduction of the tariff after having been clamoring for such a reduction since the memorable session of 1909.

Taft snickered at what he thought would be their discomfiture at having the ground cut from under them:[2]

I hope I am above advocating a policy so fraught with important consequences to my country on the mere ground that it puts some of my unscrupulous opponents in the hole; but it would be contrary to human nature not to smile at the plight that Clapp, Cummins, La Follette and the insurgent delegations from Minnesota, Iowa and Wisconsin find themselves in at the present time after the bitter attacks they made on you and me in what they called the interest of the "ultimate consumer." I don't know what they are going to do, but probably they will oppose the agreement really because they fear loss of support in their own states and because they cannot find in their hearts to support any measures coming from me, and ostensibly because as they will contend, this

1 *Reciprocity with Canada*, p. 51.
2 William Howard Taft to Nelson W. Aldrich, January 29, 1911.

is a farmers' agreement ignoring the interest of the farmer and seeking to put the whole burden of the change on him. But it is pretty hard for these valiant " defenders of God's patient poor " to step safely along the narrow ledge of such a fence.

The senatorial Insurgents were disposed to lie low and await developments in the House. As with the Payne-Aldrich tariff, reciprocity was rushed through the House by gag tactics with little opportunity for comment, except through the medium of the Appendix to the *Record,* that great repository for undelivered orations to the folks back home.

Lindbergh of Minnesota, in a letter to the *Little Falls Herald,* made the first full analysis of the effects of the reciprocity plan.[3] " It is wrong to remove the farmer's protection on what he sells and retain protection to the monopolies that sell to him," he protested. He recognized the injustice of admitting live animals free, and then placing protection upon meats dressed in the hands of packers. He pointed out that the American prices of wheat, barley, dairy products, etc., would be depressed by Canadian competition, while free timber would directly benefit the railroads of this country. Volstead of Iowa soon joined Lindbergh as a critic, but the bill carried the House on February 14, 221-93.[4] Scores of Republicans abstained from voting, and of the regulars who voted, seventy were for and seventy against reciprocity. Among the habitual rebels, eighteen favored and nine opposed the bill.

As the Sixty-first Congress passed out of existence, on March 4, 1911, there were several changes in the personnel of the Insurgent group. Beveridge had been defeated in Indiana. But Beveridge's defeat was no loss for the Insurgents, because during the short session ending March 4 he had taken the lead in defending Taft's proposal both on the floor of the Senate and in *The Saturday Evening Post.*[5] The mid-term elections

3 Charles A. Lindbergh to *Little Falls Herald,* February 3, 1911.

4 *Congressional Record,* 61 : 3 : 2563-2564.

5 Claude G. Bowers, *Beveridge and the Progressive Era,* pp. 404-405.

of 1910 resulted in a few additions to the Insurgent group of progressive Republicans, although they did not make a tremendous difference in the final accounting on reciprocity. John Works of California came in as an acknowledged progressive, yet he was a steady supporter of the proposed measure. Miles Poindexter of Washington, who had played a prominent part in rules reform and other Insurgent issues in the House, was elevated to the Senate in the 1910 election and supported Canadian reciprocity for an interesting reason. Poindexter wrote a few weeks before the final vote:[6]

I believe it is a mistake to oppose the reciprocity bill although in itself it is unjust. However, it can be made the beginning of an irresistible assault upon tariff excess and extortions under which we have labored so long and for that reason it should be passed without delay and the advance then taken up upon the Aldrich "tariff citadel."

The other Insurgents were inclined to feel that if any advance upon the tariff citadel was to be made, it was unjust that it should start with a reduction of duties on farm products.

But in spite of their failure to enlist Works and Poindexter against reciprocity, the Insurgents gained two new progressive adherents from the 1910 campaign. After the giant Dolliver had been laid to rest in Iowa, the Insurgents received a fleeting slap in the interim gubernatorial appointment of the standpat editor of the *Des Moines Capital*, Lafayette Young; but the Iowa legislature soon rectified this by electing William Kenyon for a full six-year Senate term. Kenyon joined the Insurgents wholeheartedly in their opposition to reciprocity. North Dakota contributed another Insurgent ally in Asle Gronna. Gronna, like Poindexter, had been an outstanding member of the House Insurgent group in their fight against Cannon. When he came to the Senate he took a leading part in the struggle against reciprocity, making two of the ablest speeches against the bill on July 6 and 7.

6 Miles Poindexter to Lewis Levy, July 6, 1911.

One of the most amusing aspects of the reciprocity struggle was the amount of close cooperation between the Insurgents and the ultra-conservative Republicans. Lorimer, whom the Insurgents had tried to purge from the Senate; Lippitt, Aldrich's successor from Rhode Island; Oliver of Pennsylvania; Burnham and Page, New England stalwarts—all became bedfellows of the Insurgents, along with the conservative Senators from the mountain states. Like Cannon and Dalzell in the House, these conservatives did not want any entering wedge for free trade.

Reciprocity also drew into the ranks of the Insurgents Knute Nelson of Minnesota, who had given the rebels considerable assistance in opposing the Payne-Aldrich tariff. Nelson early became convinced of the injustice of Canadian reciprocity, and joined with Hale, Smoot, Warren, and some of the older Senators in aiding the Insurgents to filibuster against a vote in the short session ending March 4.[7] Regarding the ultra-conservatives, Nelson noted: [8]

They could readily see that if there was to be free-trade in farm products the farmers would insist upon free-trade in manufactured products, and hence these Standpatters were as eager as any of us to prevent action on the reciprocity agreement.

Taft called the new Congress into special session a month after the old one had died, and immediately urged the passage of the reciprocity measure. Most of the Insurgents, however, voted against the bill when it passed the House a second time on April 21, 268-89.[9]

Reciprocity now entered a stormy seven-week session in the Senate committee on finance, to be followed by an equally stormy seven weeks on the floor of the Senate. The committee on finance reported the bill on June 13, with no recommenda-

7 Knute Nelson to Ole Canestorp, March 9, 1911.
8 *Ibid.*
9 *Congressional Record*, 62 : 1 : 559-560.

tion but individual reports.[10] Among these was a brilliant criticism by La Follette.[11] La Follette attacked reciprocity as embodying neither the Republican principles of protection nor the Democratic doctrine of tariff for revenue, and challenged the position of men of both parties who would support an outright move toward free trade. He showed that the railroad lines of the great "empire builder" James J. Hill had a score of branches into the wheat-producing areas of Canada. Transportation interests such as these would benefit from the increased importations of wheat, he declared. The main criticism was directed at the huge profits that would accrue to the railroads, millers and the beef trust. The milling interests, La Follette protested, were protected by a rate of 50c a barrel on flour and would be able to reach into Canada and get free wheat. The beef trust would be similarly benefited by free livestock and dutiable dressed meats. Advancing to the effect that reciprocity would have upon the farmer, La Follette concluded:

It singles out the farmer and forces free trade upon him, but it confers even greater benefits upon a few of the great combinations sheltered behind the high rates found in the Payne-Aldrich tariff.

From La Follette's committee report on June 13 until the final passage of reciprocity on July 22, the Insurgents trained their full fire on the scheme.

Bristow and Gronna attacked reciprocity mercilessly. "I am willing that we shall take our share of tariff reductions," Bristow insisted, "but I want the same rule applied to the products of the factory that is applied to the products of the farm." [12] Replying to the charge that the Insurgents were inconsistent in opposing the Payne-Aldrich tariff while they refused to support reciprocity, Bristow brought to light the attitude of all

10 U. S. Senate Report, Sixty-second Congress, 1st Session, Rept. 63, Pt. 2.
11 *Congressional Record*, 62: 1: 1963.
12 Joseph L. Bristow to John M. Barnes, July 13, 1911.

the Insurgents when he once again pledged allegiance to the principle of protection: [18]

But the progressives have never advocated free trade. They took the Republican national platform of 1908 seriously, and declared that tariff duties should be fixed so as to measure the difference in the cost of production at home and abroad, and that the rule should apply to all industries,—manufacturing, agriculture, etc. . . . Taft ignored it two years ago when he unreservedly supported the Payne-Aldrich tariff bill, in contending for the high protectionists and defending their greed and avarice. He flopped completely and went to the Democrats and started a free trade propaganda, when he started his Canadian reciprocity scheme, for that is free trade for the farmer and protection for everybody else.

Gronna's two-day speech against reciprocity was one of the star orations of the session.[14] The North Dakota Senator, whose unassuming manner quickly won the sympathy of his colleagues, quietly demonstrated that the treaty could not possibly effect many reductions in the cost of living, as its advocates maintained. Gronna argued that the reduced prices of natural products could not directly aid the consumers, since the consumer purchases chiefly secondary food products that have gone through the hands of the processors and upon which the import duties have been retained. Thus the treaty would take money from the pockets of the farmers to enrich the processors without benefiting the consumers. He challenged the framers of the treaty: [15]

How different the treatment of the woolen interests the duties on whose products the President has characterized as indefensible, but which, it is now given out, must not be touched until the Tariff Board has made a thorough investigation, lest a change based on deficient knowledge injure the industry!

13 Joseph L. Bristow to J. R. Harrison, June 19, 1911.
14 *Congressional Record,* 62: 1: 2676-2710.
15 *Ibid.,* 62: 1: 2681.

La Follette drew the Insurgent debate on reciprocity to a close on July 21 with one of the most magnificent speeches of his career. He showed in incontrovertible terms the gross iniquity of the form that Canadian reciprocity had taken. He showed that the inevitable result of allowing cheaper Canadian wheat to cross the border would be not only to force down American wheat prices, but to draw Canadian wheat in preference to American wheat to the Minneapolis miller. He pleaded for the barley growers of Minnesota, Wisconsin, Iowa and the Dakotas, who would suffer from the competition of the rich barley fields of Ontario, while the Buffalo brewers and maltsters were laughing behind their backs. He showed the effects of allowing the free importation of lower priced Canadian flaxseed when the Canadian growers could produce almost double the number of bushels per acre. Cheaper and more virgin land, cheaper labor and feed, and more yield per acre, equally favorable transportation rates—how, he asked, could the American farmer hope to battle against this competition, especially when he was given no compensating benefits in lower prices for products that he himself had to buy?

La Follette castigated the press for its support of free wood pulp and print paper. He denounced the Democrats for cutting the farmers to the bone at one slash, merely to create an issue for the 1912 campaign. He berated those near-Insurgents who looked upon reciprocity as a step in the right direction. " I say it is a step in the wrong direction," the "little giant" thundered. " Your first step results in still greater tariff oppression." [16]

This was Insurgency at flood tide. But it failed to overflow the bulkhead simply because Taft enlisted the aid of the Democrats to plug up and reenforce the structure. On July 22, reciprocity passed the Senate, 55-27, with all but three Democrats supporting it, and twenty-four Republicans in opposition.[17] The Republicans who voted " nay " on the final accounting were the following:

16 *Ibid.*, 62 : 1 : 3151.
17 *Ibid.*, 62 : 1 : 3175.

Eastern Regulars	Western Regulars	Near-Insurgents	Insurgents
Burnham, N. H.	Curtis, Kansas	Crawford, S. D.	Borah, Idaho
Lippitt, R. I.	Clark, Wyoming	Gamble, S. D.	Bourne, Oregon
Page, Vermont	Heyburn, Idaho	Nelson, Minn.	Bristow, Kansas
Oliver, Penna.	Lorimer, Ill.		Clapp, Minn.
	McCumber, N. D.		Cummins, Iowa
	Smith, Michigan		Dixon, Montana
	Smoot, Utah		Gronna, N. D.
	Warren, Wyoming		Kenyon, Iowa
			La Follette, Wis.

It is not an exaggeration to say that no issue disorganized the Republican Party so much as the Canadian reciprocity agreement of 1911, which never went into effect because the voters of Canada repudiated the government sponsoring it. The Insurgents hoped through their tactics to corral enough votes to block the agreement entirely. Failing this, they conceived it their duty to conduct a campaign of education against reciprocity, and to take up a cause that the newspapers refused to sponsor—justice to the American farmer.

2. THE "POP-GUN" TARIFF BILLS

During the special session of 1909, the Insurgents had sweated and slaved in a vain effort to redeem the campaign pledges of the Republican Party to revise the tariff downward. Within a month after the passage of the Payne-Aldrich tariff, Taft himself admitted at Winona, Minnesota, that the wool schedule was hardly defensible. However, the President roused the angry resentment of the country by claiming it to be " the best bill that the Republican Party ever passed." [18]

Since the special session of 1909, the tariff revisionists had kept the issue alive in their speeches on the floor of Congress. On June 13, 1910, Senator Dolliver, in the last Senate speech he made before his untimely death, summarized the terrific fight that he and his western colleagues had waged for lower duties and attacked President Taft and the regular Republicans

18 Henry F. Pringle, *The Life and Times of William Howard Taft*, Vol. I, pp. 454-456.

for their supine disregard of the consumers throughout the country.[19]

The congressional campaign of 1910 gave the Insurgents additional opportunities to bring the tariff issue to the fore. In fact, the tariff was in most localities the leading issue of the 1910 campaign, with conservation running a close second. Throughout the Insurgent stamping ground in the Middle West, the revisionists inserted ringing denunciations of the Payne-Aldrich tariff in their state platforms. With the progressives dominating most of the state conventions, these gatherings became springboards for the opponents of the existing tariff. The issue was clearly defined on the hustings, and in the Republican primaries and in the general election the people returned an unmistakable verdict against the sponsors of the Payne-Aldrich tariff.

The regular forces met a veritable holocaust in the November elections. The control of the House passed into the hands of the Democrats, who had hammered upon the tariff issue throughout the campaign. Maine, Massachusetts, Connecticut, New York, New Jersey, Ohio, Indiana and Oregon went Democratic. Yet it is significant in analyzing the results of the 1910 election that although 98 Republican Congressmen went down to defeat, the Republicans lost only three in the nine most progressive states of Wisconsin, Iowa, Kansas, Nebraska, North Dakota, South Dakota, Minnesota, California and Washington; however, in the four standpat states of New York, New Jersey, Ohio and Pennsylvania, the Republicans lost 26 Congressmen.

This popular support for the Insurgents encouraged them to consider revising the tariff during the congressional session of 1911, and the Canadian reciprocity project furnished them with a useful vehicle. The Republican revisionists reasoned that if they crystallized their ideas in the form of amendments to the reciprocity measure, Taft would not dare to veto the entire bill and thus throw out his reciprocity baby along with the

19 *Congressional Record*, 61 : 2 : 7908-7920.

downward revision bath water. This was undoubtedly sound reasoning, yet it failed to take into account the tactics of the Democratic Party, which now controlled the House of Representatives and was gazing fondly ahead to the presidential campaign of 1912. The Democrats wanted an issue for 1912, and they certainly were not disposed to allow a small segment of the Republican Party to claim the sole right to champion the interests of the American farmer.

Accordingly, Chairman Oscar Underwood of the House committee on ways and means made the first move to attack the tariff. Early in April, Underwood introduced the farmers' free list bill, a measure designed to admit duty-free about one hundred articles which the farmer bought but did not sell, such as agricultural implements, cotton bagging, cotton ties, leather, boots and shoes, wire for bailing, barbed fence wire, wire rods. sewing machines and all parts thereof, salt, and other articles. On May 8, the farmers' free list measure passed the House, 236-109,[20] aided by the votes of twenty-four bolting Republican Insurgents. However, the coalition did not hold in the Senate. The Democratic Senators refused to support it on the ground that its addition might mean the defeat of reciprocity, and the entire farmers' free list was rejected as an amendment to the reciprocity agreement without a roll-call on July 12.[21]

Schedule K was the next object of attack. Here, as in the case of the farmers' free list, the Democrats of the House took the lead in proposing a drastic downward revision. The Republican Insurgents in the Senate tried to steal some thunder by attaching their names to amendments, but again the Senate Democrats got cold feet and refused to jeopardize reciprocity by supporting any amendments.

On June 20, the House passed the Underwood wool bill by the rousing vote of 221-100, but all Insurgent efforts to attach the wool bill as an amendment to reciprocity were defeated in the Senate.

20 *Ibid.*, 62: 1: 1121.
21 *Ibid.*, 62: 1: 2867.

In the closing days before the final passage of reciprocity, scores of Insurgent amendments were overwhelmingly rejected. July 22 was a day of terror for the Insurgents. More than sixty amendments to the reciprocity bill were smothered under majorities averaging 4-1. Occasionally four or five Democrats or two or three regular Republicans would join the Insurgents upon measures which interested them locally, but in most instances the Insurgents were without any company as they were ground into submission.

Following the passage of the reciprocity agreement, the Insurgents enjoyed a brief period of triumph. The tables were now turned, and it seemed certain that the coalition with the Democrats would be perfected, since the Democrats now had no excuse for opposing tariff revision when it was not attached to reciprocity. Still, there was one obstacle in the way of Democratic cooperation. Bristow wrote on July 7: [22]

The Democratic organization here, in my judgment, does not want the Senate to pass the House bills, because if it did and Taft should happen to sign them, the Democratic Party would be " in the soup," because Taft would have pulled its teeth. It could not fight him, because he would have approved the measures which it passed. It just dawned on a few of them yesterday,—such a possibility—and since Taft is such an unknown quantity, it startles them to think of the possibility of his signing these Democratic bills, if they should happen to be passed.

And the progressives, who are fighting for something they believe in, that they want accomplished, will probably have a good deal of fun with the fellows who are jockeying for political position before it is over.

Probably the Democrats concluded that the possibility of Taft's signing the bills was remote. In any event they plunged ahead eagerly under the leadership of Senator La Follette and the Insurgents in their attack upon the wool schedule of the Payne-Aldrich tariff. Representative Underwood held out for a 20% duty on raw wool, but when the conference committee

22 Joseph L. Bristow to Fred C. Trigg, July 7, 1911.

met, La Follette announced that he was determined to preserve adequate but not extortionate protection, and insisted on a 35% rate. Interestingly enough, the standpat Republican members of the conference committee refused to have anything to do with this wool measure, and the entire work of ironing out a compromise between the Underwood and La Follette figures was turned over to the two principals. After two weeks of sweating and straining, during which firm statements were issued to the press, a 29% rate on raw wool was set. The other rates on cloths, knit fabrics, trimmings and lace, blankets and flannels were reduced substantially from the Payne-Aldrich duties.

On August 14 the House quickly approved the conference report on the wool bill, 205-90,[23] and the next day the Senate fell into line, 38-28.[24] Eight Insurgents, Bristow, Brown, Clapp, Crawford, Cummins, La Follette, Poindexter and Works bolted the Republicans to aid in passing the bill. Meanwhile both houses had passed the farmers' free list bill in substantially the same form in which it had been offered as an amendment to reciprocity.

The revision of Schedule K and the passage of the farmers' free list bill may be regarded as the major victories of Senator La Follette and the Insurgents in the post-reciprocity tariff developments. The Insurgents successfully contended for revision of a schedule that President Taft himself had termed indefensible, and also provided a counter-balance for the unjust treatment accorded to the farmers by Canadian reciprocity.

But the story was entirely different on the revision of the cotton schedule. Here, as in the case of the amendments to the reciprocity bill, jealousy and political maneuvering got the better of the Democrats and they spent their efforts in discrediting the Insurgents. On August 3, the House passed the Underwood cotton bill, 202-91,[25] reducing the average duty on goods

23 *Congressional Record*, 62: 1: 3919.
24 *Ibid.*, 62: 1: 3963.
25 *Ibid.*, 62: 1: 3584.

from 48.12% ad valorem to 27.06%. The low figure of the House bill was unacceptable to the Senate Insurgents, and they indicated as much. The Democrats held two wrangling caucuses on August 15, at which dissension appeared over how far cooperation with the Insurgents should proceed. Martin, the Democratic leader, insisted at the caucuses that the party remain solidly behind the coalition, and various Democratic moguls assured La Follette on the morning of the 16th that the bipartisan combination would remain intact.

But the Insurgents were neatly double-crossed on August 17, and according to a Democratic newspaper, " they were given the most sensational drubbing ever witnessed in the upper branch of Congress." [26] Senator Bristow ducked downstairs for a ham sandwich, and when he returned he overheard Senator Johnston of Alabama asking Senator Penrose of Pennsylvania to stop the regular Republicans from voting, so the Democrats could shove through the low-duty House cotton bill to which the Insurgents objected. Bristow denounced the scheme, Works confirmed Bristow's charges when Penrose hedged, and finally Penrose admitted that the regular Republicans had decided either to refrain from voting or to absent themselves from the chamber. As a result, the House cotton bill rode through, 29-24,[27] with a few hasty amendments to the chemical and metal schedules attached as riders. Cummins stormed in vain, and attempted to invoke an old rule that Senators present must either vote or explain their reasons for not voting. But on another division Penrose was excused from voting and the Insurgent humiliation was complete.

The President promptly vetoed all three of the " pop-gun " tariff bills, and the House by votes of 226-127 and 227-129 was unable to muster the two-thirds vote necessary to override the vetoes of the the farmers' free list and wool bills.[28] Taft

26 *New York World*, August 18, 1911.
27 *Congressional Record*, 62 : 1 : 4067.
28 *Ibid.*, 62 : 1 : 4170, 4174.

realized full well that a veto of amendments to schedules that
he had publicly condemned was not exactly an astute political
move. He took the position that these measures should wait
until the Tariff Board had made its report after a scientific
investigation of the subject.[29] Just after the wool bill had passed
the Senate, Taft revealed his inner thoughts on the subject in a
letter to his wife: [30]

The Democrats in the Senate and the insurgents yesterday came
together and agreed on a modified form of the La Follette wool bill
. . . I shall have to veto the bill because I have not had time to hear
from the Tariff Board who are engaged in studying the wool question and will make full report on it in December. I am inclined to
think that this is a clever move on the part of the insurgents and
the Democrats and that it will involve me in a loss of prestige
which I gained in the reciprocity fight. It will be said that I criticized
the wool schedule in my Winona speech and yet when an opportunity is presented to modify it I veto it. However it is plainly my
duty to defend the great manufacturing interests of the country
engaged in making woolens as well as the farmers in raising wool
at least to the extent of delaying action until we can get at the
facts. The interval of only three months is a short one and the
country could certainly better stand the burden than to do something
that might ruin an industry that should be protected . . .

Taft's position that the farmers' free list and wool bills were
not based upon " scientific investigation " was vulnerable. The
Insurgents quickly pointed out that there had not been very
much scientific investigation underlying the reciprocity agreement which the President had jammed through with Democratic aid. The President himself acknowledged that the report
of the Tariff Board would point toward a reduction of the
cotton and woolen schedules.[31]

29 William Howard Taft to J. M. Dickinson, July 29, 1911.

30 William Howard Taft to Mrs. H. H. Taft, July 28, 1911.

31 William Howard Taft to J. C. Hemphill, July 28, 1911; William
Howard Taft to J. M. Dickinson, July 29, 1911.

After the smoke of the 1911 session had cleared, the Insurgents, although bruised and battered, appeared to the public to be the only group in Congress that was sincerely interested in carrying out the 1908 pledge of the Republican Party to revise the tariff downward in a fashion that would be equitable to the interests of both farm and factory.

CHAPTER X

"I HOPE WE CAN ORGANIZE"

INSURGENCY was associated with the preservation of individual expression. It was a revolt against stereotyped action, and a protest against the use of the caucus system to ride roughshod over the opinions of individual Congressmen. Conseqently, it was rather anomalous that the Insurgents should think about how they should bind themselves together.

The necessity of achieving unity of thought and action became sorely evident in the early days of the movement. The regular Republican machine was at this period unusually well organized. Speaker Cannon in the House and Majority Leader Aldrich in the Senate had built up a smoothly functioning hierarchy whose power had its basis in the intense loyalty of its supporters and the outstanding ability of its key lieutenants.

A more obvious reason why the Insurgents needed to throw up a connected series of breastworks was their failure to achieve any results through haphazard individual effort. The experience of the rules reformers certainly demonstrated this shortcoming prior to the Sixtieth Congress. The isolated assaults of Cushman, Hepburn, Cooper, Nelson, and other ardent individualists had rebounded harmlessly.

Just as there was a conflict between unified organization and the preservation of the pristine individualism of the average Congressman, so were there practical difficulties in working out the details of the operations of the Insurgent machine. The Insurgent was a rebel from party discipline because he believed that every Congressman was a king, unanswerable to Danville, Illinois, or to Rhode Island. It was too much to expect him suddenly to abandon his personality and become answerable to McCook, Nebraska, or to Wisconsin. Time and again tempers became frayed as individual Insurgents insisted upon standing for their convictions against the wishes of their associates who were trying to map a cohesive program of action.

This inherent trait of being unamenable to discipline of any sort would have wrecked the entire Insurgent program had it not been for the great surge of popular support which underlay the entire movement, and the unifying effect of the ideals for which they were battling.

Soon after the 1908 election President-elect Taft, before he decided upon the policy of passive acquiescence in the rule of Cannon in the House, gently hinted that the opponents of the Speaker should organize.[1] Five days after the opening of the short session of the Sixtieth Congress, twenty-five Insurgents met in Hepburn's committee room in what one of those present termed a " profitable conference." [2] The Insurgent leaders had considerable difficulty in persuading those interested in rules reform to take action outside of the regular caucus. It was only through the use of the headquarters of Hepburn, a dyed-in-the-wool machine man on other issues, that most of the twenty-five consented to attend.[3] A committee consisting of Hepburn, Hayes, Townsend, Cooper and Foster was designated to draw up changes in the rules.

The organizational set-up of the Insurgent group was not perfected immediately, but grew by degrees. The chief instigators of the movement were quick to see the defect of centralizing power and authority in one leader, as this would be aping the very organization that they were fighting in the House. In addition, the dispersion of control was consciously designed to attract luke-warm Insurgents who were willing to oppose the regulars only within polite limitations.

After several meetings in January, 1909, John M. Nelson of Wisconsin became permanent secretary of the House Insurgents. Upon Nelson's shoulders fell the duty of calling meetings, arranging for the meeting place, taking elaborate minutes of the proceedings, and checking up on drifting members.[4]

1 William Howard Taft to Halvor Steenerson, November 30, 1908.
2 Edmond H. Hinshaw to William Howard Taft, December 12, 1908.
3 Victor Murdock, interview, September, 1938.
4 John M. Nelson, interview, February, 1939.

Victor Murdock was named chairman of the publicity committee. Murdock's experience as a Kansas editor, his flaming red hair and striking aptness of expression enabled him to make this office singularly useful to the Insurgent cause. Ernest Pollard, a lame duck from Nebraska, was named chairman of the committee on procedure.[5]

Ordinarily the Insurgents met two or three times a week.[6] Their most important meeting was held on January 19,[7] when out of a welter of propositions to reform the rules emerged the two principles that the House should elect its standing committees and also establish a calendar day for the alphabetical call of committees. The conservative Insurgents grumbled considerably at the first of these principles, but Gardner was appointed as chairman of a committee of three, including Madison and Nelson,[8] to draw up a resolution conforming with these two proposals. Committees were appointed to sound out the newcomers who would take office on March 4, 1909.

When the Sixtieth Congress expired, the Insurgents lost their chairman, the veteran Hepburn, and his place was taken by Gardner. Records show, however, that the chairmanship was rotated frequently after March 4, 1909, with Hayes or Madison occasionally taking over the reins. In any event, the chairman neither attempted to dictate policy, nor acted as more than a mere presiding officer.

Early in the session, Gardner, Madison and Nelson were constituted a permanent steering committee,[9] to which were soon added Hubbard and Hinshaw to aid in mapping out policy and procedure.[10]

---

5 *Wichita Eagle*, January 19, 1909.

6 G. W. Norris, "The Secret of His Power," *La Follette's Magazine*, January 8, 1910.

7 Ernest M. Pollard to William Howard Taft, January 20, 1909.

8 John M. Nelson to E. M. Keyes, January 21, 1909.

9 *Washington Times*, March 8, 1909.

10 *Ibid.*, March 12, 1909.

After the initial decision upon the type of approach to rules reform, many other questions of policy arose to be threshed out by the steering committee and the entire Insurgent group. Chief among these was the attitude to be taken toward the tariff bill and the balance of the Taft program. Largely because of the influence of Gardner and the more conservative of the Insurgents, it was unanimously decided to give the tariff bill the right of way and not to allow rules revision to interfere.[11] This decision was arrived at over the objections of a few radical Insurgents who wanted to use the threat of delaying the tariff as a club to force Taft to support the anti-Cannon movement. Another puzzling problem was the amount of cooperation with the Democrats that should be undertaken, but this was worked out fairly successfully by the steering committee. During the crisis of March 15, 1909, the Insurgents held numerous caucuses, or "conferences" as they preferred to call them, in a desperate effort to offset the defection of the Tammany Democrats to the Cannon Republicans.

Following the collapse of the revolt of March 15, 1909, the elaborate mechanism which the rules revisionists had built up fell into disuse. It was revived for the appointment of the Pinchot-Ballinger investigating committee in January, 1910, and again with dramatic suddenness when the Norris resolution created the crisis of March, 1910. The remnants of the Insurgent organization were inherited by the tariff revisionists, who constituted a smaller group of progressive westerners striving to do their bit for downward revision.

Throughout the remainder of the Taft administration, the Insurgents held numerous conferences on railroad rate regulation, postal savings bank legislation, and reciprocity, but never was there so unified and elaborately organized a group as that fighting for revision of the rules from December, 1908 until March, 1910.

The organization maintained by the Insurgents back home was in many cases developed to a very high degree. In re-

11 *Ibid.*

sponse to a request from Robert P. Bass, the leader of the progressive movement in New Hampshire, Senator Bristow revealed the type of organization he had built up in Kansas.[12]

I selected as best I could the names of the leading Republicans in every voting precinct, in a general list, and then a number of the active, progressive leaders in the precincts. I carried on a personal correspondence with the leaders, and sent my literature to the larger list. I wrote a very large number of personal letters to the Republican leaders who were in sympathy with my ideas. It was very burdensome to cover a state as large as ours in this way, but I found it very effective. Then I found it easier to interest the young men than old ones. The old soldier and the young man were usually the most enthusiastic—the old soldier because you could arouse in him a patriotism, and the young man because he was full of ambition, and new and progressive ideas. I have a list of about 60,000 Republicans and 5,000 Democrats in Kansas now that I keep in communication with by sending them bulletins and speeches, etc.

In the Senate, the Insurgents organized more loosely, as spontaneous agreement was simpler with a small group. In so far as leadership was exerted, La Follette was considered by his colleagues as *primus inter pares*. The Insurgents would never have tolerated the personal manner in which La Follette guided the destinies of his native state of Wisconsin. But if leadership can be measured by breadth of ideas and spirited courage in battle with parliamentary adversaries, " Fighting Bob " had no equal among the Insurgent Senators. Bowers claims for Beveridge the general leadership of the little bloc,[13] but no evidence exists to support his claim. Upon Bristow's arrival in 1909, the Kansas Senator gravitated toward Cummins and at first regarded him as the outstanding personality,[14] while recognizing La Follette as the ablest in crusading zeal and mastery of factual detail. As the tariff battle progressed, and the individual qualities of each Senator became apparent,

12 Joseph L. Bristow to Robert P. Bass, June 4, 1910.
13 Claude G. Bowers, *Beveridge and the Progressive Era*, p. 339.
14 Joseph L. Bristow to C. B. Kirtland, March 20, 1909.

La Follette came to be recognized as the spearhead of the entire movement. He was the man whom his progressive associates originally selected to lead the Republican Party out of the wilderness in the presidential campaign of 1912.

The Insurgent meetings of the Senate were less formal than those in the House. Much of the strategy was mapped out at fortnightly stag dinners at La Follette's house,[15] attended often by Representatives, newspaper men, and occasionally by prominent outside speakers. Beveridge's apartment on Sixteenth Street,[16] or the Indiana Senator's committee room [17] or Bourne's home [18] often provided a convenient place for the gatherings on late evenings after consideration of the tariff bill on the floor. However, most of the conferences were arranged on the spur of the moment, took place in any office that was convenient, and included only those Senators immediately concerned with the problems at hand.[19] After the retirement of Aldrich from the Senate, it became a source of much amusement to regular Senators to see his former committee rooms used by the Insurgents as a meeting place. The initial impulse for such a meeting was usually the exit from the Senate chamber of La Follette, beckoning with his finger for his twelve associates to follow him.[20] The committee rooms of Clapp [21] and Cummins [22] were also used occasionally as meeting places.

It was on the question of an income tax amendment to the tariff bill that the Insurgents had their first real chance to present an organized front: [23]

---

15 Robert M. La Follette, Jr., interview, December, 1938.
16 *Indianapolis Star*, July 5, 1909, cited in Bowers, *op. cit.*, p. 359.
17 Bowers, *op. cit.*, p. 363.
18 Colonel John Hannan, interview, February, 1939.
19 Colonel John Hannan, interview, February, 1939.
20 Butt, *op. cit.*, Vol. II, p. 684.
21 Robert M. La Follette to Joseph L. Bristow, April 2, 1911.
22 Albert B. Cummins to Joseph L. Bristow, July 1, 1912.
23 Joseph L. Bristow to E. C. Manning, April 23, 1909.

Referring to the income tax, I take pleasure in forwarding to you a copy of an amendment of Senator Cummins. I am glad to say that I had something to do with the framing of this amendment, as it was done by a number of conferences at which Senators Cummins, La Follette, Brown, Borah and myself were present, and a number of the provisions were my suggestion, but, of course, in concolidating (sic) and conferring with a number of men differences must be adjusted so as to get the best possible measure in which all could agree . . .

The tariff bill itself drew the Insurgents together and necessitated an organized program. The schedules were parceled out, not by any one individual,[24] but by an almost instinctive sense of the field in which each man was the best qualified to do battle.

Senator Bristow explained: [25]

I had lead and sugar, Cummins steel and glass, La Follette and Dolliver cotton and wool, Brown paper and wood pulp, Nelson lumber, and then on the other things every fellow got in wherever he felt that he could expose the rotten or undesirable features of the bill, and we think it has been pretty well shown up.

This technique of division of labor was most fortunate, as no other human being, had he been concerned with the minutiae of every schedule, could have hoped to match Aldrich's mastery of the tariff. Certainly the magnificent treatment that Dolliver gave to Schedules I and K could not have been achieved if he had been forced to spread himself thin over the entire field.

Throughout the torrid summer of 1909, the Insurgents met, argued, planned and discussed, and achieved a rare unity on the Senate floor as a result.

After the adjournment of Congress, the ties of the group were maintained through correspondence. Scarcely a month had elapsed before Bristow began to make preparations for a meeting of the progressives to lay plans for the regular session

24 Norris Brown, interview, September, 1938.
25 Joseph L. Bristow to Fred C. Trigg, June 21, 1909.

in December. His first attempt was to round up the Insurgents for a voyage down the Mississippi.[26] " If La Follette and you and Cummins and Beveridge could go," he wrote Clapp, " we might have an interesting and valuable conference in regard to the winter's work." Bristow cautioned Cummins to confer with La Follette in any case,[27] lest the railroad legislation which they were both preparing contain conflicting provisions, and thus split the Insurgents on the floor. He posed the issue to La Follette in the following terms: [28]

We have got to get together—the seven of us and as many more as will join us—and work as one man, because it is a tremendous struggle, and the battles that you and Cummins have had in your respective states for the last six or eight years have been the preliminary skirmishes. The real contest is ahead of us.

When the plans for the Mississippi trip failed to materialize, Bristow started a move to hold a meeting of the Insurgent Senators in Chicago during late October, and induced Cummins to round up the likely prospects.[29] Beveridge and some of the other Insurgents manifested a rather weary indisposition to go out of their way for such a meeting,[30] and accordingly the idea collapsed, despite Bristow's continued drumming upon the necessity for organization: [31]

... I hope we can organize, and get Brown with us, which will make eight, pick up as many strays as will come in, map out our own course, and not only fight against what those fellows propose, by offering amendments in harmony with our views, but take the initiative ourselves, wherever opportunity affords. And with eight or ten of us, alert and watchful, always " on the job," we will at-

26 Joseph L. Bristow to Moses E. Clapp, September 7, 1909.

27 Joseph L. Bristow to Albert B. Cummins, September 7, 1909.

28 Joseph L. Bristow to Robert M. La Follette, September 20, 1909.

29 Albert B. Cummins to Joseph L. Bristow, October 1, 1909.

30 Albert J. Beveridge to Albert B. Cummins, October 7, 1909; Bowers, op. cit., p. 373.

31 Joseph L. Bristow to Albert B. Cummins, October 4, 1909.

tract the attention of the country, which is with us, and then our
numbers will gradually grow.

A number of extra-congressional organizations were dominated by Insurgents, notably the National Progressive Republican League, formed in January, 1911, with Jonathan Bourne,
Jr., as its president. The Insurgent Congressmen who participated in the National Progressive Republican League included
Senators Clapp, Dixon, Beveridge, Bourne, La Follette,
Gronna, Bristow, Cummins, Poindexter, and Works; and Representatives Cooper, Cary, Davis, Hubbard, Haugen, Lenroot,
Madison, Morse, Murdock, Nelson and Norris. The League
subscribed to the principles of direct election of Senators, direct
primaries, direct election of delegates to national conventions
and preferential primaries to instruct such delegates, the initiative, referendum and recall, and corrupt practices acts.
Although the League declared that it was formed neither to
embarrass President Taft nor to promote the candidacy of " any
man," it had the effect of unifying Insurgent sentiment opposed
to the administration and in favor of the 1912 presidential
candidacy of Senator La Follette. Taft and Chauncey Depew
scoffed at the new group as " Bourne's salvation army," but
through a program of speeches, resolutions and meetings all
over the country, this organization gave a great impetus to
the Insurgent cause.

When the special session of the Sixty-second Congress met
in April, 1911, the Insurgents of both House and Senate held
organizational meetings to determine what demands they would
pose to the regulars. A caucus of progressive Republicans in the
House was attended by forty-six Insurgents, and it was decided
not to oppose the candidacy of James R. Mann, whom the
regulars were supporting for minority leader of the House.[32]
In the Senate, the Insurgents were more unified and militant
in their demands. Twelve progressive Republicans held a conference, and announced that inasmuch as they constituted a

32 *Des Moines Register and Leader*, April 4, 1911.

well-defined group within the Republican Party, they should
be entitled to at least one-quarter of the committee posts distributed by the leadership.[33] In addition, these Insurgents speci-
fied that La Follette should be placed on the committee on
interstate commerce, Bristow on the committee on foreign relations, Cummins on the committee on finance, and that Bourne
should be designated chairman of the committee on appropriations. The ultimatum of the Insurgents was summarily rejected
by the regulars. However, the incident demonstrated the feeling
of solidarity between the senatorial Insurgents, and their con-
sciousness that they were virtually a separate political party.

Of vast importance in the Insurgent organization and tactics
was the amount of cooperation between the various members
of the group during the campaigns. La Follette paved the way
for Bristow's election to the Senate by speaking against Chester
Long, Bristow's primary opponent, during the summer of 1908,
and by declaiming against the close association between Long
and the Aldrich clique in the Senate. After Miles Poindexter
had made his mark as a House Insurgent, he entertained
senatorial ambitions which were eventually realized with the
assistance of the Insurgent Senators. Poindexter wrote: [34]

I attended a dinner at Senator La Follette's residence the other
evening at which were the leading progressive Senators and newspaper men here. This is entirely confidential, but it was the unanimous consent to support each other.

In 1910, while Senator Beveridge, handicapped by a split
state organization, was striving to retain his seat against the
whirlwind campaign of his Democratic opponent, John W.
Kern, three of the Insurgents, Cummins, Bristow and Clapp,
entered the losing battle in Indiana, despite the strenuous objections of their own state campaign committees.

Rendered helpless by recurring attacks of gallstones, La
Follette was flat on his back during the Wisconsin primary

33 *Ibid.*, April 21, 1911.
34 Miles Poindexter to O. C. Moore, January 13, 1910.

campaign of 1910, and so was unable to tell his constituents of his conflicts with the Aldrich regime in Washington. In this critical situation, the strength of the Insurgent ties was once again revealed. Cummins, Dolliver, Clapp, Borah and Bristow all campaigned for La Follette. Bristow expressed the sentiment of unity when he wrote to Cummins: [35]

I hope that as many of our friends as can will go in and help him. This little band of patriots must stand by each other and lend a helping hand wherever it is needed.

And so it was throughout the country wherever an Insurgent Senator was tested at the polls. Not only were the Insurgents loyal to their ideals, but they were firmly loyal to each other. It was this binding force that made their assaults upon the regulars so telling. It was useless for Aldrich's crowd to dismiss the Insurgents with the sneer and sarcasm that had greeted La Follette before he was joined by a determined band of crusaders from the Middle West.

35 Joseph L. Bristow to Albert B. Cummins, August 18, 1910.

CHAPTER XI

MARRIAGE WITHOUT BENEFIT
OF CLERGY

"I AM a Republican; send this to one of your own party," was the angry notation which one of Senator Bristow's Kansas constituents penned on a tariff speech gratuitously sent to him.[1]

The rivalry between factions of the Republican Party was far more bitter than that between the Republicans and the Democrats. It was but natural that the Insurgents in seeking to achieve their ends should at various times form working arrangements with the Democrats.

This practice, however, was not nearly so widespread as the regulars claimed. Although the Insurgents were willing to cut party lines on specific issues, they still maintained a deep distrust of the Democratic Party and its conservative southern leadership. On the other hand, while the Democrats were eager to see the Republicans split asunder, they were sufficiently partisan to shun an alliance that might share the glory of Democratic achievement with some other group.

Fundamentally, the Insurgents were sanguine in their attempts to capture control of the Republican Party. Convinced that the rank and file of Republicans were progressive, they believed that only the leadership had to be overthrown to enact equitable tariff legislation, and to achieve railroad regulation, conservation and other progressive policies.[2] Their constituencies were too solidly Republican for them to switch party allegiance. They were not willing to traffic with the Democrats and thus lose their political identity entirely. It was only after they became completely disillusioned with the Republican Party at the close of the Taft administration that the Insurgents even considered the notion of setting up a separate party as the best means of realizing their aims.

1 Bristow papers.
2 Robert M. La Follette, Jr., interview, December, 1938.

In his memoirs Champ Clark admits candidly that with the aid of the Insurgents, he used the rules question largely as a tool to split the Republican Party. He was, however, a firm believer in the virtues of party government, and snorted contemptuously at Burleson, who was an advocate of wide-open cooperation with the Insurgents.[3] Likewise Clark was a personal admirer of the Speaker, and constantly made it clear that it was Cannonism rather than Cannon that he was fighting.[4] On the final day of the fight the Democratic leader was visibly moved by sympathy for the Speaker when it became apparent that Cannon was losing.[5]

Burleson was clearly the leader of that faction of the Democrats which believed in the expediency of uniting with the Insurgents. In March, 1909, he persuaded Clark and Underwood to promise the Insurgents that a unified Democratic vote would be cast against Cannon if enough Insurgents would make a similar pledge.[6] A committee of Insurgents brought the proposals of the Republican rebels in writing, signed by thirty Representatives; Clark then drew a pencil line through the names of four members whom he refused to trust. Inasmuch as the Insurgents mustered a minimum strength of twenty-nine and a maximum strength of thirty-one on the ballots of March 15, 1909, while the Democratic ranks were completely broken by the deals that Cannon had arranged with Tammany, Clark might better have examined the list of his own party when passing judgment as to which individuals could be trusted.

On the Insurgent side, the chief negotiator was John M. Nelson of Wisconsin. As secretary of the Insurgent group, Nelson was commissioned to make most of the arrangements with the Democrats. The preliminary negotiations were completed chiefly by Burleson and Nelson. Then they were passed on by the Insurgent steering committee, by Clark and Underwood

3 Champ Clark, *My Quarter Century of American Politics*, Vol. II, p. 269.
4 *Ibid.*, p. 279.
5 *New York World*, March 20, 1910.
6 Clark, *op. cit.*, p. 269.

for the Democrats, and finally by the entire group of Insurgent and Democratic Congressmen.

During the preliminaries to the first Insurgent uprising over the rules in 1909, there were frequent formal conferences between the Insurgent and Democratic leaders, to supplement the work done by Burleson and Nelson. Early in the negotiations, it was rumored that if the Insurgents would promise to stay out of the Republican caucus when the vote for Speaker took place, the Democrats would unite behind Murdock for the speakership.[7] Murdock himself scotched this plan by refusing to accept the post, and the proposal never reappeared. Four days before the culmination of the 1909 fight, Clark was closeted with Nelson and Gardner, with the result that they agreed to carry on the effort for revision of the rules. But they all denied that the Democrats and Insurgents had entered any iron-bound agreement as to voting for any specific rule.[8] Two days later the entire steering committee of the Insurgents, including Gardner, Madison, Nelson, Hubbard and Hinshaw, held an extended two-hour conference with Clark and Underwood at which the final plans of strategy for March 15 were perfected.[9]

When the revolt of March 15, 1909 collapsed, nearly all contact between the Insurgents and Democrats of the House ceased. Even on the tariff issue, when a group of downward revisionists proposed to fight for special instructions to the conference committee, and later against the conference report, no cooperative action with the Democrats was taken. Although the two groups were in substantial agreement on the question of rules revision, and unity was essential lest parliamentary blunders win the day for the regulars, the Insurgents and Democrats did not see eye to eye on the tariff. The Democrats were for the most part wedded to a tariff for revenue only, while

7 *Washington Times*, March 6, 1909.

8 *Wichita Eagle*, March 11, 1909.

9 *Ibid.*, March 13, 1909.

the Insurgents still maintained their faith in a moderate protective tariff.

Prior to the offering of the Norris resolution, which eventually proved Cannon's undoing in March, 1910, there were no conferences between the Insurgents and the Democrats, as no individual except Norris sensed that the crisis was at hand. When it became apparent that Norris and his band were about to let down the drawbridge and storm the castle of the regulars, unity of action, as in 1909, became a parliamentary necessity. Numerous conferences were held between the Insurgents and Democratic chieftains, during which the nature of the Norris resolution was altered to bring it into conformity with the will of the Democrats. As a result, during the dénouement the Democrats backed the Insurgents solidly in both the debates and the divisions. Nelson made it clear that the arrangement with the Democrats was only temporary, and that outside of the question of rules revision, there was no *anschluss* between the two groups. "We have formed no permanent alliance," Nelson claimed on the floor.[10]

Nevertheless, after the victory that the Insergents and the Democrats scored over the Cannonites had been finally realized, additional negotiation was completed by Nelson:[11]

I just made an agreement with the Democrats, acting for my fellow insurgents, that we would declare an armistice for the entire next month, in order to get at the so-called Taft policies. Before Congress adjourns we may take another crack or two at the rules.

In the Senate, Insurgent-Democratic cooperation was far more subtle than in the House. The Democrats seemed disposed to allow the Insurgents to take the lead in ripping into the Payne-Aldrich tariff bill, and occasionally they taunted the Insurgents for not joining the Democrats outright. But on the question of an income tax amendment to the tariff bill, there

10 *Congressional Record*, 61 : 2 : 3305.
11 John M. Nelson to E. M. Keyes, March 28, 1910.

was a vast amount of cooperation between the two groups, with overtures advanced from both sides.

Senator Bailey of Texas introduced the income tax amendment to the tariff bill on April 15, and Cummins six days later proposed a graduated income tax. To secure a more strategic position, the Insurgents and Democrats decided to pool forces in support of a consolidation of the two amendments, which thenceforth was known as the Bailey-Cummins amendment.[12]

In the middle of June, when the President delivered a smashing blow against the move for congressional income tax legislation by proposing a corporation tax in its stead, the coalition dissolved. It was the Democratic wing of this alliance that brought about the rupture, for Bailey swallowed Taft's compromise proposal and left the Insurgents high and dry.[13]

Considerable friction existed in connection with the income tax coalition. Although Bailey for the Democrats and Cummins for the Republicans agreed tolerably well for a while, the rank and file of both groups were inimical and hard to bring together. Since the Democratic platform of 1908 had declared in no uncertain terms for the enactment of an income tax, a number of the Republican Insurgents shied away from voting for a proposal that would carry out the Democratic pledges and would look like a Democratic bill. Likewise the Democrats did not feel any enthusiastic disposition to vote for a measure sponsored by Republicans, and both of these difficulties balked the efforts of the coalition leaders.

Throughout the tariff fight, the Insurgents were suspicious of the Democrats because some of the latter occasionally cut their own party lines to vote with Aldrich for higher duties upon products in their own states.[14] Apparently the Insurgents expected the Democrats to line up with them for the sake of principle, and so made no attempt to influence the other side

12 S. H. Acheson, *Joe Bailey, The Last Democrat*, p. 264.
13 *Ibid.*, pp. 268-269.
14 Joseph L. Bristow to J. F. Roebuck, May 29, 1909.

of the aisle.[15] When the Democrats and Insurgents happened to vote on the same side of a question, it was only a fortuitous occurrence, with no prearrangement of the details.

One Democratic Senator went so far as to write to President Taft suggesting a coalition of Democrats and Insurgent Republicans to achieve the pledges of downward revision which the conservative Republicans were sabotaging. Taft must have snickered to himself as he replied to this opportunistic suggestion in serious tones:[16]

. . . The difficulty about the union of the Republicans with the Democrats to reduce duties is that the Democrats have not enough who are in favor of a reduction of duties to make that possible. The vote on iron ore yesterday was an instance. They call it a revenue tariff, but that does not make it any different from a protective tariff. The same sort of tariff they have on lumber, which is voted for the purpose of protecting lumber. And so I doubt not we shall find enough Democratic votes on each of these disputed articles to prevent a reduction. I do not see any hope from such a coalition as you suggest.

During the furore over Canadian reciprocity in the summer of 1911, the Insurgents and Democrats took opposite sides and hence there was even less opportunity for cooperation. The House Insurgents and Democrats amended the reciprocity bill by reductions in the cotton and woolen schedules, and in products purchased by the farmer (the farmers' free list). However, the Senate Democrats, despite the entreaties of the Senate Insurgents, declined to support these reciprocity amendments lest Taft veto the entire measure. Closer cooperation between the Democrats and Insurgents was in evidence after the passage of the reciprocity bill, when the farmers' free list and woolen bills were repassed by the House, and this time received the support of the Senate Democrats. La Follette and Underwood connived openly in arranging the details of these bills

15 Joseph L. Bristow to A. L. Parker, July 1, 1909.
16 William Howard Taft to Francis G. Newlands, May 14, 1909.

after they went to the conference committee. But when the cotton bill came to a vote in the Senate, the Democrats deserted the alliance and jammed through a revenue measure which did not jibe with the protectionist theories of the Insurgents, and the latter angrily refused to support it. The cooperation was carried on almost entirely by the parties who were jockeying for political position, since the Democrats were seeking an adequate campaign issue for 1912. Hence the collaboration was not upon as genuine a basis as were the arrangements for rules revision and the early stage of the income tax fight. Never in the Senate, especially after the rupture that attended the sudden shift of the Democrats to support Taft's corporation tax, did cooperation proceed as successfully as in the House. There was apparently greater hostility toward the Insurgents on the part of the Democrats.[17]

When Senator Bristow ruminated over La Follette's tariff plans, he did not express any admiration for the motive that would move the Democrats to vote for the reduction in duties, but mused: " We will put up to our Democratic friends some very embarrassing roll calls." [18]

17 Joseph L. Bristow to Fred C. Trigg, June 26, 1911.
18 Joseph L. Bristow to Fred C. Trigg, July 7, 1911.

CHAPTER XII

THE REGULARS BOLSTER THEIR DEFENSES

In the eyes of the regular leaders, party bolting is a disease. But regarding the prevention and cure of that disease there are generally as many doctors as bolters, and many different schools of thought arise as to the proper treatment that should be accorded to party rebels. The less farsighted of the regulars regard party rebellion as a temporary matter, which can be quickly dissipated by surface measures; this group of doctors meets with little success because they would simply apply ice-bags to the fevered patient without seeking the cause of his fever. Others regard party revolt as such a deep-seated evil that drastic action is necessary; they would cut out the diseased flesh like a tumor. Then there are those who advocate an extensive program of party upbuilding to encourage a bodily resistance to the germs of party rebellion, some who think that the patient can be pampered back to health by giving him enough publicity and personal influence, and even those who apply the medieval theory that bolting is a form of insanity curable by clubbing and whipping with patronage until the evil spirit departs.

During the Taft administration, the regular leaders tried all of these methods in an effort to close the ranks and bring the straying rebels back into line. In a surprising number of cases, the regulars were successful with those Insurgents whose convictions were not very deeply ingrained. But in the case of dyed-in-the-wool Insurgents, the efforts of the regulars only spread the epidemic. Poindexter related early in the rules fight:[1]

A great deal of pressure and persuasion of various kinds was exerted on me when I arrived here to induce me to be " regular " with the party and to abide by the caucus vote upon the speakership . . .

1 Miles Poindexter to L. A. Vincent, March 17, 1909.

Poindexter's colleagues from Washington repeatedly approached him during the session and urged that his political future would be ruined if he persisted in breaking the bonds of party regularity. Threats were not used as much as gaudy pictures of a successful career if he stayed within the regular fold.[2]

A new Congressman usually finds it difficult to remain outside the party breastworks unless he has many companions. One of the most hardened of the Insurgents, Lindbergh of Minnesota, admitted that a queer feeling of bewilderment encompassed him in 1907 when a vote arose on the rules question and the re-election of Speaker Cannon. Although this incident took place before the large body of rules Insurgents became organized, it is illustrative of the feelings of a new Congressman. Lindbergh was emphatically anti-Cannon when he came to Congress, but he was convinced that it would be futile to register his opposition. In explaining his first vote for the Republican regulars in favor of Cannon and the House rules, Lindbergh years later asked: " Will you tell me how a new man, listening to such a skirmish for the first time, can understand the significance of it all? "[3] For some freshmen in Congress, however, it is somewhat easier to be an Insurgent, because no ties and connections have been established with the regular organization, and the long climb toward the top of a committee has not yet started. Thus when Bristow started to rebel in the Senate, he wrote:[4]

I have been congratulated quietly, in whispers, by a good many Senators who have been here from six to twelve years, who say they would like to do the same thing, but they have interests at stake and can't afford it.

But as a general rule, the first-termer likes to look over the scene before doing anything too much out of the way, and thus

2 Miles Poindexter, interview, November, 1938.

3 Lynn Haines, *The Lindberghs*, p. 117.

4 Joseph L. Bristow to Alex Mitchell, May 13, 1909.

he is more susceptible to the blandishments of the party leaders
than is one familiar with the methods by which the regulars
operate.

Another weapon of the regular machine to prevent Insurgency, is the use of ridicule or insult. It may seem that such a
weapon would be weak if used upon a man of convictions, as
indeed it is; but on the floor of the House or Senate it becomes
tremendously powerful. It is easy enough for a man to preach
Insurgent ideals upon the campaign platform, or even in set
speeches upon the floor of Congress. But when the final vote
comes and the party membership has its collective eyes glued
on an individual to discover whether he has cast his vote in line
with the rest of the party, then Insurgency becomes extremely
difficult.[5] Smarting with indignation, Senator Bristow wrote:[6]

When I rise, or does any other man who is not subservient to the
gang that runs the Senate, we are greeted with sneers and insulting
remarks from the Aldrich coterie. There never was a machine convention in the worst days of the machine supremacy in Kansas that
was more intolerant than this Senate machine, and I never have
seen a convention in either state or county in Kansas where the par-
ticipants in political controversy were so discourteous and insulting in their attitude.

However, Bristow was strong enough an Insurgent to be
able to withstand the hooting that he received for his views:[7]

But fortunately, their methods irritate me and increase my determination to fight this out during the six years, and if they can be
any more disagreeable to me than I will be to them as this fight
progresses, they are welcome to the satisfaction they get out of it.

These personal weapons of the regulars were always sharp-
ened immediately before a vote, by means of high appeals to
the great ideal of Republicanism and allusions to the dangers

5 John M. Nelson, interview, February, 1939.
6 Joseph L. Bristow to Harold T. Chase, May 22, 1909.
7 *Ibid.*

that lay in store for those who flirted with the Democrats. When a high party mogul rang out this plea in stentorian tones just before the roll-call, it emphasized the fact that he who bolted was losing caste. Unless the Insurgent was fairly well entrenched with his constituents, in these instances he thought twice before leaving the reservation.

Before the regulars brazenly came out in the open with their threats and punishment, numerous subtle attempts were made to convince the Insurgents that dire results would follow their desertion. When the hurricane of outright recrimination burst upon the Insurgents, it included deprivation of patronage and of key committee posts, failure to share in the pork barrel of local river and harbor and public building legislation, the withholding of money by the national committee during campaigns, and often indirect aid to Democratic opponents of Insurgents.

In 1909, after the first Insurgent uprising in the House, Speaker Cannon started the ball rolling by effecting a sweeping reorganization of committee posts. Cooper was removed from the chairmanship of the committee on insular affairs, Fowler lost the chairmanship of the committee on banking and currency, Murdock plunged toward the bottom of the committee on post offices and post roads, Norris was removed from the committee on public buildings and grounds, Morse lost his place on the committee on Indian affairs, Lovering was taken from the committee on interstate commerce, and Haugen lost his chairmanship of the committee on expenditures in the Interior Department,—to mention only a few of the Insurgents who were disciplined because of their opposition to Cannonism. The Speaker did this with the apparent acquiescence of the President, who wrote after Cooper had refused to vote for a $25,000 traveling appropriation for the President: [8]

Such a policy on his part reconciles me to the dull thud with which he will strike the bottom of an unimportant committee in the next assignment of committees by the Speaker, instead of being put at the head of the Insular Committee.

8 William Howard Taft to Mrs. H. H. Taft, July 17, 1909.

Early in the consideration of the tariff bill, when it was still pending in the House on April 4, Taft and Sherman held a lengthy discussion about the efficacy of using the patronage power to whip the Insurgents into line. The Vice-President was quite emphatic in his contention that Postmaster General Hitchcock should shut off the appointments of postmasters until the tariff bill was passed. " I hate to use the patronage as a club," protested the President.

" It is your only club," replied Sherman. " You have other weapons, but the appointing power is your only club."[9]

Throughout the special session of 1909, although many rumors were afloat about the consequences that the Insurgents would eventually suffer, their patronage was not touched. When the regular session of the Sixty-first Congress opened in December, 1909, Taft switched his views on the patronage question: [10]

. . . I propose to separate the sheep from the goats. These gentlemen who profess to be Republicans and will yet do everything to bring the Democratic Party into power can not expect me to assist them with patronage, and I hope to make this as plain as I can before I get through.

Early in January the storm broke. The House Insurgents were thrown into great excitement and intense anger when the news was confirmed that Postmaster General Hitchcock was holding up post office appointments that the Insurgents had recommended. This was being done because the Cannon organization had insisted that the administration give no recognition to the Insurgents in the form of patronage.[11] Miller of Minnesota was given this information by Hitchcock in flat terms and when he circulated it among his fellow Insurgents, there was great gnashing of teeth.

Norris immediately protested to Taft in two devastatingly logical letters which denied that the Insurgents had taken any

9 Archie Butt, *Taft and Roosevelt: The Intimate Letters of Archie Butt*, Vol. I, p. 41.

10 William Howard Taft to Otto Bannard, December 20, 1909.

11 *Des Moines Register and Leader*, January 5, 1910.

stand against the administration, and claimed that their whole purpose was to reform the rules of the House.[12] Taft squirmed, and although he replied at length, failed to answer Norris' assertion that the Insurgents were more loyal to the platform pledges than were the regulars.[13] The hue and cry against the Insurgents reached its height when the Republican Congressional Campaign Committee, in its regular weekly news letter, stated that it would oppose to the full extent of its power the principle of Insurgency, advocating the nomination and election of regular and loyal Republicans.[14] Dwight, the House whip, struck most of the Insurgents from the list of Republicans to be summoned to the floor in emergencies.[16] Late in February the regulars attacked the Insurgents in their home states. Hepburn, an old rules Insurgent, took the lead in organizing the campaign to overthrow the influence of Senators Dolliver and Cummins in Iowa.[15] Aldrich promised to get some of his friends to help finance the campaign of the stalwarts. The President himself pledged his financial assistance, and gave a private dinner for the Iowa conspirators in Washington on February 30.[17] A statewide federation of Republican Clubs for Taft sprang up, and patronage was rerouted through standpat ex-Congressmen who were striving to regain their seats from the Insurgents. The recrimination of the regulars extended even to the local battle for the Iowa governorship, when Taft withdrew the names of two postmasters who had announced they would support the progressive candidate, Garst, against the stalwart, Carroll.[18]

12 George W. Norris to William Howard Taft, January 6, 10, 1910; cf. Alfred Lief, *Democracy's Norris*, pp. 98-99; Henry F. Pringle, *The Life and Times of William Howard Taft*, Vol. II, pp. 612-613.

13 William Howard Taft to George W. Norris, January 7, 11, 1910.

14 *Des Moines Register and Leader*, January 10, 1910.

15 *Ibid.*, January 11, 1910.

16 Butt, *op. cit.*, Vol. I, pp. 300-01.

17 William Howard Taft to William P. Hepburn, February 7, 1910; *Official Functions*, p. 115.

18 *Des Moines Register and Leader*, June 17, 1910.

The same procedure was instituted in Wisconsin.[19] A new state central committee and state executive committee were set up to combat La Follette and his satellites, since the latter already had control of the regular Republican committees within the state. Speaker Cannon and his lieutenants invaded Kansas to stamp out the flames and to campaign actively against the Insurgents in the party primaries. By the fall of 1910 there was open war within the Republican Party, with the rabid stalwarts dictating a policy of absolute extermination as the only cure for Insurgency.

At this juncture came the famous Norton letter, in which Taft's private secretary openly admitted that patronage had been used as a club against the Insurgents, but that now it was time to start reuniting the party for a greater war on the Democrats: [20]

While Republican legislation pending in Congress was opposed by certain Republicans, the President felt it to be his duty to the party and to the country to withhold federal patronage from certain senators and congressmen who seemed to be in opposition to the administration's efforts to carry out the promises of the party platform.

That attitude, however, ended with the primary elections and nominating conventions which have now been held and in which the voters have had opportunity to declare themselves.

The primary defeats had chastened the party leaders and once again put the moderates in charge. But after the mid-term elections in 1910, recrimination again broke out with a rash of patronage wars against the Insurgents continuing throughout the remainder of the Taft administration.

The regulars made some concessions in legislative provisions and procedure. Scores of minor amendments were conceded by Aldrich during the consideration of the Payne-Aldrich tariff

19 George F. Mowry, *Theodore Roosevelt and the Progressive Movement,* p. 205.

20 *Philadelphia North American*, September 17, 1910.

bill, and more significant concessions to the rising sentiment were made in the railroad rate bill of 1910. During the Cannon revolt, some of the Insurgents were won over by compromises granted by the regular machine in March, 1909. This, after all, was what the Insurgents were fighting for. Far more of their number were brought into line by these basic methods than by viewing Insurgency as if it were a personal disquietude that could be quelled by such temporary expedients as withdrawal of patronage or switching of committee assignments.

In fact, the use of these minor correctives served as a spur rather than a deterrent to Insurgency, for it made the individual Insurgents feel like martyrs to a cause. Poindexter threw down a defiant challenge to Postmaster General Hitchcock for trying to control the opinions and votes of Representatives through the patronage, and made it clear that his vote was not for sale in exchange for federal jobs.[21] Lenroot testifies that the removal of patronage bound the Insurgents closer together, and made it more apparent to them that they were battling for ideals.[22] Likewise Murdock and Nelson, although bothered slightly by lack of patronage in one or two cases, were greatly strengthened by the conviction that their Insurgency lay deeper than a mere purchasable commodity.[23]

21 Miles Poindexter to Frank Hitchcock, June 1, 1910.

22 Irvine Lenroot, interview, November, 1939.

23 Victor Murdock, interview, September, 1938; John M. Nelson, interview, February, 1939.

CHAPTER XIII

CONCLUSION

" THE insurgent movement was nothing in God's world but political implementation of the deepening moral intelligence of the American people," writes one of its leading journalistic protagonists.[1] Insurgency aimed at wresting control of the Republican Party from the conservative representatives of the large industrial and financial interests of the country, who were enacting legislation beneficial to those interests and detrimental to the agrarian Middle West. It aimed to establish the responsibility of government to the popular will, and then to curb the natural and artificial privileges enjoyed by profit-hungry railroads, corporations, and despoilers of natural resources. As William Allen White so cogently put it, " The movement has two objectives, political and economic; first, to get the gun, and second to hit something with it." [2]

The destructive phase of Insurgency gradually merged into a constructive period with the perfection of the Mann-Elkins Act. The agitating zeal of the reformers was not abated, but they became soberly conscious of their new rôle as the effective balance of power between the Democrats and the regular Republicans.

The effects of Insurgency were far more pervasive than the alteration of a tariff schedule or the defeat of an administration bill. While clouding party responsibility through the shattering of party lines, Insurgency insured a greater degree of responsiveness on the part of political leaders. In our form of government, we always face the challenge of the democratic ideal of interpreting public opinion and directing it into the proper legislative channels. If artificial barriers are erected to divert the current of representative government, whether they are interposed by arrogant party leaders or unprincipled economic

1 William Allen White to Kenneth W. Hechler, September 5, 1939.

2 William Allen White, " The Insurgence of Insurgency," *American Magazine*, December, 1910.

interests, it becomes necessary for the preservation of democracy to demolish those barriers and repurify and redirect the flow into its natural channels. This was one of the tasks and accomplishments of Insurgency.

During the Taft administration, the interest of the people in the operation of government rose to a high pitch. In analyzing the thousands of letters that congressional leaders, cabinet members, presidents and vice-presidents received, the author was greatly impressed by the unusual grasp that the public had of the governmental problems of the day. There is where Insurgency played its greatest role. Something extraordinary, like a war, a depression, or a vigorous personality, is required to stimulate thinking upon the problems of government among the masses of our people. And Insurgency aided in the political education of the electorate by bringing to bear a more enlightened interest in the conduct of government.

Wilsonian liberalism and the New Deal were born of Insurgency, although many of the individual Insurgents would vigorously disown these progeny. Wilson himself felt that the Insurgent movement was too much a crusade of " anti " sentiment, and that it sorely lacked effective leadership.[3]

Senator Bristow claims:[4] " I believed that Mr. Wilson was in thorough sympathy with our ideas at the beginning of his administration. Indeed, in interviews I had with him, he so expressed himself. As time passed during the first administration, his mind was diverted, and he apparently became less interested in the things we were contending for."

Representatives Hayes of California, Woods of Iowa, and Nelson of Wisconsin feel that the Wilson-Franklin Roosevelt theories of presidential power do not jibe with the ideals of the Insurgents.[5] Likewise Miles Poindexter, a prominent figure in

3 Ray Stannard Baker, *Woodrow Wilson, Life and Letters*, Vol. III, p. 39.

4 Joseph L. Bristow to Kenneth W. Hechler, December 9, 1939.

5 J. O. Hayes to Kenneth W. Hechler, August 30, 1939; Frank P. Woods to Kenneth W. Hechler, September 9, 1939; John M. Nelson to Kenneth W. Hechler, September 8, 1939.

the movement, denies that either the New Freedom or the New Deal stem from Insurgency, and adds: [6]

The cardinal principle of the so-called " insurgents " was the dignity and inalienable rights of the individual citizen. The cardinal principle of the New Deal is the opposite one, namely, that of the totalitarian state, that the individual citizen has no rights which the government, as controlled by the New Deal, is bound to respect.

During the Wilson administration, deep splits occurred in the ranks of the men who as Insurgents had been well unified in their fight against special privilege in the Taft regime. The conservative Insurgents rejoined the regular Republicans immediately and lined up against Wilson on nearly every issue; the remnants of the Progressive Party of 1912, led by Murdock in the House, were generally in opposition to the details rather than to the philosophy of Wilson; the Wisconsin Insurgents, who refused to join the Progressives because of Theodore Roosevelt's treatment of Senator La Follette, pursued an independent course and regarded Wilson's domestic program as a vacillating attempt to solve basic problems by the use of high-sounding phrases.

The Underwood tariff bill received the support of La Follette and Poindexter in the Senate, but Bristow, Gronna and the other Insurgents vigorously objected to alleged discriminations against grain farmers of the West, and in favor of the tobacco, sugar and rice interests of the South. In the House, the former members of the Insurgent group were solid in their opposition to a " free trade " bill that was framed in secret and jammed through with a minimum of debate. Murdock and his Progressive followers continued to agitate for tariff revision schedule by schedule, instead of through an omnibus bill. However it cannot be denied that the Underwood bill was a sincere effort to repair the injustice of the Payne-Aldrich tariff, while retaining the main principles of protection, and La Follette termed its

6 Miles Poindexter to Kenneth W. Hechler, September 4, 1939.

passage "the winning of the first battle which must be waged against industrial monopoly." [7]

The Progressive Representatives supported the Federal Reserve Act, but felt that it was only a weak blow against the "money trust." Other ex-Insurgents like Lenroot, Nelson, Cooper, Kinkaid and Haugen were more enthusiastic in their approbation, but in the Senate a huge majority of the old Republican rebels declined to go along with Wilson. Bristow led the opposition to a Federal Reserve Board composed of political appointees.

On anti-trust legislation, however, most of the Insurgents backed the Wilson program unqualifiedly. Cummins said during the debate over the establishment of a Federal Trade Commission: [8]

I am not half-hearted in my support of this measure. I believe in it thoroughly. I look forward to its enforcement with a high degree of confidence.

All of the Insurgents backed the Federal Trade Commission, but a few of them shied at the Clayton Anti-Trust Act on the grounds that the teeth which it professed to put into the Sherman Anti-Trust Act were not sufficiently sharp. Thus Norris, who voted for the Senate version of the anti-trust bill, declined to back the conference report because[9]

If it is enacted into law in its present form, it will have the appearance of having passed through John D. Rockefeller's Sunday School class, rather than the Congress of the United States.

Among the "little group of willful men" who filibustered against the armed merchant ship bill in 1917 were Norris, La Follette, Gronna, Cummins, Clapp, Works and Kenyon—all survivors of the Insurgent era. All of the Insurgents opposed the peace treaty, while Poindexter, Borah, Gronna, Johnson and

7 *Congressional Record*, 63 : 1 : 5252.

8 *Ibid.*, 63 : 2 : 14770.

9 *Ibid.*, 63 : 2 : 16043.

La Follette were uncompromising in their bitter opposition to our entering the League of Nations.

During the 1920's, when American business was riding on a wave of post-war prosperity, the Insurgents took many different political roads. Beveridge, in an unsuccessful attempt to return to the Senate in 1922, made a right-about face and in his campaign defended the excessively high Fordney-McCumber tariff, called for the substitution of a sales tax for an income tax, and filled his speeches with blatant anti-labor utterances. In the Senate, Poindexter, Lenroot, and Cummins swung to the right, or perhaps the times marched ahead of them.[10] Finally in 1926 a fresh new Republican rebel, Smith Brookhart, defeated Cummins in the Iowa primaries and a few months later this great leader of the Insurgents died, a bitter man.

La Follette and Norris easily adjusted their Insurgency to meet new situations. The Wisconsin Senator kept up his uncompromising battle against monopoly, opposed the Fordney-McCumber tariff, and in 1924 made a vigorous presidential campaign on the Progressive ticket with a platform involving far-reaching reforms in labor, agricultural, tax, tariff and public ownership legislation. After La Follette's death in 1925, Robert M. La Follette, Jr. donned his father's toga in the Senate and in 1930 conducted against the high Hawley-Smoot tariff rates a long struggle directly comparable to his father's stand in 1909; the younger La Follette was also sympathetic with the domestic policies of the New Deal, and there is no doubt that his father would have taken a similar position

10 An admirer of Cummins comments on the author's view as follows: " The reference to Cummins and his subsequent career, does him rank injustice. . . . He was never radical or vindictive. His insurgency went to the point of demanding the same fairness for the railroads as for all others. He always did believe the La Follette attitude was destructive of the railroads and not helpful. Cummins never wanted to destroy or cripple the railroads. His work in 1920 and after was with a view to saving the American railroad system from the complete destruction threatened by the railroad baiters, and to forestall the drive to establish American communism by socializing the railroad business." Ora Williams to Kenneth W. Hechler, September 14, 1939.

In 1940, Norris remained the lone Insurgent survivor still in Congress. While many of his colleagues were settling back into the partisan regularity and conservatism of old age, the sad-eyed Nebraskan constantly erected new ramparts of reform and never forsook his political independence. Throughout the 1920's he was a constant critic of reactionary tendencies within the Republican Party and held aloft the banner of progressivism. Norris attacked the oil scandals of the Harding regime, led the movement for government operation of Muscle Shoals, participated in the farm bloc efforts to achieve parity through the McNary-Haugen bill and other means, and helped frame an act limiting the use of anti-labor injunctions by the federal courts. In the New Deal program, Norris frowns upon the "spoils machine" built by James A. Farley, but warmly supports the labor, agricultural, tax, relief, security, housing, banking, and business control policies of Franklin D. Roosevelt. Norris has properly been called the father of the TVA, and in the last three elections he has bolted the Republican Party to support presidential nominees whom he considered more sympathetic with his power policies. Roosevelt in turn has repeatedly praised Norris' statemanship and in 1936 successfully urged the voters of Nebraska to draft the silver-haired Senator for his fifth term.

In the political confusion of the Insurgent era, with its meaningless party labels, Franklin D. Roosevelt received his initiation. "Thank you so much for your telegram," a young candidate for the New York State Senate wrote, "I have a big majority to overcome, but there are indications of a big defection from the local Republican stand-pat machine." [11] After his triumphant election, young Roosevelt in Albany followed the pattern established by the La Follettes and Norrises at Washington. "A struggle of insurgent Democrats in the New York Legislature, led by young Senator Roosevelt, has attracted wide attention," Ray Stannard Baker reported.[12]

11 Franklin D. Roosevelt to Francis Burton Harrison, October 10, 1910.

12 Ray Stannard Baker, "The Meaning of Insurgency," *American Magazine*, May, 1911.

In view of the divergent opinions of the surviving Insurgents, it cannot be stated with any conclusiveness that the New Deal represents a realization and extension of their aims. Yet the independence and individualism for which the Insurgents fought thirty years ago was staunchly opposed by those conservative Republicans who claimed that they themselves were striving for an even more rugged individualism. The reactionaries wanted high tariff rates, but they clamored for individual freedom to exploit the natural resources of the country, individual freedom for corporations to extort profits through monopolies, and individual freedom to make money without bothersome income taxes. The use of this symbol of freedom as a cloak for anti-social action, and as a defense against governmental regulation, naturally roused the ire of the original Insurgents. Consequently, it seems rather quaint that many of the old Insurgents should dust off the arguments once used against their own cause, and employ them against an administration whose governmental control is theoretically aimed at achieving a more abundant life for the individual citizen.

Perhaps the architect of the New Deal himself should be allowed a final word on this subject. He writes: [13]

I think you are entirely accurate in comparing the fight in the Republican Party against Cannonism and Aldrichism with the general principles and ideals of the New Deal.

13 Franklin D. Roosevelt to Kenneth W. Hechler, September 8, 1939.

BIBLIOGRAPHY

A. Letters and Manuscripts

The ideal manuscript collection of letters is not found neatly catalogued and indexed in the fire-proof vaults of an endowed building. It rests in the hands of private individuals and must be disinterred from some dusty attic or damp basement. For the Insurgent period, this type of collection becomes more valuable for several reasons, aside from the obvious one that no previous research student has made an examination of its contents. In the first place, the owner of the collection can furnish a running interpretation of the why and wherefore behind the letters he has written and received, which is an invaluable aid in probing motives and intentions. Secondly, letters in private hands are free from the embarrassing restrictions which have necessarily been placed by the larger libraries upon their use. Thus the investigator is doubly rewarded when he stumbles upon such a rich collection as that of Senator Joseph L. Bristow or Senator Miles Poindexter.

1. *Allison, William Boyd*

> Location: Historical, Memorial and Art Department of Iowa, Des Moines, Iowa
>
> Custodian: O. E. Klingaman, Curator

Hundreds of volumes arranged by strict chronology, with very few copies of letters written by Allison, since the latter was addicted to hand-written letters when he had anything personal to say. Although he died seven months before Taft's inauguration, Senator Allison's correspondence is valuable because the letters written to him give a comprehensive picture of the gradual shift in the early twentieth century from conservatism to puzzlement to liberalism. There are some significant letters from James Blythe, political boss of the Chicago, Burlington & Quincy Railroad, Senator Spooner of Wisconsin, Secretary of the Treasury Leslie M. Shaw, and other leading conservatives.

2. *Bonaparte, Charles J.*

> Location: Library of Congress, Washington, D. C.
>
> Custodian: St. George L. Sioussat, Chief, Division of Manuscripts

A huge collection, with much extraneous material. Not useful for the period except to indicate the sentiment of an ex-cabinet member toward the increasing difficulties of the Taft administration.

3. *Bristow, Joseph Little*

> Location: Basement of National Bank of America Building, Salina, Kansas
>
> Custodians: Joseph L. Bristow, Fairfax, Virginia and Frank B. Bristow, Salina, Kansas

This is one of the most important collections of letters used in this study, as is apparent from the frequent references. It is contained in a score of large chests, roughly alphabetical and chronological as filed in the office, and consists of a complete set of letters received and carbon copies of letters written. The candor of Senator Bristow's correspondence makes it indispensable for both the Kansas and national aspects of the whole Insurgent movement and its aftermath.

4. *Burkett, Elmer J.*

> Location: Home of Mrs. Fannie W. Burkett, Lincoln, Nebraska
>
> Custodian: Mrs. Fannie W. Burkett

A small series of letters of Senator Burkett remains, but they are all important, including some outstanding ones from Vice-President Charles W. Fairbanks, Roosevelt and Taft. Burkett's letters on the Payne-Aldrich Tariff were useful in this study.

5. *Carter, Thomas Henry*

> Location: Library of Congress
>
> Custodian: St. George L. Sioussat

The letters of Senator Carter are revealing in connection with both the Postal Savings Bank Bill of 1910, which he piloted through the Senate, and the manifestations of Insurgent sentiment among his Montana constituents. Several boxes for the Taft period.

6. *Chandler, William E.*

> Location: New Hampshire Historical Society, Concord, N. H., and Library of Congress
>
> Custodians: Otis Gray Hammond, Director, and St. George L. Sioussat

Theoretically, this collection is divided between Concord and Washington upon a basis of that portion pertaining to New Hampshire politics and that portion pertaining to national politics. However, there are many of Senator Chandler's letters at Concord from La Follette and his Wisconsin associates, Bryan, Congressman Currier, and other national figures. Taken together, the Chandler collections give good sidelights upon the eastern reaction against railroad-dominated politics of the era, and the tieup between eastern and western Insurgency.

7. *Clapp, Moses E.*

> Location: Alexandria, Virginia, and Washington, D. C.
>
> Custodians: Mrs. Harvey Clapp and Mrs. Rosalyn Nash

Unfortunately, most of Senator Clapp's letters have disappeared, and only a few scattered items remain in the hands of his daughter-in-law, Mrs. Harvey Clapp, and Mrs. Rosalyn Nash, the sister of his late secretary, Miss Gertrude B. Spaulding. Photostatic copies of the items in Mrs. Clapp's hands have been duplicated and are in the possession of the Minnesota

Historical Society, Saint Paul, Minnesota. The existing material provides a broad picture of Senator Clapp's life and interests.

8. *Cochran, W. Bourke*

> Location: New York Public Library
> Custodian: Victor H. Paltsits

Cochran's letters give an interesting picture of a sympathetic Democratic reaction to Insurgency, but since Cochran was in Ireland during much of the Insurgent period, the collection cannot be termed indispensable.

9. *Cummins, Albert Baird*

> Location: Historical, Memorial & Art Department of Iowa
> Custodian: O. E. Klingaman

The Cummins collection is voluminous, but disappointing in two respects. Unlike Bristow, Senator Cummins was formal and reserved in his correspondence; further, there is a strange gap in the letters from 1909 to 1912. But for illustration of the development of progressive sentiment for trust control and tariff revision during Cummins' governorship, the letters have distinct value.

10. *Davidson, James O.*

> Location: The State Historical Society of Wisconsin, Madison, Wisconsin
> Custodian: Miss Alice E. Smith, Curator of Manuscripts

Governor Davidson's papers provide only a meager amount of material upon national politics, and are burdened with much that is inconsequential, but they are useful in interpreting conditions within Wisconsin.

11. *Deemer, Horace*

> Location: Historical, Memorial & Art Department of Iowa
> Custodian: O. E. Klingaman

Judge Deemer's correspondence is devoted in large part to his efforts to reach the United States Supreme Court, but there are a number of letters from the leading conservatives of Iowa, like Representative Walter I. Smith.

12. *Dodge, Grenville M.*

> Location: Historical, Memorial & Art Department of Iowa
> Custodian: O. E. Klingaman

The huge Dodge collection is valuable in its revelation of the alliance between the railroads and politics, and particularly regarding the attempt of the leading railroads to influence the form of the Mann-Elkins Act of 1910.

13. *Embree, Lucius*

> Location: Indiana Historical Society, Indianapolis, Indiana
> Custodian: C. B. Coleman

In this collection are a few letters showing the conservative opposition to Senator Beveridge.

14. *Foulke, William Dudley*

> Location: Indiana Historical Society and Library of Congress
> Custodians: C. B. Coleman and St. George L. Sioussat

The portion of the Foulke collection at the Library of Congress is concerned with the civil service activities of Foulke, and contains little of value on Insurgency. The Indianapolis branch of the collection includes some letters of tremendous significance from Senator Beveridge to Foulke.

15. *Gallinger, Jacob H.*

> Location: New Hampshire Historical Society
> Custodian: Otis Gray Hammond

This collection is not remarkable, but is helpful in mirroring the standpat New England attitude toward Insurgency, as exemplified by a president pro tem of the United States Senate.

16. *Gleed, Charles S.*

> Location: Kansas State Historical Society, Topeka, Kansas
> Custodian: Kirke Mechem, Director

Gleed, President of the Southwestern Bell Telephone company, was an intelligent exponent of conservative doctrine, and his letters contain a few pertinent comments upon Kansas politics.

17. *Harrison, Francis Burton*

> Location: Library of Congress
> Custodian: St. George L. Sioussat

There are a few illuminating letters on the tariff and rules fights in the House of Representatives; but for the Taft period the Harrison papers are by no means complete.

18. *Haugen, Nils P.*

> Location: The State Historical Society of Wisconsin
> Custodian: Miss Alice E. Smith, Curator of Manuscripts

The Governor Haugen letters are very valuable in illustrating the powerful backing that La Follette and Insurgency received among the Scandinavian elements of Wisconsin. There are a number of outstanding letters to and from Senator La Follette and Representative Irvine Lenroot.

19. *Hoover, Irwin H. (Ike)*

> Location: Library of Congress
> Custodian: St. George L. Sioussat

This material consists largely of notes which form the basis of Hoover's autobiography, *42 Years in the White House*. The notes are personal, but necessarily heavily restricted, even as to those which have already appeared in published form.

20. *Hull, Colonel John A. T.*

> Location: Historical, Memorial & Art Department of Iowa
> Custodian: O. E. Klingaman

A small collection of letters which supplements several similar collections in illustrating the reaction of Congressman Hull and his constituents to the rising Insurgency in Iowa.

21. *Kasson, John A.*

> Location: Historical, Memorial & Art Department of Iowa
> Custodian: O. E. Klingaman

Valuable in showing Iowa's sentiment toward tariff revision, in the letters of a man who played a foremost part in pushing reciprocity at the turn of the century.

22. *Keyes, E. M.*

> Location: The State Historical Society of Wisconsin
> Custodian: Miss Alice E. Smith

Few politicos are so pungently frank on paper as was Colonel Keyes, for many years the postmaster of Madison, Wisconsin, and thus his letters are of great value for this period. There are a number of outstanding letters to and from Senator La Follette, Henry Casson, Sergeant-at-arms of the House of Representatives, and Representative John M. Nelson of Wisconsin.

23. *Knox, Philander C.*

> Location: Library of Congress
> Custodian: St. George L. Sioussat

A disappointingly small collection which is incomplete, yet helpful regarding Taft's cabinet appointments and the issue of reciprocity with Canada in 1911.

24. *Lacey, John C.*

> Location: Historical, Memorial & Art Department of Iowa
> Custodian: O. E. Klingaman

Like the Hull collection, the letters of Representative Lacey show clearly the conservative reaction to the rise of Insurgency in Iowa.

25. *Lindbergh, Charles A.*

> Location: Minnesota Historical Society, Saint Paul, Minn.
> Custodian: Miss Grace L. Nute, Curator of Manuscripts

This collection is still not generally open to researchers, and is as yet unarranged. Included are photostats of important comments written from

Washington by Lindbergh to his home-town newspapers in Little Falls, Minnesota, discussing frankly various phases of Insurgency.

26. *Lyford, James O.*

> Location: New Hampshire Historical Society
> Custodian: Otis Gray Hammond, Director

This collection yielded little except a significant letter from Congressman Currier written immediately after the conclusion of the Insurgent overthrow of Speaker Cannon in 1910.

27. *Mann, James R.*

> Location: Library of Congress
> Custodian: St. George L. Sioussat

A small series of letters, with scores of scrapbooks kept by Congressman Mann; significant in revealing Mann's Insurgency on the Payne-Aldrich Tariff, and the measures of retaliation taken against the anti-Cannon Insurgents.

28. *Marshall, Thomas E.*

> Location: Indiana Historical Society
> Custodian: C. B. Coleman

Vice-President Marshall's letters do not give an intimate picture of Insurgency, but illustrate the widening split in the Indiana Republican ranks.

29. *Nelson, Knute*

> Location: Minnesota Historical Society
> Custodian: Miss Grace L. Nute

A large collection filling nearly 300 boxes, incomplete for several phases of Senator Nelson's career, yet clearly portraying the Minnesota disaffection with the eastern Republican leadership. There are some excellent letters upon the Canadian reciprocity and conservation issues.

30. *Nichols, Jeannette P. and Stephenson, Nathaniel W.*

> Location: Library of Congress
> Custodian: St. George L. Sioussat

Miscellaneous notes and interviews compiled in the preparation of the late N. W. Stephenson's biography of Nelson Aldrich; heavily restricted, but useful.

31. *Olney, Richard*

> Location: Library of Congress
> Custodian: St. George L. Sioussat

Letter-books and incoming-letters, apparently incomplete for the Insurgent period, but showing in a sketchy manner the viewpoint of an elder statesman on the Insurgent movement.

32. Perkins, George

Location: Historical, Memorial & Art Department of Iowa

Custodian: O. E. Klingaman

An admirably arranged and carefully indexed collection of real significance for this period. Letters to and from Speaker Cannon, Congressman William P. Hepburn, and Director of the Mint George E. Roberts.

33. Platt, Orville H.

Location: Connecticut State Library, Hartford, Connecticut

Custodian: James E. Brewster

Small and incomplete, nevertheless the papers of Senator Platt are very useful in showing the rising sentiment for tariff revision. Significant letters to and from Aldrich, Spooner, and Roosevelt are contained herein.

34. Poindexter, Miles

Location: Although examined at the home of Senator Poindexter, in Greenlee, Virginia, the Poindexter collection has now been transferred to the Alderman Library of the University of Virginia, Charlottesville, Virginia

Custodian: W. Edwin Hemphill, Acting Archivist

This is beyond doubt one of the outstanding collections of the period, both in scope and detail. The size is staggering, but industry is rewarded with inside accounts of every aspect of the Insurgent movement in the House of Representatives, as well as the senatorial manifestations of Insurgency after 1911, and the formation of the Progressive Party of 1912.

35. Rainey, Henry Thomas

Location: Library of Congress

Custodian: St. George L. Sioussat

Although consisting largely of letters written to and from Rainey in the final months of his life, there are a few letters of value, including a long appraisal of Bryan's part in the progressive movement, written by Rainey in 1911, along with a description of the Democratic participation in the revolt against Speaker Cannon.

36. Roosevelt, Theodore

Location: Library of Congress

Custodian: St. George L. Sioussat

This voluminous collection is indispensable for a study of Insurgency. Although Roosevelt was in Africa during a large part of the rise of the movement, the reports to him from the United States are illuminating; also invaluable for tracing the relationship between Roosevelt and Taft after the former's return, Roosevelt's participation in the election of 1910, and his contribution toward stirring Insurgent sentiment.

37. Sherman, James Schoolcraft

> Location: New York Public Library
> Custodian: Victor H. Paltsits

The letters of Vice-President Sherman constitute a virgin field for research, as they are complete and unculled for this period. There are many letters to and from the outstanding conservatives of the party, like Speaker Cannon, Lucius N. Littauer, William L. Ward, James A. Tawney, Henry Loudenslager and others. They illustrate the inside working of the regular machine in adjusting the schedules of the Payne-Aldrich tariff, the defense of the speakership, the fight against Theodore Roosevelt in the 1910 New York State Convention, and many other episodes of the times.

38. Sickles, Daniel Edgar

> Location: Library of Congress
> Custodian: St. George L. Sioussat

Mostly confined to military matters in the early period before Sickles became a Congressman, this collection cannot be said to be valuable for the Insurgent movement.

39. Swift, Lucius

> Location: Indiana Historical Society
> Custodian: C. B. Coleman

The Swift collection is not as valuable as the Foulke letters, but gives a few sidelights upon Insurgency within Indiana. The Taft-Swift letters are not open to researchers at present.

40. Stubbs, Walter Roscoe

> Location: Kansas State Historical Society
> Custodian: Kirke Mechem

The official papers of Governor Stubbs are housed at the Kansas State Historical Society, and although there is a quantity of routine chaff included, a few important personal letters have crept into the official correspondence. They include a series of exchanges between Stubbs and E. P. Ripley, President of the Atchison, Topeka, and Sante Fe Railroad, in debating the iniquities of the long and short haul discriminations.

41. Taft, William Howard

> Location: Deposited in Library of Congress
> Custodian: Taft family

The Bristow, Poindexter, Roosevelt and Taft letters are the four most significant collections used in this study. The Taft collection deals in detail with every issue arising during Taft's administration, and includes valuable letters revealing the trend of public sentiment in every state in the union. The gradual development of Taft's attitude toward the Insurgents is unfolded, along with his relationship with Roosevelt. Outstanding are the letters from Taft to Mrs. Taft and to his brother, Horace Taft. Included in the Taft papers are various diaries and engagement books, such as Archie Butt's compilation, *Official Functions,* and the diaries of Taft's secretaries, Mischler and Carpenter.

42. *Tawney, James A.*

> Location: Minnesota Historical Society
>
> Custodian: Miss Grace L. Nute

The Tawney letters are valuable in connection with the reaction of the conservative House leadership against Theodore Roosevelt, the stalwart position on the House rules, the attitude of the moderate revisionists toward the tariff, and the circumstances surrounding Taft's speech defending Tawney at Winona, Minnesota in September, 1909. The collection is large and detailed.

43. *Weaver, James Baird*

> Location: Historical, Memorial & Art Department of Iowa
>
> Custodian: O. E. Klingaman

The Weaver papers are meager for this period.

44. *White, William Allen*

> Location: Emporia, Kansas
>
> Custodian: William Allen White

Termites have destroyed many of the earlier letters of Mr. White, but remaining is a series of important letters to and from Taft and Roosevelt.

45. *Williams, John Sharp*

> Location: Library of Congress
>
> Custodian: St. George L. Sioussat

The Williams letters are more complete for the later phases of his career. During the period of the Insurgent movement, this collection is not particularly valuable.

46. *Young, Lafayette*

> Location: Historical, Memorial & Art Department of Iowa
>
> Custodian: O. E. Klingaman

The Young collection, as yet unarranged, is nevertheless important in showing the Iowa Insurgent sentiment. Young, the editor of the *Des Moines Capital,* was in the United States Senate for a few months by gubernatorial appointment following Dolliver's death, was a close friend of President Taft, and an influential figure in Iowa politics.

* * * * *

CONFIDENTIAL MANUSCRIPT SOURCES

Several complete manuscript collections and portions of other collections of letters were examined under the pledge that their identity and location be kept confidential for the present. These collections provided invaluable background material for this study, and they will become available for general use of researchers at a future date.

B. UNPUBLISHED THESES

Cooper, Vernom, *William Boyd Allison*, MS. biography in possession of State Historical Society of Iowa, Iowa City, Iowa.

Dolliver, Frances Pearsons, *Speeches of Tribute—Jonathan Prentiss Dolliver*, Master's essay, State University of Iowa Library, Iowa City, Iowa (1931).

Harrington, Elbert W., *The Political Ideas of Albert B. Cummins*, Master's essay, State University of Iowa Library, Iowa City, Iowa (1930).

Knibbs, Joseph Charles, *The Political Map of Nebraska, 1900-1934*, Master's essay, University of Nebraska, Lincoln, Nebraska (1935).

Lyman, Burton E., *Voting Behavior of Kansas Counties*, Master's essay, University of Kansas Library, Lawrence, Kans. (1937).

McCue, Claire Frances, *The Taft-Roosevelt Break*, Master's essay, Columbia University, New York, N. Y. (1936).

Mowry, George, *Theodore Roosevelt and the Progressive Movement*, Doctoral dissertation, University of Wisconsin Library, Madison, Wis. (1938).

Mulvey, Claire, *Republican Party in Nebraska, 1900-1916*, Master's essay, University of Nebraska, Lincoln, Neb. (1934).

Poland, Eleanor, *Reciprocity Negotiations Between Canada and the United States, 1866-1911*, Radcliffe College thesis (1932).

Raphael, Jacob Howard, *The Fight Against Cannonism in the House of Representatives*, Master's essay, Columbia University, New York, N. Y. (1936).

Smith, Grace Hamilton, *Notes for a Study of the Canadian Reciprocity Agreement of 1911*, Swarthmore College thesis, Swarthmore, Pa. (1936).

Wilcox, Burton Harris, *A Reconsideration of the Character and Economic Basis of Northwestern Radicalism*, Doctoral dissertation, University of Wisconsin Library, Madison, Wis. (1933).

C. PUBLISHED WORKS

Abbott, Lawrence F., *Impressions of Theodore Roosevelt*, Garden City, Doubleday, Page, 1919.

Acheson, Sam Hanna, *Joe Bailey, The Last Democrat*, New York, Macmillan, 1932.

Alexander, De Alva Stanwood, *History and Procedure of the House of Representatives*, Boston, Houghton Mifflin, 1916.

Ashley, Percy, *Modern Tariff History*, London, J. Murray, 1920.

Atkinson, Charles Raymond, *The Committee on Rules and the Overthrow of Speaker Cannon*, New York, Columbia University, 1911.

Baker, Ray Stannard, *Woodrow Wilson, Life and Letters,* Vol. 3, Garden City, Doubleday, Doran, 1931.

Barry, David S., *Forty Years in Washington,* Boston, Little, Brown, 1924.

Barton, Albert Olaus, *La Follette's Winning of Wisconsin,* Madison, Wis., 1920.

Bates, Ernest Sutherland, *The Story of Congress, 1789-1935,* New York, Harper, 1936.

Beveridge, Albert Jeremiah, *The State of the Nation,* Indianapolis, Bobbs-Merrill, 1924.

Bishop, Joseph Bucklin, *Charles Joseph Bonaparte, His Life and Public Services,* New York, Scribner's, 1922.

Bishop, Joseph Bucklin, *Theodore Roosevelt and His Time,* 2 vols., New York, Scribner's, 1920.

Bizzell, William Bennett, *The Green Rising: An Historical Survey of Agrarianism,* New York, Macmillan, 1926.

Bogart, Ernest Ludlow, *Economic History of American Agriculture,* New York and Chicago, Longmans, Green, 1923.

Bogart, Ernest Ludlow, *Economic History of the American People,* New York and London, Longmans, Green, 1935.

Bowden, Robert Douglas, *Boies Penrose: Symbol of an Era,* New York, Greenberg, 1937.

Bowers, Claude Gernade, *Beveridge and the Progressive Era,* Boston, Houghton Mifflin, 1932.

Brandeis, Louis Dembitz, *Other People's Money,* New York, Frederick H. Stokes, 1934.

Briggs, John Ely, *History of Social Legislation in Iowa,* Iowa City, The State Historical Society of Iowa, 1915.

Briggs, John Ely, *William Peters Hepburn,* Iowa City, The State Historical Society of Iowa, 1919.

Brooks, Robert Clarkson, *Political Parties and Electoral Problems,* New York and London, Harper, 1933.

Brown, George Rothwell, *The Leadership of Congress,* Indianapolis, Bobbs-Merrill, 1922.

Brown, George Rothwell, *The Speaker of the House: The Romantic Story of John N. Garner,* New York, Brown, Warner and Putnam, 1932.

Buck, Solon Justus, *The Agrarian Crusade,* New Haven, Yale, 1920.

Buck, Solon Justus, *The Granger Movement,* Cambridge, Harvard, 1913.

Busbey, L. White, *Uncle Joe Cannon,* New York, Holt, 1927.

Butler, Nicholas Murray, *Across the Busy Years,* New York, Scribner, 1939.

Butt, Archie, *The Letters of Archie Butt,* ed. by Lawrence F. Abbott, Garden City, Doubleday, Page, 1924.

Butt, Archie, *Taft and Roosevelt: The Intimate Letters of Archie Butt,* 2 vols., Garden City, Doubleday, Doran, 1930.

Capper, Arthur, *The Agricultural Bloc,* New York, Harcourt, Brace, 1922.

Chamberlain, John, *Farewell to Reform,* New York, Liveright, 1932.

Chamberlain, Joseph P., *Legislative Processes—National and State,* D. Appleton-Century, New York and London, 1936.

Chiu, Chang-Wei, *The Speaker of the House of Representatives Since 1896,* New York, Columbia University, 1928.

Clark, Champ, *My Quarter Century of American Politics,* 2 vols., New York, Harper, 1920.

Clark, Victor S., *History of Manufactures in the United States,* 3 vols., New York and London, McGraw-Hill, 1929.

Cole, Cyrenus, *I Remember, I Remember; A Book of Recollections,* Iowa City, State Historical Society of Iowa, 1936.

Connelley, William Elsey, *The Life of Preston B. Plumb,* Chicago, Browne and Howell, 1913.

Coolidge, Louis A., *An Old-Fashioned Senator, Orville H. Platt of Connecticut,* New York, Putnam, 1910.

Cotton, Edward, *William Howard Taft, A Character Study,* Boston, Beacon, 1932.

Croly, Herbert David, *Marcus Alonzo Hanna, His Life and Work,* New York, Macmillan, 1912.

Croly, Herbert David, *The Promise of American Life,* New York, Macmillan, 1909.

Cullom, Shelby Moore, *Fifty Years of Public Service,* Chicago, A. C. McClurg, 1911.

Darling, Arthur B., ed., *The Public Papers of Francis Newlands,* 2 vols., Boston and New York, Houghton Mifflin, 1932.

Davis, Oscar King, *Released for Publication,* New York, Houghton Mifflin, 1925.

Depew, Chauncey M., *My Memories of Eighty Years,* New York, Scribner's, 1922.

Dewey, Davis Rich, *Financial History of the United States,* New York and London, Longmans, Green, 1934.

DeWitt, Benjamin Parke, *The Progressive Movement,* New York, Macmillan, 1915.

Douglas, Paul Howard, *The Coming of a New Party,* New York and London, Whittlesey House, McGraw-Hill, 1932.

Dreier, Thomas, *Heroes of Insurgency,* Boston, Human Life, 1910.

Duffy, Herbert S., *William Howard Taft,* New York, Minton, Balch, 1930.

Duncan-Clark, S. J., *The Progressive Movement; Its Principles and Its Programme,* Boston, Small Maynard, 1913.

Dunn, Arthur Wallace, *From Harrison to Harding,* Vol. 2, New York and London, G. P. Putnam's, 1922.

Faulkner, Harold Underwood, *American Economic History,* New York and London, Harper, 1924.

Faulkner, Harold Underwood, *The Quest for Social Justice, 1898-1914,* New York, Macmillan, 1931.

Fine, Nathan, *Labor and Farmer Parties in the United States, 1828-1928,* New York, Rand School, 1928.

Follett, Mary P., *The Speaker of the House of Representatives,* New York, Longmans, Green, 1909.

Folwell, William Watts, *A History of Minnesota,* 4 vols., Saint Paul, Minnesota Historical Society, 1921-1930.

Foraker, Joseph Benson, *Notes of a Busy Life,* Vol. 2, Cincinnati, Stewart and Kidd, 1916.

Ford, Henry Jones, *Representative Government,* New York, Holt, 1924.

Ford, Henry Jones, *The Rise and Growth of American Politics,* New York, Macmillan, 1914.

Ford, Worthington C., *The Letters of Henry Adams,* Vol. 2, Boston and New York, Houghton Mifflin, 1938.

Foulke, William Dudley, *A Hoosier Autobiography,* New York and London, Oxford University, 1922.

Foulke, William Dudley, *Lucius B. Swift, a Biography,* Indianapolis, Bobbs-Merrill, 1930.

Fowler, Charles H., *The National Issues of 1916,* New York, Harper, 1916.

Fuller, Herbert Bruce, *The Speakers of the House,* Boston, Little, Brown, 1909.

Fuller, Robert Higginson, *Jubilee Jim: The Life of Colonel James Fisk, Jr.,* New York, Macmillan, 1928.

Griffin, Solomon Bulkeley, *People and Politics,* Boston, Little, Brown, 1923.

Griffin, Solomon Bulkeley, *W. Murray Crane, a Man and a Brother,* Boston, Little, Brown, 1926.

Gue, Benjamin F., *History of Iowa,* 4 vols., New York, The Century History Co., 1903.

Hacker, Louis M. and Kendrick, Benjamin B., *The United States Since 1865,* New York, F. S. Crofts, 1939.

Haines, Lynn, *Lawmaking in America,* Bethesda, Lynn Haines, 1912.

Haines, Lynn, and Haines, Dora B., *The Lindberghs,* New York, Vanguard, 1931.

Haines, Lynn, *The Minnesota Legislature of 1911,* Minneapolis, Lynn Haines, 1911.

Haines, Lynn, *The Senate from 1907 to 1912,* Washington, The National Capital Press, 1912.

Haines, Lynn, *Your Congress,* Washington, The National Voters' League, 1915.

Hansbrough, Henry Clay, *The Wreck: An Historical and Critical Study of the Administrations of Theodore Roosevelt and of William Howard Taft,* New York, Neale, 1913.

Hapgood, Norman, *The Advancing Hour,* New York, Boni and Liveright, 1920.

Hasbrouck, Paul De Witt, *Party Government in the House of Representatives,* New York, Macmillan, 1927.

Haynes, Fred Emory, *James Baird Weaver,* Iowa City, State Historical Society of Iowa, 1919.

Haynes, Fred Emory, *Social Politics in the United States,* Boston, Houghton Mifflin, 1924.

Haynes, Fred Emory, *Third Party Movements Since the Civil War,* Iowa City, State Historical Society of Iowa, 1916.

Heaton, John Langdon, *The Story of a Page,* New York and London, Harper, 1913.

Hendrick, Burton J., *Age of Big Business,* New Haven, Yale, 1919.

Hendrick, Burton J., *The Life of Andrew Carnegie,* 2 vols., Garden City, Doubleday, Doran, 1932.

Hibbard, Benjamin Horace, *A History of the Public Land Policies,* New York, Macmillan, 1924.

Hicks, John D., *The Populist Revolt,* Minneapolis, University of Minnesota, 1931.

Hoover, Irwin H. (Ike), *42 Years in the White House,* Boston and New York, Houghton Mifflin, 1934.

Howard, Sir Esme, *Theatre of Life,* London, Hodder and Stoughton, 1936.

Howe, Frederic C., *Confessions of a Reformer,* New York, Scribner's, 1925.

Howe, Frederic C., *Wisconsin: An Experiment in Democracy,* New York, Scribner's, 1912.

Howe, Mark Antony De Wolfe, *George von Lengerke Meyer, His Life and Public Services,* New York, Dodd, Mead, 1920.

Howe, Mark Antony De Wolfe, *Portrait of an Independent, Moorfield Storey,* Boston and New York, Houghton Mifflin, 1932.

Howland, Harold, *Theodore Roosevelt and His Times,* New Haven, Yale, 1921.

Jessup, Philip Caryl, *Elihu Root,* 2 vols., New York, Dodd, Mead, 1938.

Johnson, Claudius O., *Borah of Idaho,* New York and Toronto, Longmans, Green, 1936.

Jones, Eliot, *The Trust Problem in the United States,* New York, Macmillan, 1922.

Kirkland, Edward Chase, *A History of American Economic Life,* New York, F. S. Crofts, 1932.

Kohlsaat, Henry H., *From McKinley to Harding,* New York and London, Scribner's, 1923.

La Follette, Robert Marion, *La Follette's Autobiography,* Madison, La Follette Co., 1913.

Laidler, Harry W., *Concentration of Control in American Industry,* New York, Thomas Y. Crowell, 1931.

Lane, Letters of Franklin K., ed. by Anne Wintermute Lane and Louise Herrick Wall, Boston and New York, Houghton Mifflin, 1922.

Leary, John J., Jr., *Talks with T. R.,* Boston and New York, Houghton Mifflin, 1920.

Lief, Alfred, *Brandeis: The Personal History of an American Ideal,* New York and Harrisburg, Stackpole, 1936.

Lief, Alfred, *Democracy's Norris,* New York and Harrisburg, Stackpole, 1939.

Lodge, Henry Cabot, *Selections from the Correspondence of Theodore Roosevelt and Henry Cabot Lodge, 1884-1918,* 2 vols., New York, Scribner's, 1925.

Longworth, Alice Roosevelt, *Crowded Hours,* New York, Scribner's, 1933.

Looker, Earle H., *The White House Gang,* New York, Fleming H. Revell, 1929.

Luce, Robert, *Congress: an Explanation,* Cambridge, Harvard University, 1926.

Luce, Robert, *Legislative Assemblies,* Boston and New York, Houghton Mifflin, 1924.

Luce, Robert, *Legislative Principles; The History and Theory of Lawmaking by Representative Government,* Boston and New York, Houghton Mifflin, 1930.

Luce, Robert, *Legislative Problems,* Boston and New York, Houghton Mifflin, 1935.

Luce, Robert, *Legislative Procedure,* Boston and New York, Houghton Mifflin, 1922.

McCall, Samuel W., *The Business of Congress,* New York, Columbia University, 1911.

McCarthy, Charles, *The Wisconsin Idea,* New York, Macmillan, 1912.

McClure, Samuel Sidney, *My Autobiography,* New York, Stokes, 1914.

McHale, Francis, *President and Chief Justice; The Life and Public Services of William Howard Taft,* Philadelphia, Dorrance, 1931.

Meany, Edward S., *History of the State of Washington,* New York, Macmillan, 1909.

Moody, John, *The Masters of Capital,* New Haven, Yale University, 1921.

Moody, John, *The Railroad Builders,* New Haven, Yale University, 1921.

Morgenthau, Henry, *All in a Life-Time,* Garden City, Doubleday, Page, 1922.

Morison, Samuel Eliot, and Commager, Henry Steele, *The Growth of the American Republic,* New York and London, 2 vols., Oxford University Press, 1937.

Muzzey, David Saville, *James G. Blaine: A Political Idol of Other Days,* New York, Dodd, Mead, 1934.

Myers, William Starr, *The Republican Party, a History,* New York, Century, 1928.

Neuberger, Richard L., and Kahn, Stephen B., *Integrity; The Life of George W. Norris,* New York, Vanguard, 1937.

Nevins, Allan, *Henry White, Thirty Years of American Diplomacy,* New York and London, Harper, 1930.

Odland, Martin Wendell, *The Life of Knute Nelson,* Minneapolis, The Lund Press, 1926.

Orcutt, William Dana, *Burrows of Michigan and the Republican Party,* 2 vols., New York, Longmans, Green, 1917.

Page, Thomas Walker, *Making the Tariff in the United States,* New York, McGraw-Hill, 1924.

Parrington, Vernon Louis, *The Beginnings of Critical Realism in America,* Vol. 3 of *Main Currents in American Thought,* New York, Harcourt, Brace, 1930.

Paxson, Frederic L., *History of the American Frontier,* Boston and New York, Houghton Mifflin, 1924.

Paxson, Frederic L., *Recent History of the United States,* Boston and New York, Houghton Mifflin, 1937.

Pinchot, Gifford, *The Fight for Conservation*, New York, Doubleday, Page, 1910.

Platt, Chester C., *What La Follette's State is Doing*, Batavia, N. Y., Press, 1923.

Pollock, Ivan L., *History of Economic Legislation in Iowa*, Iowa City, The State Historical Society of Iowa, 1918.

Pringle, Henry F., *The Life and Times of William Howard Taft*, 2 vols., New York, Farrar and Rinehart, 1939.

Pringle, Henry F., *Theodore Roosevelt, a Biography*, New York, Harcourt, Brace, 1931.

Regier, Cornelius C., *Era of the Muckrakers*, Chapel Hill, University of North Carolina, 1932.

Rhodes, James Ford, *The McKinley and Roosevelt Administrations, 1897-1909*, New York, Macmillan, 1923.

Riegel, Robert Edgar, *The Story of the Western Railroads*, New York, Macmillan, 1926.

Ripley, William Z., *Railroads: Rates and Regulation*, New York, Longmans, Green, 1912.

Robinson, Doane, *South Dakota, Sui Generis*, 3 vols., Chicago and New York, The American Historical Society, 1930.

Robinson, Edgar E., *The Evolution of American Political Parties*, New York, Harcourt, Brace, 1924.

Roosevelt, Theodore, *Autobiography*, New York, Macmillan, 1916.

Rosewater, Victor, *Backstage in 1912: The Inside Story of the Split Republican Convention*, Philadelphia, Dorrance, 1932.

Russell, John Andrew, *Joseph Warren Fordney, An American Legislator*, Boston, Stratford, 1928.

Sanford, Albert Hart, *The Story of Agriculture in the United States*, Boston and New York, D. C. Heath, 1916.

Schmidt, Louis Bernard, and Ross, Earle Dudley, eds., *Readings in the Economic History of American Agriculture*, New York, Macmillan 1925.

Scott, James Brown, *Robert Bacon, Life and Letters*, Garden City, Doubleday, Page, 1923.

Seager, Henry R., and Gulick, Charles A., *Trust and Corporation Problems*, New York and London, Harper, 1929.

Seligman, Edwin R. A., *The Income Tax*, New York, Macmillan, 1921.

Sheldon, Addison E., *Nebraska, The Land and the People*, 3 vols., Chicago and New York, Lewis, 1931.

Stahl, Rose M., *The Ballinger-Pinchot Controversy*, Smith College Studies in History, vol. ix, Northampton, Smith College, 1926.

Steffens, Lincoln, *Autobiography of Lincoln Steffens*, 2 vols., New York, Harcourt, Brace, 1931.

Steffens, Lincoln, *The Letters of Lincoln Steffens*, Vol. i, 1889-1919, New York, Harcourt, Brace, 1938.

Stephenson, George M., *John Lind of Minnesota*, Minneapolis, University of Minnesota, 1935.

Stephenson, Isaac, *Recollections of a Long Life*, Chicago, T. R. Donnelley, 1915.

Stephenson, Nathaniel Wright, *Nelson W. Aldrich: A Leader in American Politics*, New York, Scribner's, 1930.

Stoddard, Henry L., *As I Knew Them*, New York and London, Harper, 1927.

Stoddard, Henry L., *It Costs to be President*, New York and London, Harper, 1938.

Straus, Oscar S., *Under Four Administrations, From Cleveland to Taft*, Boston and New York, Houghton Mifflin, 1922.

Sullivan, Mark, *The Education of an American*, New York, Doubleday, Doran, 1938.

Sullivan, Mark, *Our Times*, Vol. 4, *The War Begins, 1909-1914*, New York and London, Scribner's, 1932.

Swisher, Jacob A., *Robert Gordon Cousins*, Iowa City, The State Historical Society of Iowa, 1938.

Taft, William Howard, *Presidential Addresses and State Papers*, New York, Doubleday, Page, 1910.

Taft, Mrs. Helen H., *Recollections of Full Years*, New York, Dodd, Mead, 1914.

Tarbell, Ida Minerva, *All in the Day's Work*, New York, Macmillan, 1939.

Tarbell, Ida Minerva, *The Tariff in Our Times*, New York, Macmillan, 1911.

Taussig, Frank William, *Free Trade, the Tariff and Reciprocity*, New York, Macmillan, 1920.

Taussig, Frank William, *Some Aspects of the Tariff Question*, Cambridge, Harvard University, 1931.

Taussig, Frank William, *The Tariff History of the United States*, New York and London, G. P. Putnam's, 1931.

Thompson, Charles G., *Presidents I've Known—and Two Near Presidents*, New York, Bobbs-Merill, 1929.

Thwaites, Reuben Gold, *Wisconsin, The Americanization of a French Settlement*, Boston and New York, Houghton Mifflin, 1908.

Tucker, Ray and Barkley, Frederick R., *Sons of the Wild Jackass*, Boston, L. C. Page, 1932.

Turner, Frederick Jackson, *The Frontier in American History*, New York, Holt, 1920.

Usher, Ellis Baker, *The Greenback Movement of 1875-1884, and Wisconsin's Part in it*, Milwaukee, E. B. Usher, 1911.

Van Hise, Charles Richard, *Concentration and Control*, New York, Macmillan, 1914.

Villard, Oswald Garrison, *Fighting Years*, New York, Harcourt, Brace, 1939.

Watson, James E., *As I Knew Them*, Indianapolis and New York, Bobbs-Merrill, 1936.

Weyl, Walter Edward, *The New Democracy*, New York, Macmillan, 1912.

White, William Allen, *A Puritan in Babylon; The Story of Calvin Coolidge*, New York, Macmillan, 1938.

White, William Allen, *Masks in a Pageant,* New York, Macmillan, 1928.
White, William Allen, *The Old Order Changeth,* New York, Macmillan, 1910.
Wilson, George Grafton, *Insurgency* (Lectures delivered at the Naval War College), Washington, Government Printing Office, 1900.

D. UNITED STATES GOVERNMENT DOCUMENTS

Sixtieth Congress, second session:

House Document No. 1505, *Tariff Hearings Before the Committee on Ways and Means of the House of Representatives, 1908-1909.* 1909.

Sixty-first Congress, first session:

House Document No. 85, *Constitution, Jefferson's Manual and Rules of the House of Representatives of the United States with a Digest of the Practice, prepared by Asher C. Hinds,* 1909.
House Document No. 91, *Conference Report on H. 1438, Tariff Act of 1909,* 1909.
House Document No. 92, *H. 1438, Tariff Act of 1909, as Agreed to by Committee of Conference,* 1909.
House Document No. 93, *Statement of Managers on Part of House on H. 1438, Tariff Act of 1909,* 1909.
Senate Document No. 72, *Shall Hides be Free?* 1909.
Senate Document No. 75, *Memorandum on Cotton Schedule of Tariff Bill of 1909,* 1909.
Senate Document No. 98, *Message of President Relating to Tax on Net Income of Corporations,* 1909.
Senate Document No. 109, *Duties on Iron and Steel Products,* 1909.
Senate Document No. 151, *Sugar Tariffs of the United States and the Dutch Standard of Color,* 1909.
Senate Document No. 153, *Votes on Tariff Bill in Senate,* 1909.
Senate Document No. 154, *Comparative Statement of Tariff Rates of Conference Committee with Act of 1897,* 1909.
Senate Document No. 155, *Comparison of Payne Tariff Bill as Agreed to by Conference Committee with Dingley Law,* 1909.

Sixty-first Congress, second session:

House Document No. 948, *Comparison of the Tariffs of 1897 and 1909 in Parallel Columns,* 1910.
Senate Report No. 125, *Postal Savings Depositories,* 1910.

Sixty-first Congress, third session:

Senate Document No. 719, *Investigation of the Department of Interior and of the Bureau of Forestry,* 13 vols., 1911.
Senate Documents Nos. 787, 828, 829, 834, 842, 849, 862, *Documents Relating to Reciprocity with Canada,* 1911.

Sixty-second Congress, first session:

House Report No. 3, *Reciprocity with Canada,* 1911.
House Report No. 4, *To Place Certain Articles on Free List,* 1911.

House Report No. 144, *Conference Report on Bill for Reduction of Duties on Wool, etc.*, 1911.

House Report No. 146, *Conference Report on Farmers' Free List Bill*, 1911.

Senate Document No. 56, *Reciprocity with Canada—Hearings before the Committee on Finance*, 1911.

Senate Document No. 77, *Chugach National Forest Lands in Alaska, a Message from the President*, 1911. (Transmitting in response to a Senate resolution of June 22, 1911, all papers and information relating to the elimination from the Chugach National Forest of certain lands fronting upon Controller Bay in Alaska.)

Senate Document No. 80, *Reciprocity with Canada*, Compilation of 1911 prepared by the Finance Committee, 1911.

Senate Report No. 63, *To Promote Reciprocal Trade Relations with Canada*, 1911.

Senate Report No. 84, *Farmers' Free List*, 1911.

Senate Record No. 85, *Schedule K*, 1911.

Congressional Record (citation 60:1:3386 refers to Sixtieth Congress, first session, page 3386).

Official Congressional Directory.

Twenty-third Annual Report of the Interstate Commerce Commission, December 21, 1909, 1910.

United States Bureau of the Census, *Thirteenth Census of the United States*, 1910, 1912.

United States Tariff Commission, *Reciprocity with Canada; A Study of the Arrangement of 1911*, 1920.

Yearbook of the Department of Agriculture, 1909-1912, 1910-1913.

E. PERIODICALS

The following periodicals, magazines and journals were useful for running interpretations of contemporary events:

American Magazine
American Historical Review
American Political Science Review
The Arena
Atlantic Monthly
The Century
Chautauquan
Collier's
Cosmopolitan
Current Literature
Everybody's Magazine
Forum
Harper's Magazine
Harper's Weekly
Independent
Iowa Journal of History and Politics

Journal of Political Economy
La Follette's Magazine
Literary Digest
Living Age
McClure's Magazine
Munsey's Magazine
Nation
North American Review
Outlook
The Palimpsest
Political Science Quarterly
Quarterly Journal of Economics
Review of Reviews
The Saturday Evening Post
Scribner's Magazine
Success
Taylor-Trotwood Magazine
Twentieth Century
The World Today
The Wisconsin Magazine of History
World's Work

F. Newspapers

The files of the following newspapers were examined and revealed a surprisingly accurate account of the day-by-day events during the Insurgent period; accuracy was checked with manuscript and printed sources, as well as personal interviews.

Des Moines Register and Leader
Emporia Gazette
Indianapolis Star
Kansas City Star
Nebraska State Capital
Nebraska State Journal
New York Sun
The New York Times
New York Tribune
New York World
Omaha World-Herald
Philadelphia Ledger
Philadelphia North American
Philadelphia Press
Philadelphia Record
Salina (Kans.) Journal
Sioux Falls (S. D.) Daily Argus-Leader
Sioux Falls (S. D.) Daily Press
Spokane (Wash.) Spokesman-Review

Topeka Capital
Washington Times
Wichita Eagle

G. Personal Interviews

The fifty men and women listed below are but a small percentage of those who have provided the life blood of this study through their recollections, interpretations, and intimate sidelights upon the personalities and politics of Insurgency:

Allen, Henry J., Editor, *Topeka State Journal,* Topeka, Kansas.

Barton, Albert O., author, Madison, Wisconsin.

Briar, John, secretary of the late Senator Albert B. Cummins of Iowa, Alexandria, Virginia.

Bristow, Frank B., son of ex-Senator Joseph L. Bristow of Kansas, Salina, Kansas.

Bristow, Joseph L., former U. S. Senator from Kansas, Fairfax, Virginia.

Brown, Norris, former U. S. Senator from Nebraska, Omaha, Nebraska.

Bryan, Charles W., former Governor of Nebraska, Lincoln, Nebraska.

Burkett, Fannie W., widow of Senator Elmer J. Burkett of Nebraska, Lincoln, Nebraska.

Capper, Arthur, U. S. Senator from Kansas, Topeka, Kansas.

Clapp, Mrs. Harvey, daughter-in-law of the late Senator Moses E. Clapp of Minnesota, Alexandria, Virginia.

Cosson, George W., former Attorney-General of Iowa, Des Moines, Iowa.

Cummins, Miss Anna B., sister of the late Senator Albert B. Cummins of Iowa, Des Moines, Iowa.

Dawson, Judge John, Chief Justice of the Supreme Court of Kansas, Topeka, Kansas.

Dean, Mrs. Virginia Dixon, daughter of the late Senator Joseph M. Dixon of Montana, New Haven, Conn.

Garrett, Judge Finis J., Presiding Judge, U. S. Court of Customs and Patent Appeals, former Representative from Tennessee, Washington, D. C.

Gore, Thomas P., former U. S. Senator from Oklahoma, Washington, D. C.

Haines, Mrs. Dora B., widow of Lynn Haines, author, Washington, D. C.

Hannan, Colonel John, secretary of the late Senator Robert M. La Follette of Wisconsin, Madison, Wisconsin.

Haynes, Fred Emory, author, Iowa City, Iowa.

Kinsler, James W., former U. S. Attorney, Omaha, Nebraska.

La Follette, Miss Fola, daughter of the late Senator Robert M. La Follette of Wisconsin, N. Arlington, Virginia.

La Follette, Robert M., Jr., U. S. Senator from Wisconsin, Washington, D. C.

Lawrence, James E., Editor, *Lincoln Star,* Lincoln, Nebraska.

Lenroot, Irvine L., former Representative and Senator from Wisconsin, Washington, D. C.

Lief, Alfred, author of *Democracy's Norris,* New York, N. Y.

McNeal, Tom A., Editor, *Capper's Farmer,* Topeka, Kansas.

Maguire, John A., former Representative from Nebraska, Lincoln, Nebraska.

March, Benjamin, Executive Secretary, People's Lobby, Washington, D. C.

Murdock, Victor, former Representative from Kansas, Editor, *Wichita Eagle*, Wichita, Kansas.

Metcalf, Richard L., former Associate Editor, *Bryan's Commoner*, Omaha, Nebraska.

Murphy, Don R., Editor, *Wallace's Farmer and Iowa Homestead*, Des Moines, Iowa.

Murray, Joseph, Editor, *Lawrence World-Herald*, Lawrence, Kansas.

Mushlitz, Earl, *Indianapolis Star*, Indianapolis, Indiana.

Nelson, John M., former Representative from Wisconsin, Madison, Wisconsin.

Nelson, William L., Representative from Missouri, member of committee on rules, 76th Congress, Washington, D. C.

Norris, George W., U. S. Senator from Nebraska, Washington, D. C.

Page, William Tyler, Clerk to the Minority, and former Clerk, House of Representatives, Washington, D. C.

Poindexter, Miles, former Representative and U. S. Senator from Washington, Greenlee, Virginia.

Robertson, John, secretary and son-in-law of Senator George W. Norris, Washington, D. C.

Rosewater, Victor, former Editor, *Omaha Bee*, Philadelphia, Pennsylvania.

Newbranch, Harvey, Editor, *Omaha World-Herald*, Omaha, Nebraska.

Sessions, Charles J., Editor, *Topeka Capital*, Topeka, Kansas.

Sheldon, Addison, author, Director, Nebraska Historical Society, Lincoln, Nebraska.

Sherley, Swagar, former Representative from Kentucky, Washington, D. C.

Souders, W. H., secretary to Senator Arthur Capper of Kansas, Topeka, Kansas.

Trimble, South, Clerk of House of Representatives, Washington, D. C.

Underwood, Mrs. Oscar, widow of Senator Oscar Underwood of Alabama, Alexandria, Virginia.

Watson, James E., former U. S. Senator from Indiana, Washington, D. C.

Waymack, W. W., Editor, *Des Moines Register and Tribune*, Iowa.

White, William Allen, Editor, *Emporia Gazette*, Emporia, Kansas.

INDEX